DESIGN OF REINFORCED CONCRETE STRUCTURES

A PRIMER WORKBOOK

PYO-YOON HONG, PH.D., P.E.

Matthias & Alex Publishing, Inc.

Design of Reinforced Concrete Structures
A Primer Workbook
Pyo-Yoon Hong

Copyright © 2020 by Matthias & Alex Publishing, Inc.

All rights reserved. Except as permitted under U.S. Copyright Act of 1976, no part of this publication may be reproduced, distributed, or transmitted in any form or by any means, or stored in a database or retrieval system, without the prior written permission of the publisher.

Publisher's address and contact information:
13570 Technology Dr. #2117, Eden Prairie, MN 55344

ISBN-10: 0989511227
ISBN-13: 978-0-9895112-2-3

Printed in the United States of America

Book Design by Pyo-Yoon Hong
Editing by Pyo-Yoon Hong

First Edition: Mar 10, 2014
10 9 8 7 6 5 4 3 2 1

This book is dedicated to

유영

성운

성준

I love you all, each and every one.

TABLE OF CONTENTS

Preface 1

Chapter 1

Concrete as Structural Material 1

1.1 Introduction 1

1.2 Advantages and Disadvantages of Reinforced Concrete 3

1.3 Materials 5

1.4 How concrete develop strength? - Hydration 6

1.5 Steel Reinforced Concrete 7

1.6 Compatibility of Concrete and Steel 8

1.7 Structural Properties of Steel 9

1.8 Steel Reinforcement 11

1.9 Structural Properties of Concrete 12

1.10 Water Cement Ratio 13

Chapter 2

Structural Analysis and Design 17

2.1 Structure 16

2.2 Loads on Structures 18

2.3 Building Codes 20

2.4 Design Specifications 21

2.5 ASD and LRFD 22

Chapter 3

Flexural Analysis of Beams 34
3.1 Introduction 33
3.2 Flexural behavior of RC Beam for different stages of loading 34
3.3 Working Stress Design - Transformed Area Method 37
3.4 Ultimate Flexural Strength of Rectangular Beams 47
3.5 Whitney Stress Block 48
3.6 Stress Design vs. Strength Design 50

Chapter 4

ACI Strength of Beams 66
4.1 Introduction 65
4.2 Beam Strength according to ACI Code 65
4.3 Ductility Considerations 66
Strain Limit for Beams (ACI 10.3.5) 67
4.4 Strength Reduction Factors (ACI 9.3.2) 67
4.5 Balanced Section (Under-Reinforced and Over-Reinforced Beams) ... 68
4.6 Maximum Reinforcement Ratio 70
4.7 Minimum reinforcement limits for beams (ACI 10.5) 70
4.8 ACI Singly Reinforced Concrete Beam Design Process 73
4.9 Summary of Design of Singly Reinforced Beam 75
4.10 Summary 76

Chapter 5

T-beams & One-way Slab 104
5.1 Floor Systems 103
5.2 One-Way Systems 103
5.3 Two-Way Systems 105
5.4 Analysis and Design of One-way Slab 107

Chapter 6

Shear Force and Diagonal Tension 118

6.1 Introduction 117

6.2 Types of Shear Cracks 118

6.3 Nominal Shear Stress 118

6.4 Current Shear Design Philosophy 119

6.5 Shear Strength of Concrete 120

6.6 Strength of Shear Reinforcement 120

6.7 Spacing of Vertical Stirrups 121

Chapter 7

Design of Columns 131

7.1 Introduction 130

7.2 Classification of columns 130

7.3 Types of Columns 131

7.4 Axial Strength of Columns 132

7.5 Resistance Factors for Columns 134

7.6 Code Requirements 135

Chapter 8

Foundations 155

8.1 Introduction 154

8.2 Pressure Distribution below Foundations 155

8.3 Allowable Bearing Capacity of Soil 155

8.4 Depth of Foundation 156

8.5 Foundation Types 157

8.6 Wall Foundation 158

8.7 Isolated Foundation 159

8.8 Retaining Walls 159

Appendix

Table 1. Reinforcing Bar Properties 203

Table 2. Areas of Groups of Strandard Reinforcing Bars 203

Table 3. Area of Bars in Slabs 204

Table 4. Minimum Web Width for Beams with Inside Exposure 204

Table 5. Steel Ratio for Tensilely Reinforced Rectangula Beams 205

Table 6. Minimum Thickness of Beams or One-way Slab 205

Table 7. Steel Ratio Table 206

Table 8. Nominal Load-Moment Strength Interaction Diagram 212

PREFACE

This book offers a concise and thorough presentation of reinforced concrete design process, application and underlying structural principles and thus is committed to developing users' problem-solving skills. This workbook makes the contents of textbooks with same subjects more visible, extractable, and relevant for an application or process. The material is reinforced with variety of structural design examples of progressively varying degrees of difficulty to illustrate structural principles and design issues that focus on practical and realistic situations encountered in professional practice. This book features many photorealistic figures that have often been depicted in 3-dimensional view to appeal to visual learners. The case study problems and group workshop are prepared to relate the verbal and visual elements to each other in an effective way. Most verbal elements are presented in categorized boxes. Some of the visual and verbal elements are deliberately left incomplete or missing so the instructor and students can complete them together in the classroom. This approach promotes problem-based learning and active participation of students, which can lead to a fundamental understanding that is more likely to be retained.

A thorough presentation of structural mechanics theory and applications includes some of these topics:

      Properties of concrete and steel
      Elastic behavior of reinforce concrete beam
      Ultimate behavior of reinforce concrete beam
      ACI Beam strength
      T-beam and one-way slab design
      Shear reinforcement design
      Compression member design
      Combined bending and axial force
      Footing design

CHAPTER 1

1. CONCRETE AS STRUCTURAL MATERIAL

1.1 Introduction

While cement has been used in various forms for a surprisingly long period since prehistoric times, the development of reinforced concrete is relatively recent. Concrete is a composite material comprised of coarse aggregates embedded in cement paste that fills the space among the aggregates and glues them together. The ancient Romans were the earliest large-scale users of concrete technology and concrete was widely used in the Roman Empire. The Coliseum was built mainly of concrete and the Pantheon is still the world's largest un-reinforced solid concrete dome. After the Roman Empire collapsed, use of concrete became scarce until the technology was re-pioneered in the mid-18th century. The origin of reinforced concrete in England is generally accepted as William Wilkinson's patent in 1854. His system was not widely adopted however and most of the early developments and successful patents came from Germany and France. The method of reinforced concrete flooring patented by Francois Hennebique in 1892 was the most widely used, such that by 1909 nearly 20,000 structures had been designed using the Hennebique system. His company helped make reinforced concrete a serious construction material in Europe. The patented system meant that the contractor paid for a structural design, license for the materials and instructions on how to build to a particular system. Reinforced concrete was used in the 19th century,

Pantheon - World's largest un-reinforced concrete dome

Ingalls Building, 1904

Marina City, 1964

Lake Point Tower, 1968

Burj Khalifa, 2009

mainly for foundation work. In the second half of the 19th century a number of ways of combining iron and concrete, and later steel and concrete, to produce more efficient, and hence, cheaper structures were developed. Today, concrete is the most widely used man-made material (measured by tonnage) in the world. Reinforced concrete was first introduced to buildings as fireproofing (reference & date) and led to a series of inventions in the following years, most of them in the US.

In the United States, William E. Ward built the first landmark building structure in reinforced concrete in Port Chester, NY (1870). The main part of the building had two stories. It did not take a very long time for enterprising engineers in the US to push the limit to 15 stories. High-rise construction in concrete progressed slowly forward from the Ingalls Building in 1904. The giants and mid-giants of the 1930s were all of steel construction. However, the Johnson Wax Tower

First RC building in US, 1870

(1936), designed by American architect Frank Lloyd Wright, provided the impetus for Bertrand Goldberg's twin towers of Marina City, though on a vastly different scale. Reinforced concrete became successful because of its strength, economy, durability, and fire resistance. Reinforced concrete has been improved significantly during the last decade of the twentieth century. The compressive strength of the concrete reached well above 10,000 psi from a typical 4,000 psi and self-consolidating concrete made casting of complicated shapes an easy task. The Chicago 60 story high-rise, erected in 1962, heralded the beginning of the use of reinforced concrete in modern skyscrapers and with it, competition for the steel frame. Place Victoria in Montreal, constructed in 1964, reached height of 624 ft utilizing 6000 psi concrete in the columns. Concretes of higher strength proved to be the key to increased height, permitting as they do a reasonable column size on the floors below. One Shell Plaza in Houston topped out at 714 ft in 1970 using 6000 psi concrete. The Chicago area, with its plentiful supply of high-quality fly ash (which helps to achieve a more workable concrete at lower water/cement ratios), has spawned the greatest concentration of tall reinforced concrete buildings. The 70-story Lake Point Towers used 7500 psi concrete to reach 645 ft in 1968. Water Tower Place reached 859 feet in 1973 with concrete strengths as high as 9000 psi thanks to a superplasticizing. In 2009, a proprietary 11,600 psi ultrahigh-strength concrete was used the world's tallest building, the Burj Khalifa.

1.2 Advantages and Disadvantages of Reinforced Concrete

Reinforced concrete structures are characterized by their strength, economy, durability and fire resistance. It is the material of choice for many structures where these characteristics are required. The **advantages** of reinforced concrete can be summarized as follows:

1. Concrete has a relatively high compressive strength.
2. Concrete is a non-combustible material which has better resistance to fire than steel.
3. Concrete is very durable and thus has a long service life with low maintenance cost;
4. Concrete is relatively inexpensive material and in some types of structures, such as dams, piers, and footings, it is the most economical structural material;
5. Concrete can be molded into almost any desired shape, making it widely used in precast structural components.
6. Concrete frames are inherently rigid as compared to steel & wood frames and yields rigid members with minimum apparent deflection. Hence, they are resistant to lateral forces such as earthquake or wind loads.

However, reinforced concrete structures have several **disadvantages** which may preclude it as a building material, including:

1. It has a very low tensile strength of about one-tenth of its compressive strength.
2. Quality control is difficult. It needs mixing, casting, and curing, all of which affect the final strength of concrete.
3. The cost of the forms used for casting concrete is relatively high than other materials.
4. It has a low strength-to-weight ratio as compared to steel (the ratio is about 1:10, depending on materials), which leads to larger and heavier member sizes of multistory buildings.
5. Cracks develop in concrete due to shrinkage.
6. Concrete is very brittle material and thus it has very low ductility.
7. Concrete construction is very labor-intensive and requires trained laborers.
8. It takes longer construction schedule due to curing time
9. Concrete has poor insulation values. Concrete expands and contracts with the changes in temperature. Hence expansion joints are to be provided to avoid the formation of cracks due to thermal movements.

10. Creep develops in concrete under sustained loads. Creep is increasing deformation that takes place when a material sustains a high stress level over a long time period. In a beam, the additional long-term deflection due to creep can be as much as two times the initial elastic creep can be as much as two times the initial elastic deflection.

Choice of Construction Materials (Steel or Reinforced Concrete)
1. The height and span of the building. – Concrete members get large and heavy.
2. The usage of the building. – Fire, Chemical Facilities.
3. Erection Time. – Steel frames can be erected more quickly than concrete structures.
4. The local material market and the local labor market.
5. The soil condition of the construction site and the local weather condition.
6. Architectural Consideration.

Steel Construction   Reinforce Concrete Construction

1.3 Materials

> **Concrete** is a mixture of
> 1. Coarse Aggregate; Gravel, Crushed Rock
> 2. Fine Aggregate; Sand
> 3. Cement Paste; Cement + Water
> 4. (Admixture)

Concrete is a composite material composed of coarse granular material (the aggregate of filler) embedded in a hard matrix of material (the cement or binder) that fills the space between the aggregate particles and glues them together.

Air: 6%
Cement: 10%
Water: 18%
Sand: 25%
Gravel: 41%

Concrete = Filler + Binder

1. Portland **Cement** – The active ingredient that "glues" the other materials together, conforming to ASTM C 150. The raw materials used in Portland cement consist mainly of limestone, and clays & shale. Different types of Portland cement include:
   Type I – General purpose
   Type II – Sulfate resisting
   Type III – High early strength
   Type IV – Low heat of hydration
   Type V – High sulfate resistance

2. **Water** – Water is necessary to create the chemical reaction of hardening the cement called "hydration." It should be clean and free from any impurities (i.e., potable).

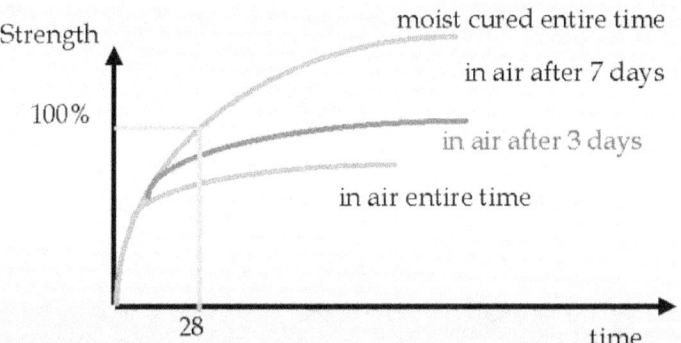

3. **Aggregates** – Aggregates typically occupy 70% to 75% of the volume of the hardened concrete mass.

a. Fine aggregate (sand) and
   b. Coarse aggregate (gravel), typically ¾" dia. max. In no case shall the aggregate size be larger than 75% of the spacing between bars.

4. **Admixtures** – Other ingredients added to enhance properties:
   a. Air Entrainment – Tiny bubbles used to reduce cracking in concrete subject to freeze-thaw cycles. Conforming to ASTM C 260 with an air content of 4% - 8% by volume.
   b. Super Plasticizers – Also called "High Range Water Reducers", used to increase concrete's flow (workability) instead of adding water.
   c. Retarders – Used to slow the hydration process.
   d. Accelerators – Used to speed-up the curing process.
   e. Insulating beads – Increases the "R" value, but diminishes strength.
   f. Fly Ash – The byproduct of coal-burning electric generating plants. Used to decrease the amount of Portland cement required. Maximum fly ash content should not exceed 25% of the volume of Portland cement.

1.4 How concrete develop strength? - Hydration

Concrete is prepared by mixing cement, water, and aggregate together to make a workable paste. It is molded or placed as desired, consolidated, and then left to harden. Concrete does not need to dry out in order to harden as commonly thought. As a matter of fact, the cement needs moisture to hydrate and cure (harden). When concrete dries, it actually stops getting stronger. Concrete with too little water may be dry but is not fully reacted. The properties of such a concrete would be less than that of a wet concrete. The reaction of water with the cement in concrete is extremely important to its properties and reactions may continue for many years. This very important reaction is call hydration. Hydration is a chemical process in which the cement powder reacts with water and then **sets** and **hardens** into a stone-like, solid mass bonding the aggregates together. This chemical change is irreversible and heat is released during the hydration process. In large masses like a dam, heat is dissipated slowly so temperature rises and volume expands. As a result, later cooling causes contraction which leads to shrinkage cracking.

Cement + H_2O + Aggregates = Hardened Concrete + Energy (Heat)

CONCRETE AS STRUCTURAL MATERIAL

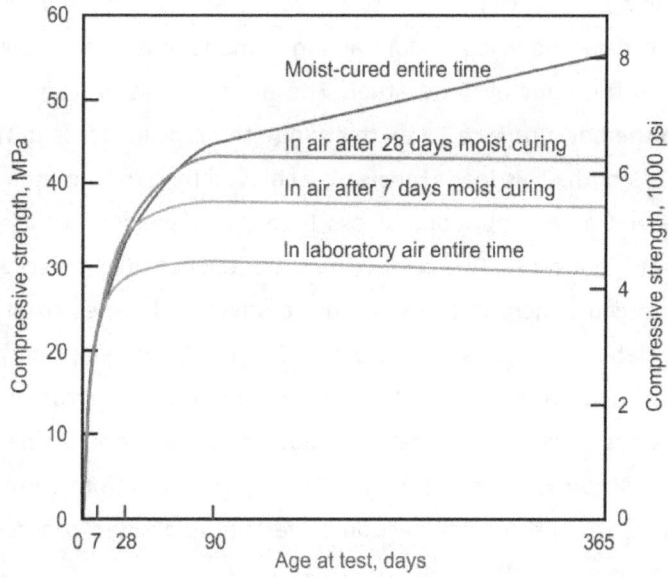

Curing of Concrete (preferably for 14 days at least 7 days)

When concrete is born—when you place fresh concrete where you want it to live out its life—it's like a baby: very sensitive and easily ruined. If you take good care of it when it's young, it will grow up to be a strong and reliable adult. Curing is all of the things that we do to keep our concrete baby happy during the first week or so of its life: maintain the proper temperature (neither too hot nor too cold) and provide enough clean water. Curing is easy to skip in the instant but that will have a major impact on the quality of the concrete structures. While curing is important for all concrete, the problems that arise from not curing are most obvious with horizontal surfaces. An uncured slab, whether decorative or plain gray, is likely to develop a pattern of fine cracks and once it's in use the surface will have low strength that can result in a dusting surface that has little resistance to abrasion.

1. Moisture   – Enough clean water that you could drink
2. Temperature   – Not too high not too cold (especially below freezing)
3. No Shocking   – Micro-crack may be formed

1.5 Steel Reinforced Concrete

As with most rock-like materials, concrete has a relatively high compressive strength but very low tensile strength. Reinforced concrete is a combination of concrete and steel. The steel reinforcement provides the tensile strength lacking in the concrete while the concrete protects steel reinforcement from fire, corrosion and buckling. The reinforcement in a RC 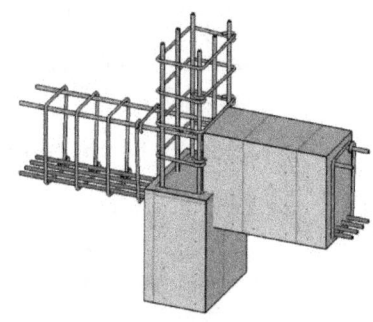 structure, such as a steel bar, has to undergo the same strain or deformation as the surrounding concrete in order to prevent discontinuity, slip or separation of the two materials under load. Maintaining composite action requires transfer of load between the concrete and steel. The direct stress is transferred from the concrete to the bar interface so as to change the tensile stress in the reinforcing bar along its length. This load transfer is achieved by means of bond (anchorage) and is idealized as a continuous stress field that develops in the vicinity of the steel-concrete interface. The relative cross-sectional area of steel required for typical reinforced concrete is usually quite small and varies from 1% for most beams and slabs to 6% for some columns. Reinforcing bars are normally round in cross-section and vary in diameter. Reinforced concrete structures sometimes have provisions such as ventilated hollow cores to control their moisture & humidity. Distribution of concrete (in spite of reinforcement) strength characteristics along the cross-section of vertical reinforced concrete elements is inhomogeneous

1.6 Compatibility of Concrete and Steel

It is notable that the advantages of one material make up the disadvantage of the other.

1. Reinforcing bars make up the great shortcoming of concrete, lack of tensile strength.
2. The coefficient of thermal expansion is similar for concrete and steel, so when reinforced concretes freezes or gets hot, the two materials contract and expand similarly. If they didn't, the combination would tear itself apart over time.
3. The bond between reinforcing steel bars (rebar) and concrete is strong and efficient. The rebar has surface deformations (ridges) to further improve that bond. Due to the strong bond, the concrete effectively transfers stresses to the steel and vice versa.
4. When the cement paste contacts the steel rebar, it forms a non-reactive surface film that inhibits corrosion. This passivation process helps rebar from corroding inside the reinforced concrete.
5. The location of the rebar in the structure depends on the use. Simple beams and slabs often only have rebar only on the tension (bottom) side. When a continuous beam spans over top of columns, the tension is at the top of the beam, so rebar is needed at the top of the beam over column supports.

Advantage/Disadvantage of Concrete and Steel

	Concrete	Steel
Advantage	Considerable **Compressive** strength Great **Resistance** to **Fire** Low-**Maintenance** required Very **Rigid** material **Durability** – Chemical, etc.	High **Tensile** & Compressive strength High **Strength**/weight ratio – Light members Formwork not required **Ductile** material High **Quality Control/Little Variation** Speedy construction
Disadvantage	Very low **Tensile** Strength Low strength/weight ratio – **Heavy** members Expensive **Formwork** necessary **Brittle** Material Difficulty in **Quality Control** Longer construction period - curing	High **Cost**/strength ratio **Vulnerable** to **Fire** – Protective cover essential Corrosion - **Maintenance** required **Flexible** material – Deformation, Vibration Low resistance to chemicals

1.7 Structural Properties of Steel

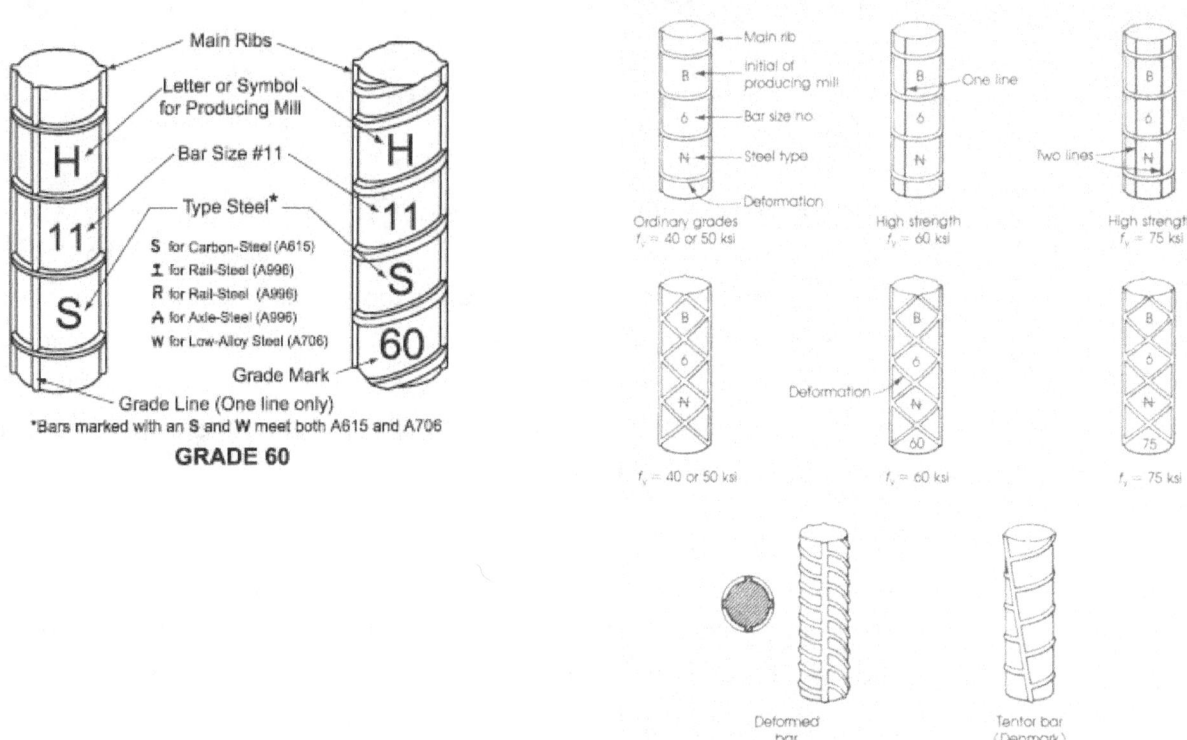

Tensile Testing

A tensile test, also known as tension test, is the most fundamental type of mechanical test to be performed on a material. Tensile tests are simple, relatively inexpensive, and fully standardized. As a tensile test specimen is being pulled, its stress and strain are continuously recorded. The resulting curve shows how the material behaves to the forces being applied. The two major points of interest on the test curve are "Yield Strength" and "Ultimate Strength" of the material.

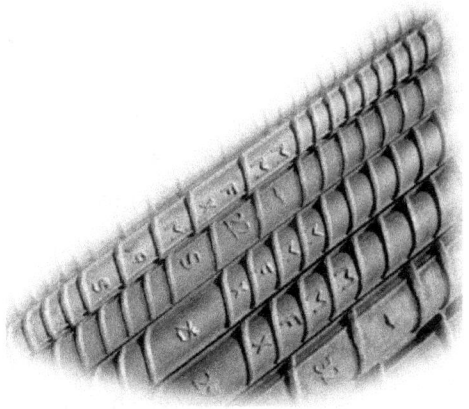

Tensile Test Curve

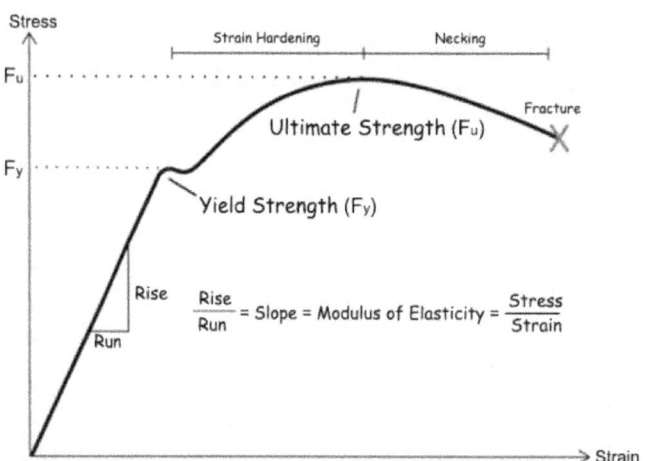

Hooke's Law

For most tensile testing of materials, it is noticed that the initial portion of the relationship between the applied force and the elongation of the specimen is linear. In this linear region, the line obeys the relationship defined as "Hooke's Law" where the ratio of stress to strain is a constant. **E** is the slope of the line in this region where stress (**f**) is proportional to strain (**ε**) and is called the "Modulus of Elasticity" or "Young's Modulus".

Modulus of Elasticity

The modulus of elasticity is a measure of the stiffness of the material, but it only applies in the linear region of the curve. If a specimen is loaded within this linear region, the material will return to its exact same condition if the load is removed. At the point that the curve is no longer linear and deviates from the straight-line relationship, Hooke's Law no longer applies and some permanent deformation

CONCRETE AS STRUCTURAL MATERIAL

occurs in the specimen. This point is called the "elastic limit". From this point on in the tensile test, the material reacts plastically to any further increase in load or stress. It does not return to its original, unstressed condition even if the load is removed.

Yield Strength

A value called "yield strength" of a material is defined as the stress applied to the material at which plastic deformation starts to occur while the material is loaded.

Ultimate Tensile Strength

The ultimate strength is the maximum stress the specimen sustains during the test before rupture occurs. This all depends on type of material.

Brittle and Ductile Behavior

The behavior of materials can be broadly classified into two categories; brittle and ductile. The two categories can be distinguished by comparing the stress-strain curves. The area under the stress strain curve represents the energy absorbed in the tensile test. If the material is capable of absorbing a lot of energy before rupture occurs, it is ductile. Steel and aluminum usually fall in the class of ductile materials. Glass and cast iron fall in the class of brittle materials. These differences are a major consideration for structural design. Ductile materials exhibit large

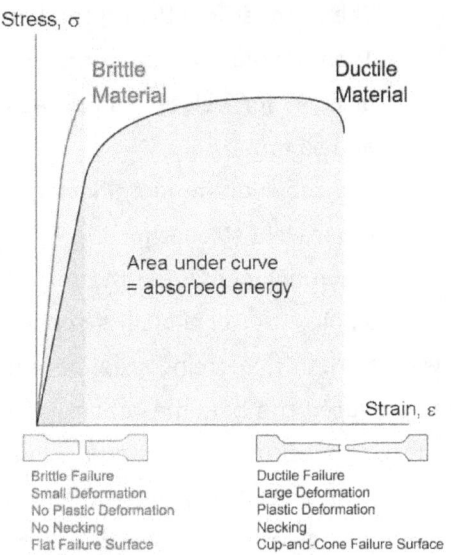

strains and yielding before they fail. On the contrary, brittle materials fail suddenly and without much warning. Thus ductile materials such as steel are a natural choice for structural members in buildings as considerable warning is desirable before a building fails. It is observed from stress-strain curves that ductile materials are capable of absorbing much larger quantities of energy before failure.

1.8 Steel Reinforcement

Reinforcing steel bars (re-bars) are used to help concrete withstand tension forces. Concrete by nature is sufficiently strong to compression forces, although tension forces can crack concrete. Deformed rebars on reinforcing steel was made a standard requirement since 1968, however, plain rebars are also used in situations where the reinforcing steel is expected to slide as usually installed in highway pavement and in segmental bridges. The deformed patter on a rebar will help the concrete to adhere to the reinforcing steel surface. The pattern on a deformed bar is not specified, however, the spacing, and the height of the 'bumps' is regulated.

Rebar: Reinforcing Steel Bar Specifications

Reinforcing bars are hot-rolled using different steel materials. Most rebars are rolled from new steel billets, while others are rolled from steel debris or railroad rails. Rebars are required to contain some sort of identification that could be used to identify the mill that produced the reinforcing steel bar. The ASTM (American Society for Testing and Materials) has created a standard identification ruling that all rebars must comply with:

1. The Number identifying the bar size.
2. Type of steel symbol, for example, means the bar was rolled from a new billet, W for weldable steel (ASTM A-706), A for Axle (M 322 / ASTM 966) and so on.
3. The rebar grade identification, either 60 or 75. This grade indicates the rebar yield strength.
4. A symbol identifying the manufacturer that rolled the bar. It is usually a single letter or a plain symbol.

Lower strength reinforcing steel bars has only three marks that identify the mill that produced the bar, the rebar size and the type of steel used. High strength reinforcing steel uses a continuous line system to show steel grade. If the rebar contains two lines it indicates that the rebar was rolled into the 75,000 psi bars, however, when a single line is present, it represents a 60,000 psi bar.

1.9 Structural Properties of Concrete

Compressive Strength (f_c') :

The compressive strength (f_c') of concrete is determined using 6 in by 12 in concrete cylinder that is 28 day old. Values of f_c' are based on 28 days of curing. The condition in which concrete cures significantly affects the ultimate strength of the hardened concrete's f_c'. Allowing the freshly-placed concrete to have continuous moisture applied will significantly increase the strength, f_c'. Conversely, subjecting the freshly-placed concrete to constant air will decrease the f_c'.

CONCRETE AS STRUCTURAL MATERIAL

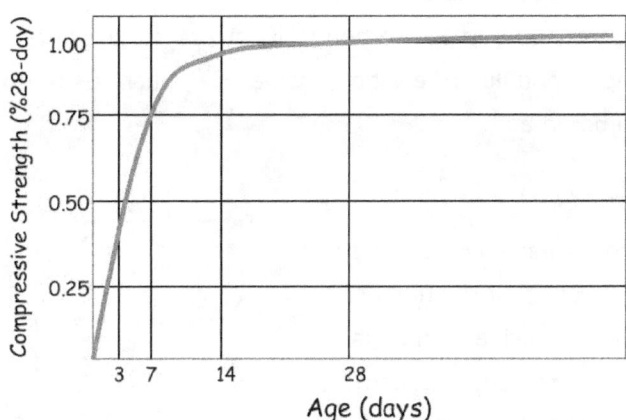

Typical ranges of f_c' are:
- a) slab-on-grade, footings, foundation walls   = 3 ksi
- b) beams, framed slabs   = 3.5 ksi – 5 ksi
- c) columns   = 4 ksi – 10 ksi

f_c' = 3 ksi or 4 ksi concrete is commonly used in most reinforced concrete structures. The specified concrete compressive strength, f_c', is actually a certain level of stress. It is the most important structural property of concrete and is decidedly dependent upon the water-to-cement ratio.

1.10 Water Cement Ratio

The water cement ratio is obtained by dividing the weight of water by the weight of cement. A low w/c ratio yields high f_c' and high w/c ratio does low f_c'. A low w/c ratio is very stiff and difficult to work with and to consolidate into formwork. Normal concrete has w/c ratios ranging from about 0.25 (very stiff) up to a maximum of about 0.50 but preferably should not exceed 0.45.

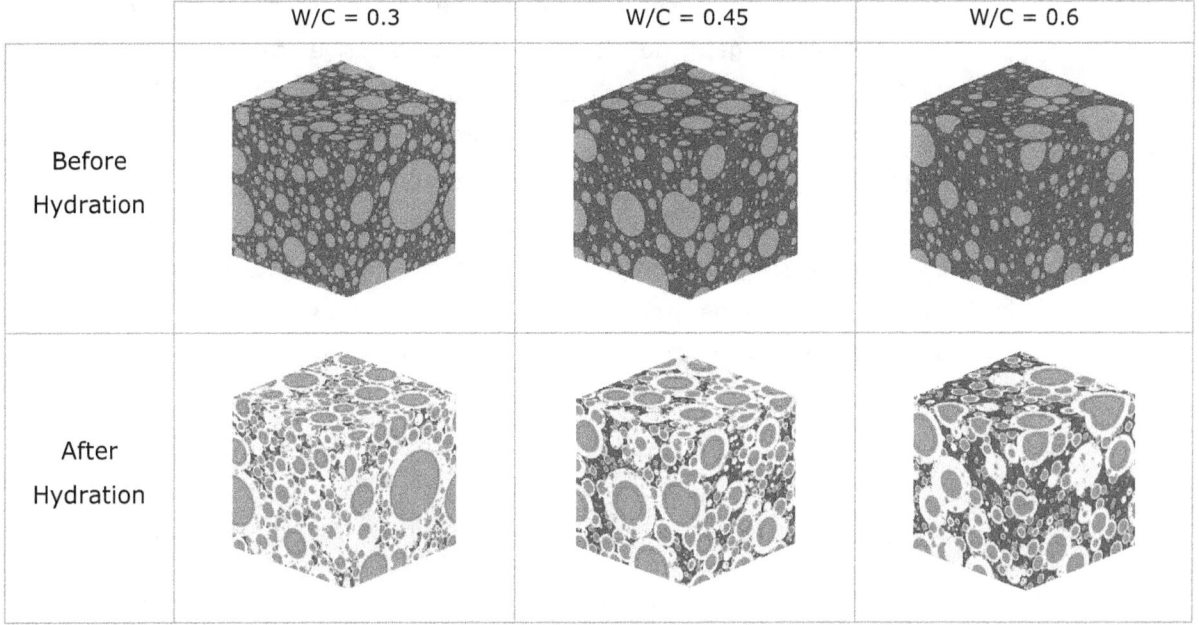

Modulus of Elasticity of Concrete

Because concrete has no linear portion to its stress-strain curve, it is difficult to measure a proper modulus of elasticity value. For concretes up to about 6 ksi it can be approximated as:

$$E_c = 57000 \sqrt{f_c'}$$

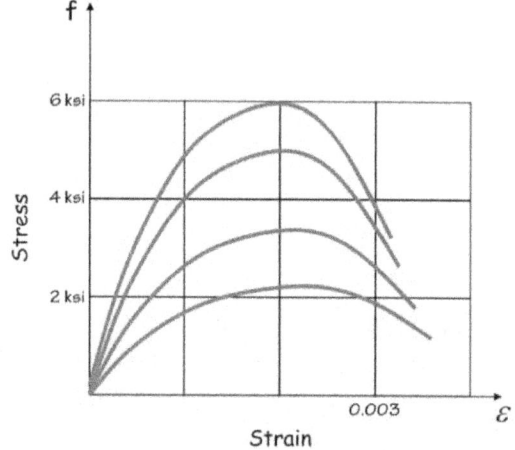

where, f_c' is the compressive strength in psi. It is important that the units of f_c' be expressed in psi and not ksi whenever the square root is taken). The weight density of reinforced concrete using normal sand and stone aggregates is about 150 lb/ft³. If 5 lb/ft³ of this is allowed for the steel and the unit weight is taken as 145 lb/ft³. E_c values computed have proven to be acceptable for use in deflection calculations.

Shrinkage

As concrete cures it shrinks because the water not used for hydration gradually evaporates from the hardened mix. For large continuous elements such shrinkage can result in the development of excess tensile stress, particularly if high water content brings about a large shrinkage. Concrete, like all materials, also undergoes volume changes due to thermal effects, and in hot weather the heat from the hydration process adds to this problem. Since concrete is weak in tension, it will often develop cracks due to such shrinkage and temperature changes. For example, when a freshly placed concrete slab-on-grade expands due to temperature change, it develops internal compressive stresses as it overcomes the friction between it and the ground surface. Later when the concrete cools land shrinks as it hardens and tries to contract, it is not strong enough in tension to resist the same frictional forces. For this reason contraction joints are often used to control the location of cracks that inevitably occur and so-called temperature and shrinkage reinforcement is placed in directions where reinforcing has not already been specified for other reasons. The purpose of this reinforcing is to accommodate the resulting tensile stresses and to minimize the width of cracks that do develop.

Creep

Creep is a continued deflection under a constant loading as time passes, e.g., sagging of wooden bookshelf. In addition to strains caused by shrinkage and thermal effects, concrete also deforms due to creep. Creep is increasing deformation that takes place when a material sustains a high stress level over a long time period. Whenever constantly applied loads (such as dead loads) cause significant compressive stresses to occur, creep will result. In a beam, for example, the additional long-term deflection due to creep can be as much as two times the initial elastic deflection The way to avoid this increased deformation is to keep the stresses due to sustained loads at a low level. This is usually done by adding compression steel.

Workability

The workability is the ability of a fresh concrete mix to fill the form/mold properly with the desired work (vibration) and without reducing the concrete's quality. Workability is measured by a standard slump test. This is a good indication of the water content of a mix and thus the workability. In this test a metal cone 12 in tall is filled with fresh concrete in a specified manner. When the cone is lifted, the mass of concrete "slumps" downward and the vertical drop is referred to as the slump. Most concrete mixes have slumps in the 2- to 5-in range.

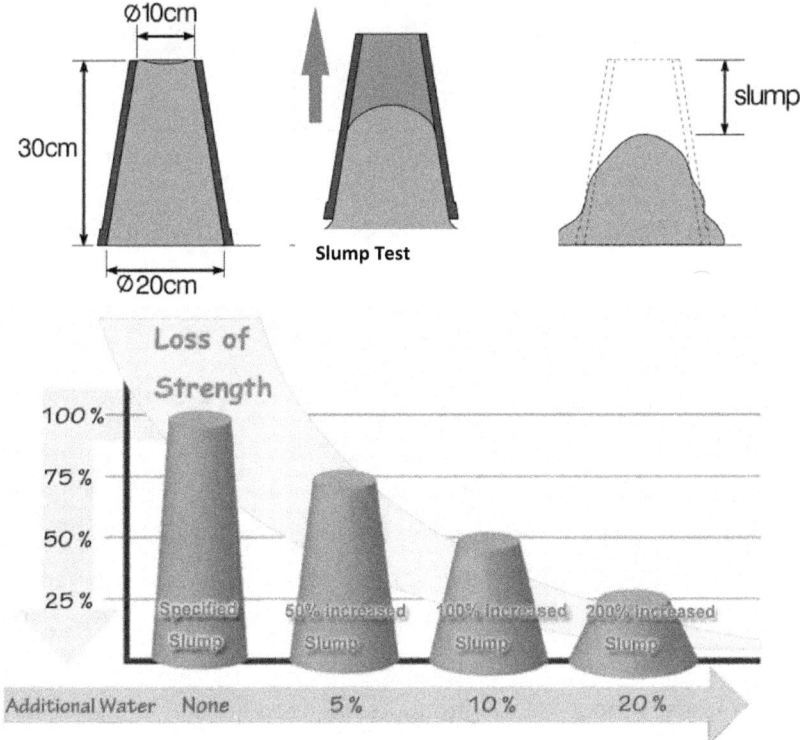

Slump Test

Water-Strength Relationship

2. STRUCTURAL ANALYSIS AND DESIGN

2.1 Structure

Structure is load-carrying system of building transmitting applied loads through the various members down into the foundations. The primary purpose of a structure is to transmit or support loads.

> **Primary Functions of Structure**
> 1. Strength
> 2. Stability
> 3. Serviceability
> 4. Economy
> 5. Aesthetics

Each structural system may be composed of one or more of the four basic types of structures:
1. Trusses
2. Frames
3. Cables and Arches
4. Surface Structures

If the structure is improperly designed or fabricated, or if the actual applied loads exceed the design specifications, the device will probably fail to perform its intended function, with possible serious consequences. A well-engineered structure greatly minimizes the possibility of costly failures. The basic objective in structural analysis and design is to produce a structure capable of resisting all applied loads without failure during its intended life.

Structural Analysis and Design

1. Structural analysis is finding out the effects (responses and behaviors) of loads on structures. The main objective of structural analysis is to determine

internal member forces, resulting stresses and deformations of structural systems under various load effects. Given a cross section, concrete strength, reinforcement size and location, and yield strength, compute the resistance or strength. In analysis there should be one unique answer.

2. Structural design is the methodical investigation of the stability, strength and rigidity of structures. With a set of forces are given, the structural elements are proportioned in a structural design process by checking the adequacy of the individual structural members. For new structures, iterative process between analysis and design is necessary because the sizes, shapes and configurations of the members are not determined yet. Given a factored design moment, normally designated as select a suitable cross section, including dimensions, concrete strength, reinforcement, and so on. In design there are many possible solutions.

Although both types of problem are based on the same principles, the procedure is different in each case. Analysis is easier, because all of the decisions concerning reinforcement, beam size, and so on have been made, and it is only necessary to apply the strength calculation principles to determine the capacity. Design, on the other hand, involves the choice of section dimensions, material strengths, and reinforcement placement to produce a cross section that can resist the moments due to factored loads. Because the analysis problem is easier, this chapter deals with section analysis to develop the fundamental concepts before considering design in the next chapter.

Classification of Structural Members

Tension Member is the simplest form of a structural member which carries tension forces along the member axis.

Beam is a flexure member of the structure and carries loads transverse to their long member axis. These loads create shear force and bending moment in the beam

Column carries compression forces along the member axis.

Beam-Column is a structural member subjected to compression as well as flexure.

Plate and Slabs – Plates are three dimensional flat structural components usually made of metal that are often found in floors and roofs of building structures. Slabs are similar to plates except that they are usually made of concrete.

2.2 Loads on Structures
Gravity Loads

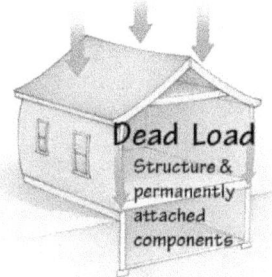

Dead Load - Gravity loads of constant magnitudes and fixed positions that act permanently on the structure. Such loads consist of the weights of the structural system itself and of all other non-structural elements and equipment permanently attached to the structural system. Weights of permanent equipment, such as heating and air-conditioning systems, are usually obtained from the manufacturer.

Live Load - Gravity loads of varying magnitudes and/or positions caused by the use of the building. Furthermore, the position of a live load may change, so each member of the structure must be designed for the position of the load that causes the maximum stress in that member. Live loads include the weights of furniture, occupants, stored materials, appliances, vehicles. (floor live load & roof live load)

Snow Load - Design snow load for a structure is based on the ground snow load for its geographic location, exposure to wind and its thermal, geometric, and functional characteristics. In most cases, there is less snow on the roof than on the ground. The effects of non-uniform drift snow load must be properly addressed.

Rain Load – When it rains over the snow accumulated on roof, the rain water may increase the roof loads. For flat roofs, where water accumulates on roof faster than it runs off thus increases the roof loads, ponding failure may occur. Typically, roofs with slopes of 0.25 in/ft or greater are not subjected to ponding unless roof drains become clogged.

Roof Live Load - A load on a roof produced during maintenance by workers, equipment, and materials and during the life of the structure by movable objects, such as planters or other similar small decorative appurtenances that are not occupancy related.

Lateral Loads
Wind Load

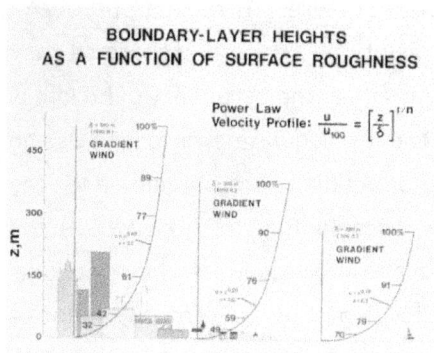

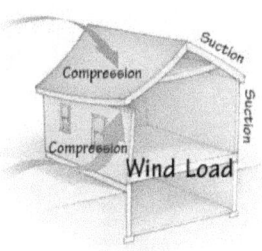

Wind loads are produced by the flow of wind around structures and create pressure on the windward surfaces and suction on the leeward surfaces including roof. When the wind blows close to the ground, obstructions near the ground create turbulence and friction, lowering the average wind speed. The higher is the obstructions, the greater the turbulence and the lower the wind speed. As a general rule, wind speed increases with height. Wind load magnitudes vary in proportion to the distance from proportion to the distance from the base of the structure, peak wind speed, type of terrain, importance factor, and side of building and roof slope.

Earthquake Load

An earthquake is a sudden undulation of a portion of the earth's surface. Although the ground surface moves in both horizontal and vertical directions during an earthquake, the magnitude of the vertical component of ground motion is usually small and does not have a significant impact on most structures. Thus, seismic loads are often simulated by a series of horizontal forces.

Other Loads
Impact Load

An impact is a high force or shock applied over a short time period. Such a force or acceleration usually has a greater effect than a static load which is applied over a proportionally longer time period of time.

Fatigue Load

Fatigue occurs when a material is subjected to repeated loading and unloading causing stress reversal. The nominal maximum stress values are less than the ultimate tensile stress limit, and may be below the yield stress limit of the material.

2.3 Building Codes

A building code is a set of law requirements that specify the minimum acceptable level of safety for buildings and structures. The main purpose of building codes is to protect public health, safety and general welfare as they  relate to the construction and occupancy of buildings and structures. The law requirements for the design and construction of buildings are obtained from the various codes applicable for the area where the construction is done. Many countries have national building codes, developed by government agencies and applied to all building and construction work across the country. Many local jurisdictions have developed their own specific codes. In America, New York and Chicago are the only two cities to use their own city-specific guidelines. The major model building codes used in the United States are developed by the International Code Council (ICC), which have 14 sets of International codes including the International Building Code (IBC) and others.

Local Codes	Building Code of the City of New York
	Chicago Building Code
	Georgia State Building Code, etc.
Regional Codes	Uniform Building Code (UBC) : west of the Mississippi
	Standard Building Code (SBC) : southeastern states
	Building Official's Conference of America (BOCA) : northeastern states
National Codes	International Building Code (IBC), ASCE7

2.4 Design Specifications

How is a structural design done? (How to achieve requirements mandated by building codes)

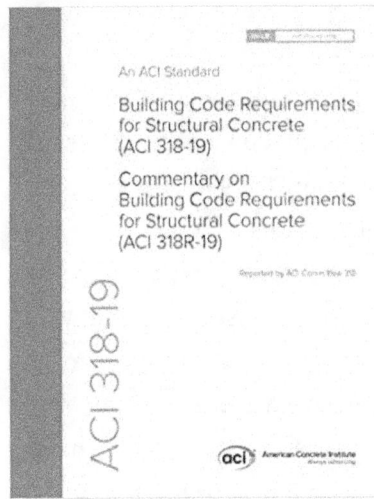

All reinforced concrete structures and structural elements must be proportioned so that no strength limit state is exceeded when subjected to all required factored load combinations. To achieve this goal efficiently, structural design is carried out by a set of design rules called specifications. The American Concrete Institute (ACI) has released ACI 318-19, "Building Code Requirements for Structural Concrete and Commentary." ACI 318-19 is a standard for all concrete design, construction, inspection, repair, and research professionals. It contains the latest code requirements for concrete building design and construction alongside the corresponding commentary, and includes many improvements and changes from the 2008 edition, ACI 318-08. The manual contains additional tables of design data and other useful design information.

Design Specifications for Reinforced Concrete

The first set of building regulations for reinforced concrete was drafted under the leadership of Professor Mörsch of the University of Stuttgart and was issued in Prussia in 1904. Design regulations were issued in Britain, France, Austria, and Switzerland between 1907 and 1909. The American Railway Engineering Association appointed a Committee on Masonry in 1890. In 1903 this committee presented specifications for Portland cement concrete. Between 1908 and 1910, a series of committee reports led to the Standard Building Regulations for the Use of Reinforced Concrete, published in 1910 by the National Association of Cement Users, which subsequently became the American Concrete Institute. A Joint Committee on Concrete and Reinforced Concrete was established in 1904 by the American Society of Civil Engineers, the American Society for Testing and Materials, the American Railway Engineering Association, and the Association of American Portland Cement Manufacturers. This group was later joined by the American Concrete Institute. Between 1904 and 1910, the Joint Committee carried out research. A preliminary report issued in 1913 lists the more important papers and books on reinforced concrete published between 1898 and 1911. The final report of this committee was published in 1916. The history of reinforced concrete building codes in the United States was reviewed in 1954 by Kerekes and Reid.

2.5 ASD and LRFD

ASD – Allowable Stress Design

ASD stands for Allowable Stress Design or, Allowable Strength Design. The Allowable Stress Design is the older or original designation which was used in the 9th Edition of the AISC Steel Construction Manual (1989 AISC) and the old ACI Concrete code (called Working Stress Design). In these codes service level loads where applied to members. The stresses in the members are determined and then checked against a code-specified allowable stress value which accounts for a safety factor. ASD may novice engineers more of a feel for the design as it is easier to better understand how the material and members where stressed. Allowable Strength Design (2005 AISC) – was mostly developed so that engineers who did not want to use LRFD could still use ASD and service level. It differs from the allowable stress design in that it is a 'Strength Design' methodology. The 2005 ASD uses safety factors on the nominal strength of the member based the particular limit state. The 2005 ASD allowable strength values maybe transformed into 1989 ASD stress values by factoring out the appropriate section property. Both ASD methods utilize Limit States Design however they are 'hidden' in the 1989 ASD code. Meaning that in the '05 ASD each limit state is checked (i.e. yielding, local buckling, lateral-torsional buckling, etc.). In the '89 ASD code the allowable stress is reduced to the lowest applicable limit state. They also both take advantage of inelastic behavior in some limit states. For allowable strength design, the design philosophy can be expressed as:

Required Strength (R_u) ≤ Design Strength (R_n/Ω)

Or,

Factored (Load Effects) ≤ Reduced (Nominal Strength)

Load Combinations for ASD

In ASD, the required strength, R_u, is determined from the following load combinations (according to the ASCE7 2010).

    D
    D + **L**
    D + (Lr or S or R)
    D + 0.75**L** + 0.75(Lr or S or R)
    D ± (0.6W or 0.7E)
    D + 0.75**L** + 0.75(0.6W) + 0.75(Lr or S or R)

$D + 0.75L \pm 0.75(0.7E) + 0.75S$

$0.6D \pm (W \text{ or } 0.7E)$

Where,

D = dead load,

L = live load due to occupancy and movable equipment

Lr = live roof load

W = wind load

S = snow load

E = earthquake load

R = initial rainwater load

Loads due to fluids with well-defined pressures and maximum heights (F), loads due to lateral earth pressure, ground water pressure, or pressure of bulk materials (H) and self-straining loads (T) are not common in building structures so that they have been omitted in the load combination for clarity. Combinations of service loads (or, working loads) are evaluated for maximum stresses and compared to allowable stresses. When wind loads are involved, the allowable stresses are typically allowed to increase by 1/3. The allowable stresses are some fraction of limit stresses.

LRFD – Load Resistance Factor Design

LRFD refers to Load and Resistance Factor Design which is also a Limit States Design methodology. This method uses a load factor to **factor up** (or down in some load combinations) service level loads and also reduce member strength based on reliability and statistical data. When using LRFD, the strength must be based on the LRFD load combinations and factors. However, deflection should be based on service level loads, so it is critical to keep track of the design loads. In the 2005 AISC both the ASD and LRFD methods for determining nominal strengths are presented side by side. The nominal strength will be the same for both methods and only the allowable strength will differ due to the fact that the safety factor (Ω) applied for ASD and the strength reduction factor, or resistance factor, (ϕ) applied for LRFD will be different. These factors have nothing to do with structural loads. Resistance factors are generally less than 1.0 to account for uncertainties involved such as:

1. Variations in member dimensions
2. Variations in material properties
3. Construction tolerances and errors
4. Effects of simplifying assumptions in analysis

In LRFD, risks involved are assessed using reliability studies. Thus, it is a more reliable and statistical based method for predicting loads and material strengths. Whereas the safety factors in ASD are based on engineering judgment and past experiences. It seems in most situations LRFD will produce a smaller sized beam based on strength but not always. Also, serviceability and deflection control many designs, in which case both methods will yield the same result as the design is not based on strength in those cases. The Manual of Steel Construction LRFD, 3rd ed. by the American Institute of Steel Construction requires that:

$$\Sigma \gamma Q \leq \phi R_n \text{ or,}$$

$\sum$ (load factors × Loads) ≤ resistance factor × resistance
where,

γ = load factor for the type of load
Q = load effects
R_n = nominal strength
ϕ = resistance factor (generally less than 1.0)

The design philosophy of LRFD can be simply expressed:

Factored **Load** Effects ≤ Reduced (or, Factored) **Resistance**

Required Strength (R_u) ≤ Design Strength (ϕR_n)

Nominal strength is defined as the capacity of a structure or component to resist the effects of loads, as determined by computations using specified material strengths (such as yield strength, F_y, or ultimate strength, F_u) and dimensions and formulas derived from accepted principles of structural mechanics or by field tests or laboratory tests of scaled models, allowing for modeling effects and differences between laboratory and field conditions. Resistance factors vary based on type of failure mode. Typical resistance factors for structural steel are:

- 0.90 for flexure, shear, compression, & tensile yielding
- 0.75 for tensile fracture

Load Factors and Load Combinations for LRFD

In LRFD, the required strength, $\Sigma \gamma Q$, of each structural element or structural assembly must equal or exceed the design strength based on the following combinations of factored nominal loads from ASCE 7 (2010):

1.4**D**

1.2**D** + 1.6**L** + 0.5(Lr or S or R)

1.2**D** + 1.6(Lr or S or R) + 0.5(L or W)

1.2**D** + 1.0W + 0.5 **L** + 0.5(Lr or S or R)

1.2**D** + 1.0E + 0.5 **L** + 0.2S

… STRUCTURAL ANALYSIS AND DESIGN

$0.9D \pm 1.0W$

$0.9D \pm 1.0E$

where:
D = dead load,
L = live load due to occupancy and movable equipment
Lr = live roof load
W = wind load
S = snow load
E = earthquake load
R = initial rainwater load

Loads due to fluids with well-defined pressures and maximum heights (F), loads due to lateral earth pressure, ground water pressure, or pressure of bulk materials (H) and self-straining loads (T) are not common in building structures so that they have been omitted in the load combination for clarity. Combinations of 'factored loads' are evaluated for maximum member forces, bending moments or stresses. These load factors take into consideration how likely the load is to happen and how often. This "imaginary" worse case load, moment or stress is compared to a limit value that has been modified by a resistance factor. The resistance factor is a function of how "comfortable" the design community is with the type of limit, i.e., yielding or rupture.

Location of re-bars

Concrete is weak in tension but relatively strong in compression. Therefore,

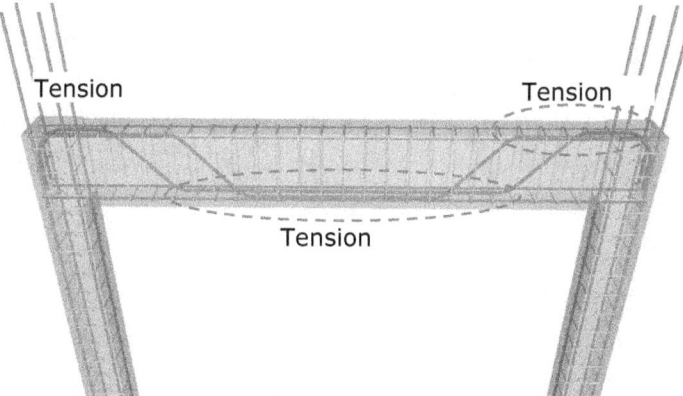

reinforcement is needed to resist the tensile stresses resulting from the bending moments. Additional reinforcement sometimes added to the compression zones to reduce long term deflection. Steel is a high-cost material compared to concrete. Thus, the two materials are best used in combination if the concrete is made to resist the compressive stresses and the steel the tensile stresses. The steel reinforcements must be placed wherever tension side of bending moment is.

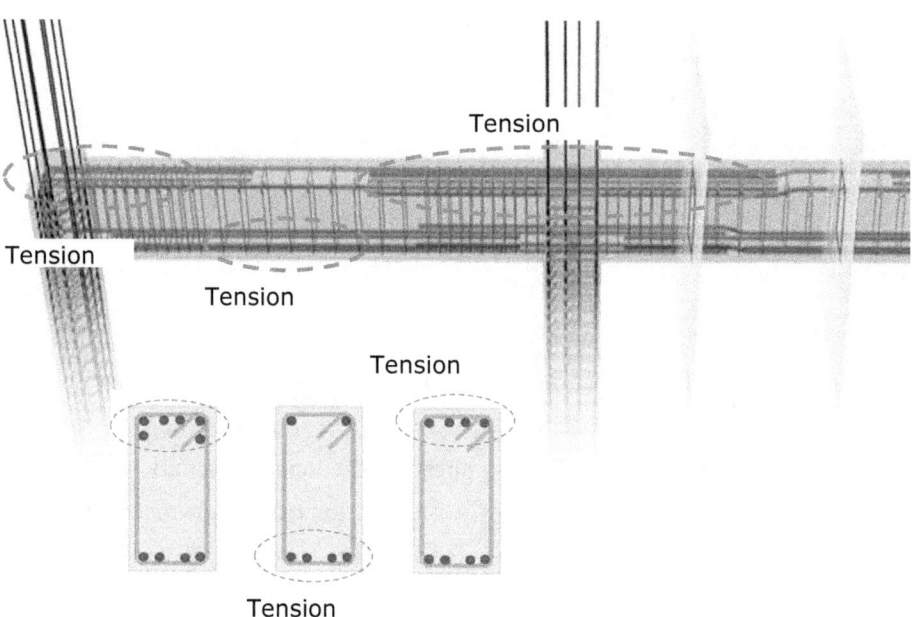

Frames where no seismic design is required

The following frame is composed by two columns and one beam and it bears 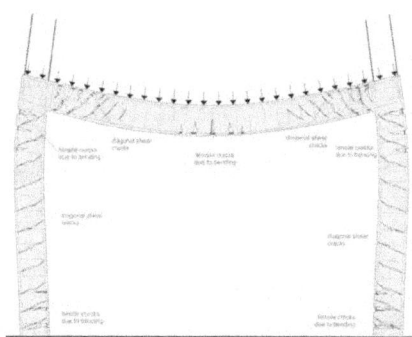 only gravity loads i.e. no seismic loading is applied. The following figure shows the concrete deformations and cracks. They are presented in a very large scale so as to thoroughly comprehend the way the members behave. In reality they are so small that they are not visible to the human eye. The tensile stresses applied to some areas of concrete cause the formation of cracks; therefore, in those areas the necessary reinforcement is placed. When the cracks are perpendicular to the axis of the member, longitudinal reinforcement is placed i.e. rebars that prevent the expansion of the hairline cracking. When the cracks are diagonal, transverse reinforcement i.e. stirrups is placed to control them. In the case where the frame is subjected to gravity loads only and seismic forces are not supposed to be applied to it, the diagonal cracking could be controlled with the use of diagonal reinforcement.

Frames where seismic design is required

The following frame is exactly the same with the frame mentioned above. Both frames will be-have in exactly the same way through their lifetime except in those few seconds during an earthquake. An earthquake ground motion causes horizontal displacements that in their turn cause horizontal inertia forces, forces generated by the sudden change in the kinetic state of the

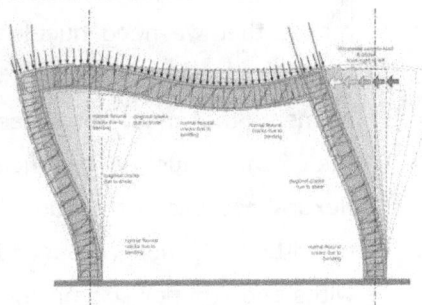

body. During the seismic action the applied horizontal forces constantly shift direction. This results in a continuous change in the frame's behavior, consequently the tensile stresses and thus the inclined cracks appear in different positions and directions. This position- direction alteration is the reason why earthquake design and reinforcement detailing are so critical in areas with high seismic activity.

Fundamental rules seismic resistant structural systems

The following rules regarding the proper placement of reinforcement, derive from the behavior of structures:

Columns:
a. Rebars must be symmetrically placed around the perimeter of the cross section since the tensile forces and therefore the inclined cracking constantly change direction.
b. There must be enough, high strength and properly anchored stirrups. This reinforcement protects the member from the large diagonal cracks of alternating direction, caused by the diagonal stressing or otherwise called shear.

Beams:
a. Rebars placed in the beams lower part must be as well anchored as those placed in the upper part. This happens because tension and therefore the resulting transverse cracking, continuously change place during a seismic action and as a consequence in critical earthquakes, tensile stresses appear to the lower fibers of the supports.
b. There must be enough, high strength and properly anchored stirrups because the high intensity of the diagonal stresses and thus the large inclined diagonal cracking, shift direction during an earthquake.

No matter how "well designed" a structure is, either because of exceeded design seismic forces or because of local conditions during the construction, one or possibly more structural members will exceed their design strength. In case of an earthquake greater than the design earthquake we don't want failure (fracture) of any member even if it remains permanently deformed, this means that we need ductile structural members. In case of an extremely intense earthquake, where failure of some members is unavoidable, the elements that must not exceed their strength are columns. This means that the columns must have sufficient capacity, over-strength. All failures must be flexural because of their ductile nature as opposed to shear failures that have a brittle behavior (i.e. sudden fracture). By designing the structure to withstand a major seismic incident, something achieved by the use of a high seismic factor, we avoid extensive failures. By providing ductility and capacity to the elements we design against local failures. Local failure may happen for various reasons and if it occurs it may lead to the progressive failure of the structure.

Ductility of Reinforced Concrete Member
Ductility is the ability of a reinforced concrete member to sustain deformation after the loss of its strength, without fracture. In both columns and beams supports, it is required to place a substantial number of stirrups not only to bear the diagonal tension but also to ensure a high level of ductility which is crucial in the case of strong earthquakes. When design seismic actions are exceeded, only one element, the most vulnerable, will overcome its strength capacity. If that element is ductile, it will continue to bear its loading and will give the second most vulnerable element the possibility to contribute its strength. If all members of the structural system have enough ductility the structure's strength will depend on the strength capacity of all the structural members, otherwise it will depend on the strength of the most vulnerable structural member. Columns and beams basically fail in the connection area. Therefore, columns and beams must be enough ductile in the connection area. Strength design ensures that the columns will have greater capacity than the adjacent beams therefore no matter how intense the seismic action will be, beam failure will precede the failure of columns. Failing beams will absorb part of the released seismic energy thus altering the structure's natural (fundamental) frequency and avoiding resonance. Generally, failure of one or more beams does not induce progressive failing. Even in an extremely strong seismic event, the structure will not collapse and will retain a minimum serviceability level allowing its evacuation and most of the times its rehabilitation.

Workshop 2-1

Determine the **Un-Factored Total Loads** for ASD and the **Factored Total Loads** for LRFD

Reality	Unfactored Loads (ASD)	Factored Loads (LRFD)
L.L.=1 k, L.L.=2 k, L.L.=3 k; D.L.=1 k, D.L.=2 k, D.L.=3 k; spans 5', 5', 6', 6'		
LL = 2 k/ft, DL = 1 k/ft; 22 ft		
LL = 4 k, LL = 5 k; DL = 2 k, DL = 3 k; LL = 2 k/ft, DL = 1 k/ft; 3', 3', 4', 3', 3'		
LL = 4 k, LL = 5 k; DL = 1 k/ft; 3', 10', 3'		

STRUCTURAL ANALYSIS AND DESIGN

Case Study 2-2a

W24x62 typical interior beams are spaced 10 ft on center and support a floor dead load of 50 lb/ft² and floor live load of 100 lb/ft². Determine the maximum combined loads in lb/ft that each beam must support. Use the AISC LRFD load combinations.

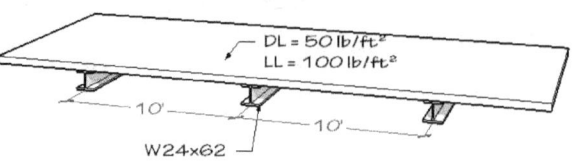

Solution

DL = (50 lb/ft²)(10 ft) + 62 lb/ft = 562 lb/ft

LL = (100 lb/ft²)(10 ft) = 1000 lb/ft

LRFD Load Combinations

1	1.4D	787							=	787
2	1.2D + 1.6L+ 0.5(Lr or S or R)	674	+	1600	+	0			=	2274
3	1.2D + 1.6(Lr or S or R) + (0.5L or 0.8W)	674	+	0	+	500			=	1174
4	1.2D + 1.6W +0.5L+ 0.5(Lr or S or R)	674	+	0	+	500	+	0	=	1174
5	1.2D + 1.0E + 0.5L +0.2S	674	+	0	+	500	+	0	=	1174
6	0.9D + (1.6W or 1.0E)	506	+	0					=	506

Answer: The governing load combination is #2 and the factored load is 2274 lb/ft.

Case Study 2-2b

W18x60 typical interior beams are spaced as shown and support a floor dead load of 50 lb/ft² and floor live load of 80 lb/ft². Determine the maximum combined loads in lb/ft that each beam must support. Use the AISC LRFD load combinations.

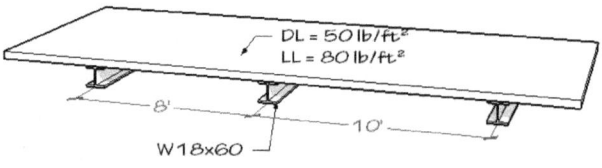

Solution

DL =

LL =

LRFD Load Combinations

1	1.4D						=
2	1.2D + 1.6L+ 0.5(Lr or S or R)		+		+		=
3	1.2D + 1.6(Lr or S or R) + (0.5L or 0.8W)		+		+		=
4	1.2D + 1.6W +0.5L+ 0.5(Lr or S or R)		+		+	+	=
5	1.2D + 1.0E + 0.5L +0.2S		+		+	+	=
6	0.9D + (1.6W or 1.0E)		+				=

Answer:

STRUCTURAL ANALYSIS AND DESIGN

Case Study 2-2a

A roof system is supported by W16x40 sections that are spaced 10 ft on center. Determine the governing factored load in lb/ft that the beam must support. The roof system supports a dead load of 35 lb/ft^2, a snow load of 30 lb/ft^2 and a wind load of 20 lb/ft^2

Solution

$$D = (35 \text{ lb/ft}^2)(10 \text{ ft}) + 40 \text{ lb/ft} = 390 \text{ lb/ft}$$

$$L = 0 \text{ lb/ft}$$

$$S = (30 \text{ lb/ft}^2)(10 \text{ ft}) = 300 \text{ lb/ft}$$

$$W = (20 \text{ lb/ft}^2)(10 \text{ ft}) = 200 \text{ lb/ft}$$

LRFD Load Combinations

#	Combination										
1	1.4D	546								=	546
2	1.2D + 1.6L + 0.5(Lr or S or R)	468	+	0	+	150				=	618
3	1.2D + 1.6(Lr or S or R) + (0.5L or 0.8W)	468	+	480	+	160				=	1108
4	1.2D + 1.6W + 0.5L + 0.5(Lr or S or R)	468	+	320	+	0	+	150		=	938
5	1.2D + 1.0E + 0.5L + 0.2S	468	+	0	+	0	+	60		=	528
6	0.9D + (1.6W or 1.0E)	351	+	320						=	671
7	0.9D - (1.6W or 1.0E)	351	+	-320						=	31

Answer: The governing factored load is 1108 lb/ft.

Case Study 2-2b

A roof system is supported by W21x50 sections that are spaced 8 ft on center. Determine the governing factored load in lb/ft that the beam must support. The roof system supports a dead load of 40 lb/ft^2, a snow load of 25 lb/ft^2 and a wind load of 10 lb/ft^2

Solution

$$D =$$

$$L =$$

$$S =$$

$$W =$$

LRFD Load Combinations

#	Combination										
1	1.4D									=	
2	1.2D + 1.6L + 0.5(Lr or S or R)		+		+					=	
3	1.2D + 1.6(Lr or S or R) + (0.5L or 0.8W)		+		+					=	
4	1.2D + 1.6W + 0.5L + 0.5(Lr or S or R)		+		+		+			=	
5	1.2D + 1.0E + 0.5L + 0.2S		+		+		+			=	
6	0.9D + (1.6W or 1.0E)		+							=	
7	0.9D - (1.6W or 1.0E)		+							=	

Answer

3. FLEXURAL ANALYSIS OF BEAMS

3.1 Introduction

When a beam is subjected to a positive bending moment, compressive strains and stresses are produced in the top portion of the beam cross section while tensile strains and stresses are produced in the bottom portion of the beam cross section. The reverse is the case for a cantilever beam which is subjected to a negative bending moment. Concrete has considerable compressive strength, but it has very little tensile strength. This can be seen quite easily at the mid-span of a non-reinforced concrete beam simply supported at its ends. At a certain level of loading, cracks start to form at the bottom of the beam, but there is still no

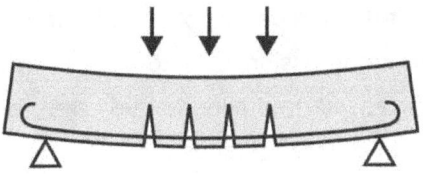 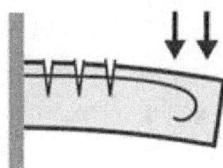

crack at the top. Under gravity loads, the top of a simply supported beam is in compression, while the bottom edge is in tension.

For a concrete flexural member (e.g. beam, slab and retaining wall) to have any significant load carrying capacity, its basic inability to resist tensile stresses must be overcome. This weakness of concrete in tension is overcome by incorporating mild steel reinforcements into the concrete wherever tension is likely to occur. The reinforcements are not necessary where the concrete is in compression, because the concrete itself is well suited to withstand compressive stresses. Therefore, the whole concrete section of a reinforced concrete beam is not effective in resisting the applied bending moment. In the tension zone, the concrete's function is to merely protect the steel from fire and rust and to enable both the steel and the concrete to act as a single unit.

3.2 Flexural behavior of RC Beam for different stages of loading

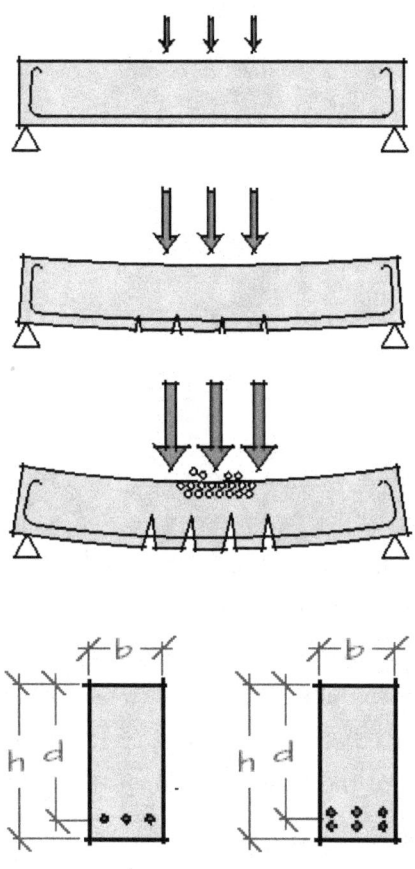

A reinforced concrete beam is a composite section which consists of two different materials, steel and concrete. The concrete can be cracked or uncracked. The load-deformation behavior of both the steel and the concrete are non-linear at failure. The figures below show characteristics of the response of a simply-supported reinforced concrete beam subjected to increasing loads. Steel reinforcing (three bars) is located near the bottom of the beam, which is the tension side. The overall depth of the beam cross section is designated "h." The effective depth "d" is measured from the compression face to the centroid of the reinforcing steel. In this example, the centroid is at the center of the single layer of bars. If there are multiple layers of bars, the effective depth "d" is measured from the compression face to the centroid of the bar group. Now, the gravity load is increased gradually to study the flexural behaviors of the reinforced concrete beam at different stages of loading.

Stage I : Un-cracked Section

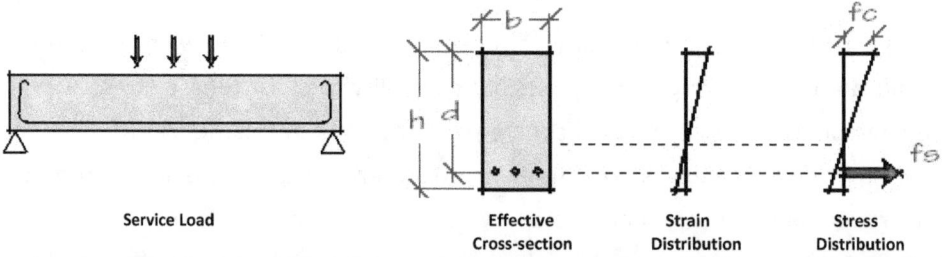

| Service Load | Effective Cross-section | Strain Distribution | Stress Distribution |

At very small loads, the concrete has not cracked and the maximum tensile stress is lower than the modulus of rupture (tensile strength of concrete). Therefore, both concrete and steel resist the tension at the bottom of the beam. This bending strength of a beam is called the cracking moment, ***M*ₐᵣ**. Concrete alone resists the compression at the top of the beam. The strain variation is linear from the neutral axis to the extreme fibers. Stresses also vary linearly from zero at the neutral axis and are proportional to strains. In this stage, stresses are distributed linearly.

FLEXURAL ANALYSIS OF BEAMS

This case is exclusively used in the design of un-cracked sections associated with water structures (when water is on the tension side of the section) using the working stress design method. The gross moment of inertia is used for this case but in most practical situations, this is not the case because the concrete under the neutral axis is in tension and is ineffective. Since the reinforced concrete beam is composite and therefore must be analyzed as such (e.g., using transformed area method).

Stage II : Linear Elastic Stage (Cracked Section)

With moderate loads applied to the beam, the tensile stress in concrete exceeds

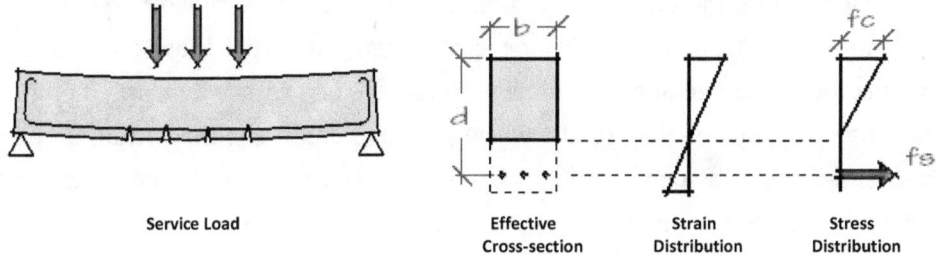

| Service Load | Effective Cross-section | Strain Distribution | Stress Distribution |

the modulus of rupture. Thus, the first of tensile cracks (hairline cracks) at the bottom extreme fiber starts to develop. The concrete cannot resist tension across a crack; the steel bars must resist all the tension. The tensile strength of concrete in the area below the neutral axis is to be neglected. The concrete compressive stress is still proportional to the concrete compressive strain. This linear compressive stress pattern is valid for concrete stresses up to $0.5f_c'$. Above a stress of $0.5f_c'$, concrete is no longer considered to behave elastically. This stage is considered the basis for design of sections subjected to bending using the working stress design method. In this case, the cracked moment of inertia is calculated taking into consideration the composite action between the concrete and steel rebar. This assumes that the concrete in the tension zone is totally ineffective, which is overly conservative. When the steel reinforcement first yields, the bending moment strength of the beam is called the yielding moment, M_y.

Stage III : Ultimate Strength (Beam Failure)

With further increase in the load, the cracks push upward moving the neutral axis in that direction until failure takes place. Depending on the properties of a beam, flexural mode of failure may be ductile or brittle as will be explained in the next section. The compressive strains and stresses in the concrete are no longer proportional. The compressive strains in the concrete continue to vary linearly from the neutral axis to the top extreme fiber. However, compressive stresses vary in a nonlinear manner, similar to the shape of the stress-strain curve. The steel bars resist all the tension.

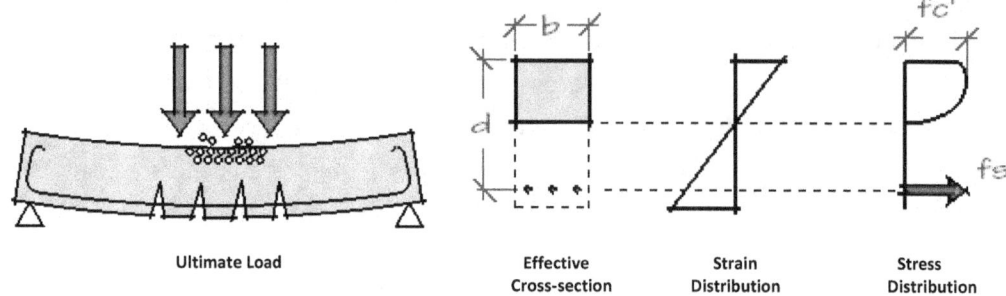

Ultimate Load   Effective Cross-section   Strain Distribution   Stress Distribution

Effective Moment of Inertia

As shown before, the effective cross-section of a reinforced concrete beam is not constant as is true in a prismatic steel beam. It varies depending on the magnitude of the bending moment which varies along with the beam. Therefore, the effective moment of inertia is typically used to determine the section property of the member at a specific point along the moment diagram. In most cases, the effective moment of inertia is used to determine the actual deflection of the member when designing against Code-specified maximums.

Assumptions in Flexure Theory

The three assumptions already made are sufficient to allow calculation of the strength and behavior of reinforced concrete elements. For design purposes, however, the following additional assumptions are introduced to simplify the problem with little loss of accuracy.

1. The tensile strength of concrete is neglected in flexural-strength calculations. The strength of concrete in tension is roughly one-tenth of the compressive strength, and the tensile force in the concrete below the neutral axis is small compared with the tensile force in the steel. Hence, the contribution of the tensile stresses in the concrete to the flexural capacity of the beam is small and can be neglected. It should be noted that this assumption is made primarily to simplify flexural calculations.

2. In some instances, particularly shear, bond, deflection, and service-load calculations for pre-stressed concrete, the tensile resistance of concrete is not neglected.

3. The section is assumed to have reached its nominal flexural strength when the strain in the extreme concrete compression fiber reaches the maximum useable compression strain, Strictly speaking, this is an artificial limit developed by code committees to define at what point on the general moment–curvature relationship the nominal strength of the section is to be calculated. The selection of a specific value for will not significantly affect the

calculated value for the nominal flexural strength of the section. Thus, design calculations are simplified when a limiting strain is assumed.

3.3 Working Stress Design - Transformed Area Method

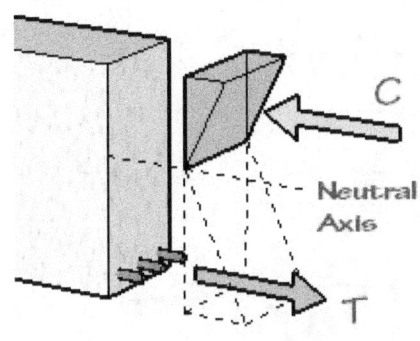

At moderate level of loading, both the stress and strain distributions are assumed to be linear along the depth of the concrete section. In other words, stress is proportional to strain in elastic stress stage. Even though reinforced concrete members are non-homogeneous, the elastic behavior approach was considered valid for concrete design and was known as the working stress design method (WSD). To analyze and design reinforced concrete members, the actual service loads are used and allowable stresses are decided depending on the safety factor. For example, allowable compressive bending stress is calculated as 0.45f'c. If the actual stresses do not exceed the allowable stresses, the structures are considered to be adequate for strength. The WSD method is easier to explain and use than other method but this method is being replaced by a more realistic and rational approach for the design and analysis of reinforced concrete. Originally called the ultimate strength design (USD) method, the method is now called the strength design method. ACI 318 Code treats the WSD method just in a small part. Basic assumptions of the WSD method include:

1. A plane section before bending remains plane after bending. This implies strains across section are linearly varying. This is true for most section of flexural member except deep beam where shear deformation is significant.
2. Hooke's law applies to both the steel and the concrete. Therefore, the strain is proportional to the distance from the neutral axis of the beam.
3. The tensile strength of concrete is zero and the reinforcing carries all of the tension.
4. The bond between the concrete and the steel is perfect, so no slip occurs.
5. The modular ratio, **n** may be taken as the nearest whole number (but not less than 6 or more than 15). In doubly reinforced sections, to consider creep of concrete in compression zone an effective modular ratio of **2n** shall be used to transform compression reinforcement for stress computation.

FLEXURAL ANALYSIS OF BEAMS

Transformed Section

Consider a rectangular beam subject to bending moments such that there are compressive stress at the top extreme fiber and tensile stress at the bottom. The beam is subject to a bending moment **M** and is reinforced in its tensile zone by a number of reinforcement bars of total cross section are **A_s**. The centroid of the

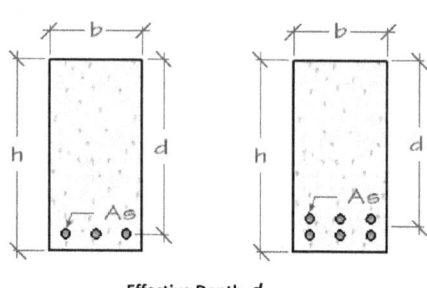

Effective Depth, *d*

reinforcement is at a depth **d** from the top surface and is identified as the *effective depth*.

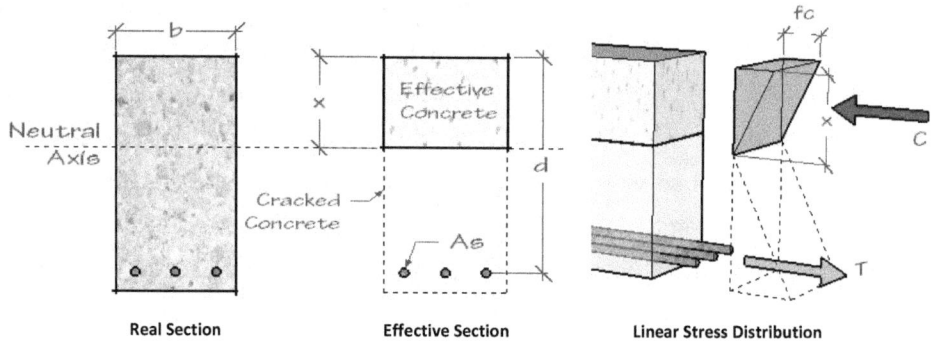

Real Section   Effective Section   Linear Stress Distribution

In elastic analysis, the bending stress is the maximum at the top and bottom extreme fibers. The bending stress varies linearly from the tensile maximum to the compressive maximum along the depth of the beam cross-section. Therefore, there is a plane where there is no stress and no strain somewhere in the middle depth of the cross-section. This plane is called the neutral plane of the cross section. The intersection of the neutral plane and the cross-section is called the neutral axis.

The concrete is assumed to only contribute to resisting the compressive stresses in the region above the neutral axis. The concrete below the neutral axis is considered ineffective and all tensile stresses are resisted by the steel reinforcements. The neutral axis of the section is at a depth **x** from the top surface. The location of the neutral axis is unknown and to be calculated using static equilibrium of the compressive and tensile stresses.

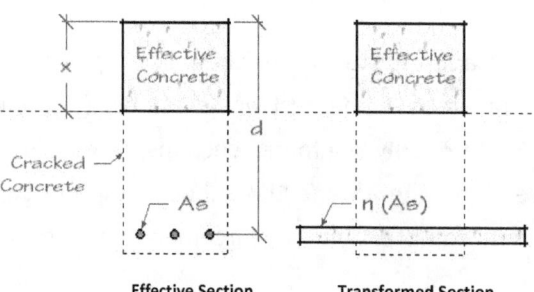

Effective Section   Transformed Section

In the analysis of composite members such as reinforced concrete members, one material (steel) is theoretically transformed into the other material (concrete). To obtain the equivalent section which is all concrete, the cross-sectional area of the steel reinforcements is multiplied by **n** (the ratio of the concrete and steel moduli of elasticity). The modular ratio $n = E_s/E_c$. Multiplying the area of the reinforcement bars by the modular ratio results in the area of reinforcement being effectively transformed into an equivalent area of concrete.

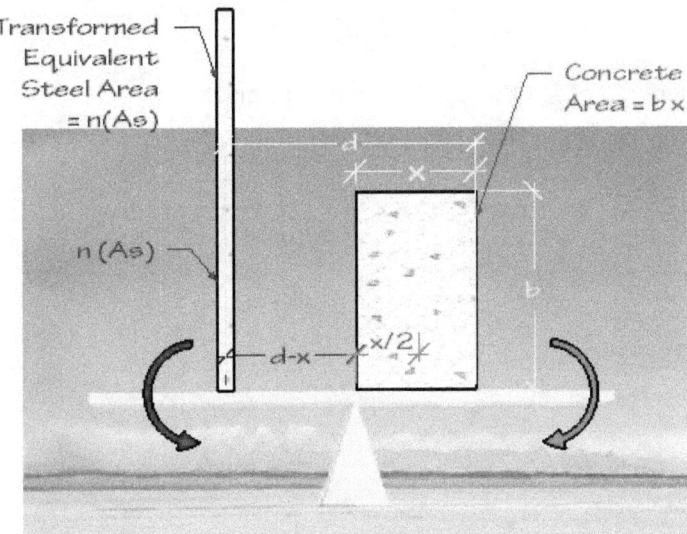

Because the area moment of the transformed cross-section about the neutral axis is zero, **x** can be solved for knowing that **d** is the distance from the top of the concrete section to the centroid of the steel. Then, the moment of inertia for the equivalent concrete section (transformed section) about the neutral axis are calculated. In order to determine the elastic stresses in the composite section, the following flexure formula is used even though the beam is non-homogeneous.

$$f = \frac{M}{I} y$$

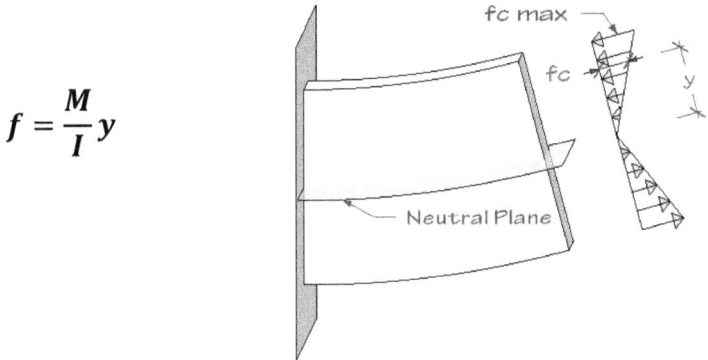

It must be noted that the mechanical properties are equivalent to the concrete material. The overall depth of the transformed section is the same as the original section. The resulting strain at any location of the transformed section must be unchanged. This approach is called the *transformed area method* and is valid if the maximum stress in each of the materials is within the relevant materials elastic limit. The transformed area method is applicable to beams with cracked section when

$$M_{cr} < M < M_y$$

,where M_{cr} = the cracking moment and
M_y = the yield moment.

FLEXURAL ANALYSIS OF BEAMS

Case Study 3-1a Transformed Area Method –singly reinforced beam

Calculate the bending stresses in the beam shown below for a bending moment of 65 kips-ft. by using the ***transformed area method***. Use ***n*** = 9 and check the bending stresses against the allowable stresses, F_s = 20 ksi. and F_c = 1350 psi.

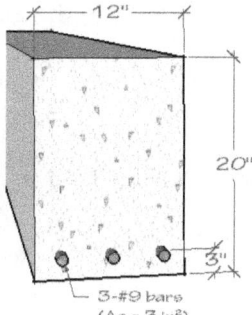

Solution)

a) Get the ***Transformed Section***.

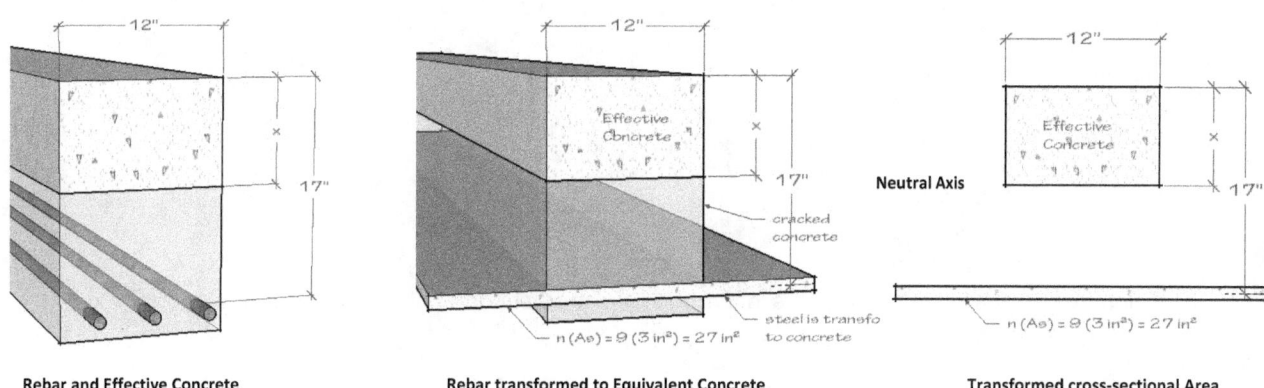

| Rebar and Effective Concrete | Rebar transformed to Equivalent Concrete | Transformed cross-sectional Area |

b) Locate the **Neutral Axis** using the area moment. (*Note : The area moment w.r.t. the N.A. is ZERO!!*)

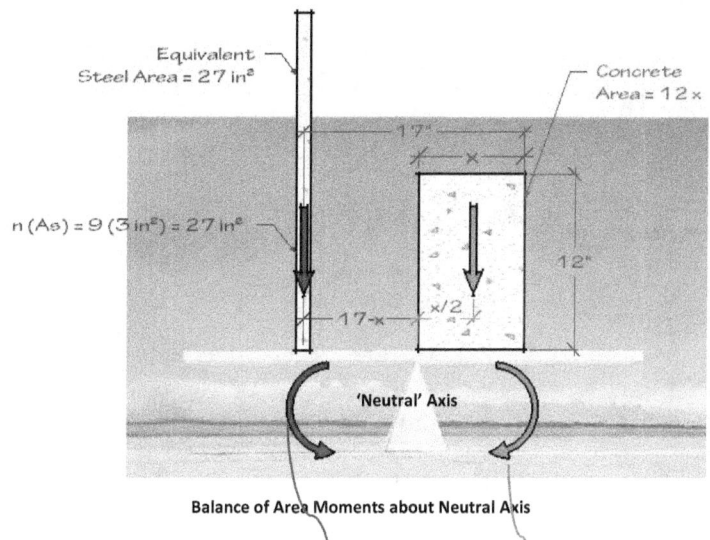

Balance of Area Moments about Neutral Axis

By taking the moments of the steel and concrete areas about the neutral axis,

$$(27 \text{ in}^2)(17-x) = (12x)(x/2)$$

This, when rearranged, results in the quadratic equation.

$$6x^2 + 27x - 459 = 0$$

FLEXURAL ANALYSIS OF BEAMS

Solving the quadratic equation gives:

$$x = \frac{-(27) \pm \sqrt{27^2 - 4(6)(-459)}}{2(6)}$$

$x = 6.78$ or $x = -11.28$ (Note : Discard the negative root since x is a distance.)

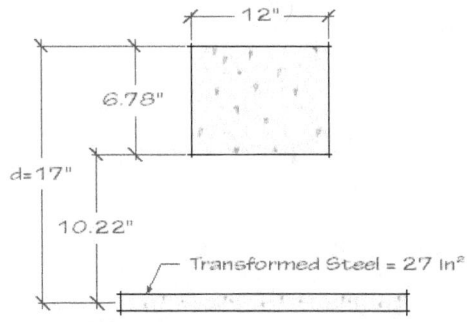

c) Calculate the **Moment of Inertia** of the transformed section with respect to the neutral axis.

$$I_c = \frac{(12)(6.78)^3}{3} = 1246.7 \text{ in}^4$$

$$I_s = (27)(17 - 6.78)^2 = 2820.1 \text{ in}^4$$

$$I_{total} = 4067 \text{ in}^4$$

d) Calculate the **Compressive** Bending Stress in the concrete.

$$f_c = \frac{M}{I} y = \frac{65(12)(1000)}{4067}(6.78) = 1300 \text{ psi}$$

$f_c = 1300 \text{ psi} < F_c = 1350 \text{ psi}.$ **O.K.**

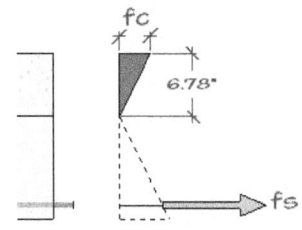

e) Calculate the **Tensile** Bending Stresses in the reinforcements.

(Note : The stress in steel is **n** (modular ratio) times the concrete stress at the same strain level.)

$$f_s = (n)\frac{M}{I} y = (9)\frac{65(12)(1000)}{4067}(10.22) = 17640 \text{ psi}$$

$17640 \text{ psi} = 17.64 \text{ ksi} < F_s = 20 \text{ ksi}.$ **O.K.**

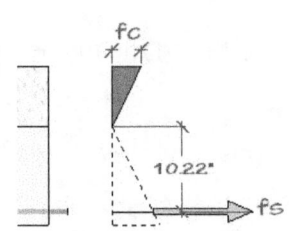

FLEXURAL ANALYSIS OF BEAMS

Reinforcement in compression zone of beam – Doubly reinforced beams

If the dimensions of a beam are limited because of architectural or other considerations, it may happen that concrete section cannot develop the compression force required to resist the given bending moment. In these cases, increasing the area of the tension reinforcement does not provide a resulting increase in the moment strength. This limitation can be overcome by adding reinforcement in the compression zone of the beam. Other effects of using compression steel include:

1. Compression steel insures that the tension steel yields before the concrete crushes and thus it helps change the failure mode to tension controlled. It makes members more ductile. Since the steel takes some of the compressive stress, the compression block depth is reduced, increasing the strain in the tension steel at failure, resulting in more ductile behavior.
2. The yield moment remains generally the same with compression steel added, but the increase in capacity after yield is significant.
3. Also, for continuous members, it is often easier to run your negative moment steel the full length of the beam rather than trying to cut it off in the positive moment regions.
4. Concrete deflects over time under sustained loads in addition to the instantaneous elastic deflection. This time-dependent deflection of concrete is called creep. Compression steel reinforcement also reduces the long-term deflections because sustained compressive stress in the concrete is reduced.
5. Compression reinforcement is also used to improve serviceability related to temperature and shrinkage.
6. Compression steel also makes beams easier to construct. With bars in the top and bottom, the shear stirrups can be kept in place when pouring the concrete.

In doubly reinforced sections, an effective modular ratio of **2n** shall be used to transform compression reinforcement for stress computation to consider creep of concrete in compression zone.

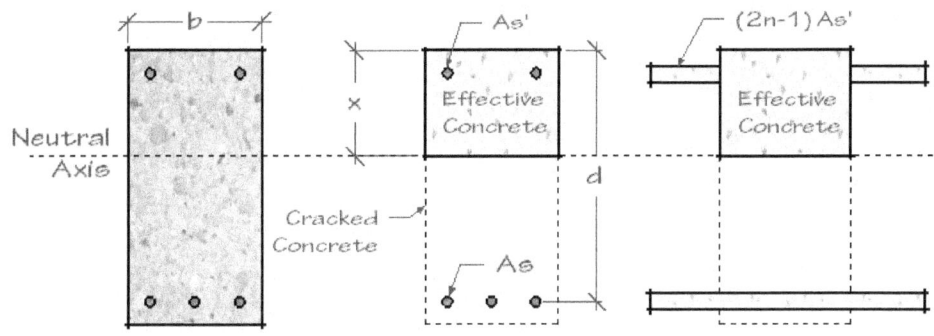

FLEXURAL ANALYSIS OF BEAMS

Case Study 3-2a Transformed Area Method –doubly reinforced beam

Calculate the bending stresses in the beam shown below for a bending moment of 118 kips-ft. by using the **transformed area method**. Use n = 10 and check the bending stresses against the allowable stresses, F_s = 20 ksi. and F_c = 1450 psi.

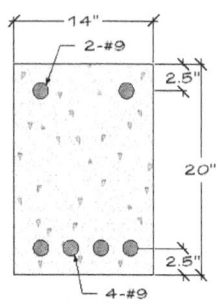

Solution)

a) Get the **Transformed Section**.

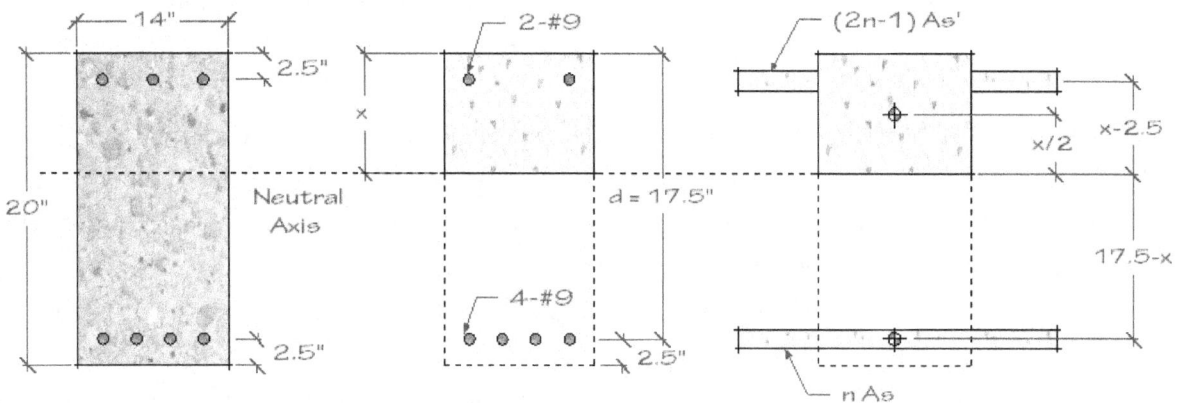

Moment of Transformed Area

	Transformed Area	Moment Lever	Area Moment
Concrete Area	14 x	x/2	14x (x/2)
Compression Steel	(2n-1) A_s' = (19)(2 in²) = 38 in²	x-2.5	38(x-2.5)
Tension Steel	(n) A_s = (10)(4 in²) = 40 in²	17.5-x	40(17.5-x)

b) Locate the **Neutral Axis**. (Note : The area moment about the N.A. is ZERO!!)

$$(14x)\left(\frac{x}{2}\right) + (38)(x-2.5) - (40)(17.5-x) = 0$$

$$7x^2 + (38x - 95) - (700 - 40x) = 0$$

$$7x^2 + 78x - 795 = 0$$

Solve this quadratic equation using your TI86 calculator to obtain;

$$x = \frac{-(78) \pm \sqrt{78^2 - 4(7)(-795)}}{2(7)}$$

x = 6.45 or x = -17.6 (Note : Discard the negative root since x is a distance.)

FLEXURAL ANALYSIS OF BEAMS

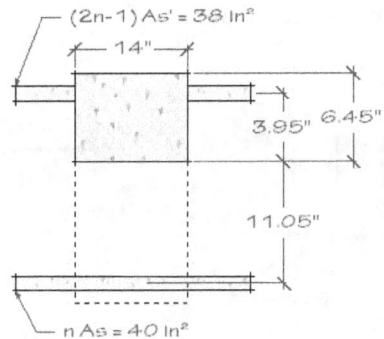

c) Calculate the **Moment of Inertia** of the transformed section with respect to the neutral axis.

$$I_c = \frac{(14)(6.45)^3}{3} = 1252.2 \text{ in}^4$$

$$I_s' = (38)(3.95)^2 = 592.9 \text{ in}^4$$

$$I_s = (40)(11.05)^2 = 4884.1 \text{ in}^4$$

$$I_{total} = 6729 \text{ in}^4$$

d) Calculate the **Compressive** Bending Stress in the concrete.

$$f_c = \frac{M}{I}y = \frac{118(12)(1000)}{6729}(6.45) = 1357 \text{ psi}$$

1357 psi < F_c = 1450 psi. **O.K.**

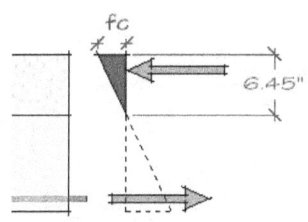

e) Calculate the *Bending Stresses* in the **Compression** steel.

(Note : The stress in steel is **2n-1** times the concrete stress at the same strain level.)

$$f_s' = (2n-1)\frac{M}{I}y = (19)\frac{118(12)(1000)}{6729}(3.95) = 15793 \text{ psi}$$

15793 psi = 15.79 ksi < F_s = 20 ksi. **O.K.**

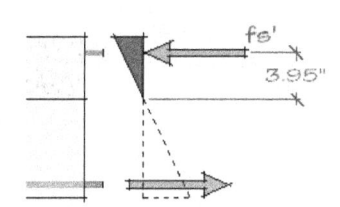

f) Calculate the *Bending Stresses* in the **Tension** steel.

(Note : The stress in steel is **n** (modular ratio) times the concrete stress at the same strain level.)

$$f_s = (n)\frac{M}{I}y = (10)\frac{118(12)(1000)}{6729}(11.05) = 23253 \text{ psi}$$

23253 psi = 23.3 ksi > F_s = 20 ksi. **N.G.**

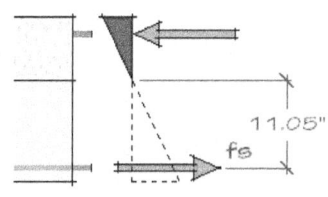

Ultimate Behavior of RC Beam

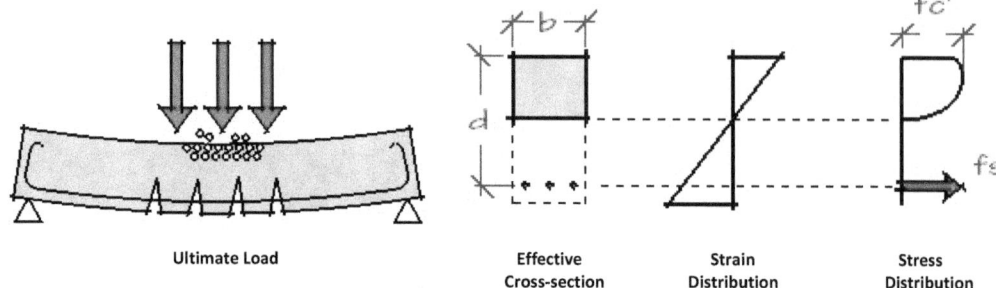

With a load level close to the ultimate load capacity of a reinforced concrete beam, the compressive strains and stresses in the concrete increase and the steel bars resist all the tension. The compressive strains in the concrete continue to vary linearly from the neutral axis to the outer fiber. However, the proportional stress-strain relationship for the compression stresses in the concrete is no longer valid because the stress in the concrete exceeded the proportional limit.

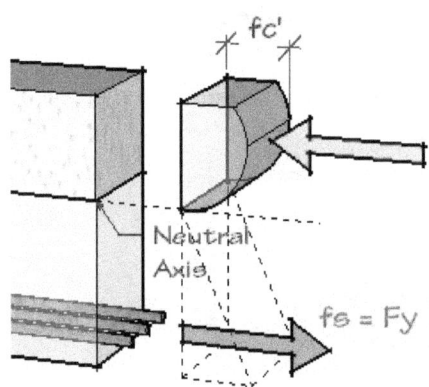

Compressive stresses vary in a nonlinear manner and thus the compressive stress block of the concrete takes a profile similar to the shape of the stress-strain curve of the concrete. The process of attaining the ultimate capacity of the reinforced concrete beam is irreversible. The beam has cracked and deflected significantly. The steel has yielded and cannot return to its original length. Structures are not designed and constructed to reach the ultimate capacities. Safety factors are introduced to provide commonly accepted margins of safety. However, ultimate capacities are the basis for reinforced concrete analysis and design. Assumptions for the strength design method are similar to those listed for the working stress design (WSD) method, with one notable exception – the nonlinear stress distribution in concrete section. The major differences between the working stress design method and the strength design method include the way in which the service loads are handled and the way in which the capacity (strength) of the reinforced concrete member is determined. In the strength design method, the service loads are amplified using load factors. Then, the member is designed so that the practical strength at failure is sufficient to resist the effects (e.g. moment, shear) of the factored loads.

3.4 Ultimate Flexural Strength of Rectangular Beams

The strains, stresses, and forces of a reinforced concrete beam subjected to its ultimate moment are now discussed. The ultimate moment of a beam is the bending moment level at time of impending failure of the beam. A reinforced concrete beam may reach its ultimate moment in the following two ways.

1. The maximum tensile steel stress equals the yield stress (i.e. $f_s = F_y$) and the maximum concrete compressive strain is 0.003 inch/inch.
2. The maximum tensile steel stress is less than the yield stress (that is, $f_s < F_y$) and the maximum concrete compressive strain is 0.003 inch/inch. Each condition implies a specific mode of failure.

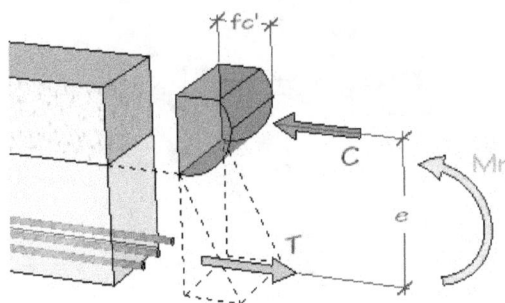

At impending failure, the stress distribution in a concrete beam is not linear any longer because the stress in concrete exceeded the proportional limit. The compressive stress distribution above the neutral axis for the beam is similar to the concrete compressive stress-strain curve. The ultimate compressive stress f_c' does not occur at the top extreme fiber. The shape of the stress curve is different for different strengths of concrete. Strains are assumed linear with the maximum strain of 0.003 occurring at the extreme outer compression fiber. The maximum concrete compressive stress f_c' develops at some intermediate level near, but not at, the extreme outer fiber. The flexural strength of a rectangular beam is developed by the internal stresses that may be represented as internal forces. C is a theoretical internal resultant compressive force representing the total internal compression above the neutral axis. T is a theoretical internal resultant tensile force representing the total internal tension below the neutral axis. These two internal forces (parallel, equal, opposite, and separated by a distance e) constitute an internal resisting couple. The maximum value of this couple is termed the nominal moment strength (M_n) of the beam member. This nominal moment strength must be capable of resisting the design bending moment induced by the applied loads. The design of a beam for a given loading condition requires proper concrete dimensions and placement of the steel reinforcement. The determination of the moment strength is complex because of the parabolic profile of the compressive stress block above the neutral axis. The resultant of the compressive stresses in the concrete, C is the volume of the stress block and difficult to evaluate. The location of C relative to the tensile steel is also difficult to establish. These difficulties can be eliminated by replacing the complex compressive stress distribution by a simplified box-shape stress block based on static equilibrium proposed by Charles Whitney in 1937. Of course, the uniform compressive stress distribution must have the same resultant force **C** (the same volume of stress block) as in the actual non-linear distribution. Also, the resultant force **C** must be applied at the same height as in the actual distribution.

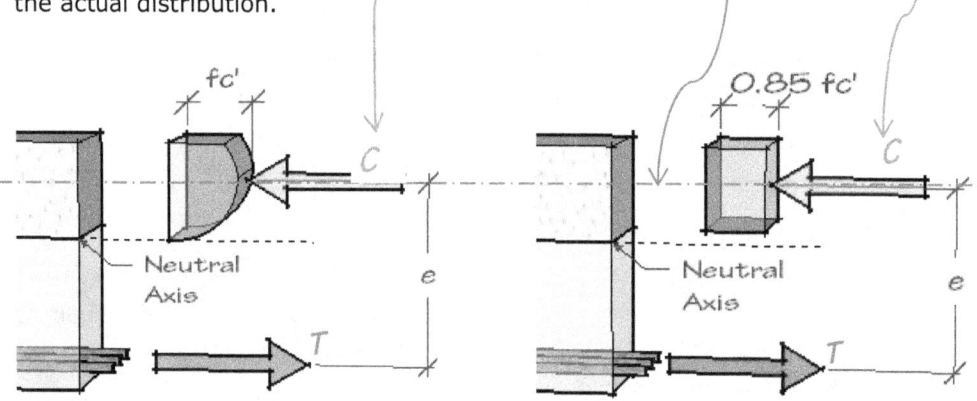

Real Stress Block (Non-linear)   Whitney Stress Block (Linear)

3.5 Whitney Stress Block

The simple rectangular stress block for concrete stress distribution proposed by Whitney became the basis for standard design by ACI code. Even though the strain varies linearly throughout the beam cross-section, the stress distribution is not linear but

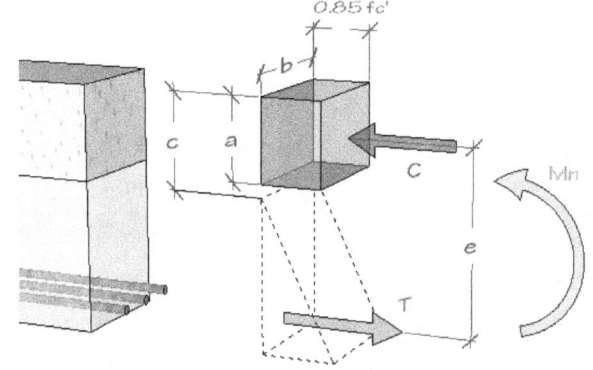

has an approximately parabolic shape. The average stress intensity is taken as **0.85f_c'**. This stress is assumed to act over the upper area of the beam cross section defined by the width **b** and a depth of **a**. It must be noted that the depth of the stress block, **a** is smaller than **c**, the neutral axis distance from the top extreme fiber.

$$a = \beta_1 c \qquad \text{where } \beta_1 = 0.85 \text{ for } f_c' = 4000 \text{ psi or less}$$

The values for β_1 are reduced for high-strength concretes as follows:

f_c'	3000	4000	5000	6000
β_1	0.85	0.85	0.80	0.75

FLEXURAL ANALYSIS OF BEAMS

This is because the location of the resultant of the compressive stresses must remain unchanged after the idealization of the compressive stress distribution. It is unlikely that the compressive stresses are actually distributed in this simplified manner. However, because of the simplicity, the rectangular shape has become the more widely used idealized stress distribution for design and analysis purposes because this equivalent rectangular distribution gives results close to those of the complex actual stress distribution. The ACI nominal moment strength, M_n of a rectangular reinforced concrete beam is determined using the Whitney stress block. Then, the nominal moment strength is reduced by a strength reduction factor, ϕ to determine the practical moment strength for the beam section. The nominal moment strength of a reinforced concrete beam, M_n, is determined as shown below:

1) Determine the **tensile force** in the reinforcing *steel*.

    $T = A_s F_y$ (Note : The steel stress at the ultimate moment is F_y.)

2) Calculate the **compressive force** in the *concrete*.

    $C = (a \times b)(0.85 f'_c)$

3) Note that the cross-section is in **horizontal equilibrium**.

    $C = T$ or, $(a \times b)(0.85 f'_c) = A_s f_y \therefore a = \dfrac{A_s F_y}{b(0.85 f'_c)}$

4) Note that C and T form a **couple moment** which resists to the applied moment.

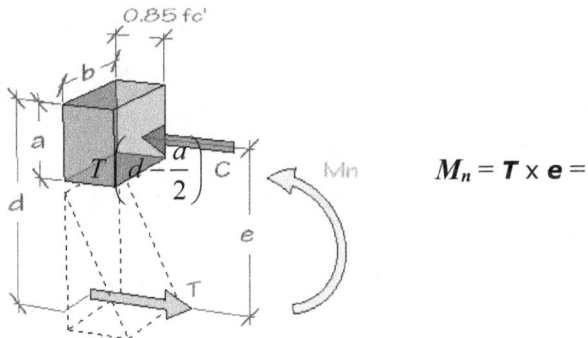

$M_n = T \times e =$

The ultimate bending strength of a concrete beam is based on the yield strength of the reinforcement of the steel in tension and the failure strength of concrete in compression both modified by a factor of safety. However, concrete is a brittle material (and thus, generally fails suddenly) while construction steel is generally ductile (and thus, fails progressively). The ultimate flexural analysis is based on the assumptions that plane sections remain plane after bending and there is no contribution of concrete in the tension zone to the bending strength of the beam.

3.6 Stress Design vs. Strength Design

ASD can mean either Allowable Stress Design or Allowable Strength Design. The Allowable Stress Design is the older or original designation which was used in the

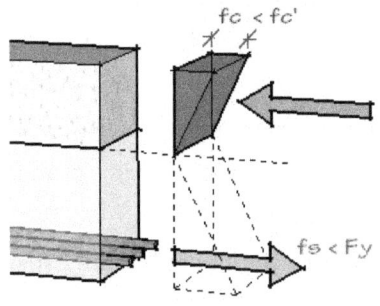

9th Edition of the AISC Steel Construction Manual (1989 AISC) and the old ACI Concrete code (called Working Stress Design. Side note: working stress design can be helpful in reducing cracks and crack size. Therefore, the method is sometimes still used in water applications). In these codes service level loads where applied to members. The stresses in the members where found and then checked against an allowable stress value which had a safety factor incorporated into it. Many 'old timers' will say that this used to give you more of a feel for the design as you better understood how the material and members where stressed. Allowable Strength Design (2005 AISC) – was mostly developed so that engineers who did not want to use LRFD could still use ASD and service level loads therefore both the '89 ASD and '05 ASD both use the same load combinations. It differs from the allowable stress design in that it is a 'Strength Design' methodology. The '05 ASD uses safety factors on the nominal strength of the member based the particular limit state. The 05' ASD allowable strength values maybe transformed into 89' ASD stress values by factoring out the appropriate section property. Both ASD methods utilize Limit States Design however they are 'hidden' in the '89 ASD code. Meaning that in the '05 ASD each limit state is checked (i.e. yielding, local buckling, lateral-torsional buckling, etc.).

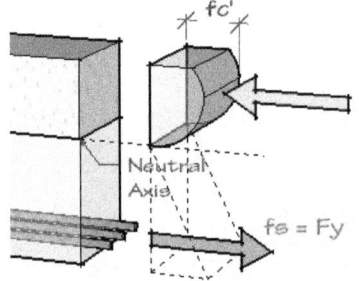

In the '89 ASD code the allowable stress is reduced to the lowest applicable limit state. They also both take advantage of inelastic behavior in some limit states.

LRFD refers to Load and Resistance Factor Design which is also a Limit States Design methodology. This method uses a load factor to 'factor up or down' service level loads and also reduce member strength based on reliability and statistical data. When using LRFD you must design the strength based on the LRFD load combinations and factors however deflection should be based on service level loads, so you must keep track of your loads.

In the 2005 AISC both the ASD and LRFD methods for determining nominal strengths are presented side by side. The nominal strength will be the same for both methods and only the allowable strength will differ due to the fact that the safety factor applied for ASD and the reduction factor applied for LRFD will be different.

It is generally accepted that LRFD is a more realistic, reliable and statistical based method for predicting loads and material strengths. Whereas the allowable stress safety factors are based on engineering judgments and past experiences. It is debated which will give you a more efficient design however it seems in most situations LRFD will produce a smaller sized beam based on strength but not always. Also, serviceability and deflection control many designs, in which case both methods will yield the same result as the design is not based on strength at that point.

Strength design in reinforced concrete refers to the redistribution of moments that occurs throughout a structure as the steel reinforcement at a critical section reaches its yield strength. Under working loads, the distribution of moments in a statically indeterminate structure is based on elastic theory, and the whole structure remains in the elastic range. In strength design, where factored loads are used, the distribution of moments at failure when a mechanism is reached is different from that distribution based on elastic theory. The ultimate strength of the structure can be increased as more sections reach their ultimate capacity. Although the yielding of the reinforcement introduces large deflections, which should be avoided under service, a statically indeterminate structure does not collapse when the reinforcement of the first section yields. Furthermore, a large reserve of strength is present between the initial yielding and the collapse of the structure. In steel design the term plastic design is used to indicate the change in the distribution of moments in the structure as the steel fibers, at a critical section, are stressed to their yield strength. Limit analysis of reinforced concrete developed as a result of earlier research on steel structures. Several studies had been performed on the principles of limit design and the rotation capacity of reinforced concrete plastic hinges. Full utilization of the plastic capacity of reinforced concrete beams and frames requires an extensive analysis of all possible mechanisms and an investigation of rotation requirements and capacities at all proposed hinge locations. The increase of design time may not be justified by the limited gains obtained. On the other hand, a restricted amount of redistribution of elastic moments can safely be made without complete analysis and may be sufficient to obtain most of the advantages of limit analysis.

Assumptions of Strength Design Method

The use of the strength design method depends on the following basic assumptions.

1. The strength analysis of RC sections in flexure is based on the principles of strain compatibility and equilibrium as out lined in ACI 318 10.2.
2. A plane section before bending remains plane after bending. Strain in the steel and concrete shall be directly proportional to the distance from the neutral axis.
3. Stress and strain are approximately proportional only up to a moderate load level. The proportionality between concrete strain and stress is valid as long as the stress does not exceed $0.5fc'$. When the load increases and approaches an ultimate load, the concrete stresses and strains are no longer proportional. At the ultimate load, the stress distribution in concrete is no longer linear.
4. The tensile strength of the concrete is neglected.
5. The strength is governed by the forces that will cause the strain in the concrete to equal the crushing strain (0.003). This value is based on extensive testing. Flexural concrete strain at failure for rectangular beams actually ranges from 0.003 to 0.004. The assumption that the concrete is about to crush when the maximum strain reaches 0.003 is slightly conservative.
6. The steel is uniformly strained. The steel strain used is the strain that exists at the level of the centroid of the steel. If the strain in the steel (ε_s) is less than the yield strain of the steel (ε_y), then the stress in the steel reinforcement is $f_s = \varepsilon_s E_s$ when $\varepsilon_s < \varepsilon_y$. If the strain in the steel (ε_s) is greater than the yield strain of the steel (ε_y), then the stress in the steel reinforcement is independent of the strain and is equal to the yield stress (F_y). Therefore, when $\varepsilon_s > \varepsilon_y$, $f_s = F_y$
7. The strain in the reinforcement is equal to the strain in the concrete at the same location. The bond between the steel and concrete is perfect and no slip occurs.

Assumptions 5 and 6 constitute what may be termed code criteria with respect to failure. The true ultimate strength of a member is slightly greater than the strength determined using these assumptions. The strength method of design and analysis of the ACI Code is based on these criteria. Although strength design is currently the philosophy employed most widely, serviceability must be maintained. Working stress is stilled required to calculate deflections and cracking of structure in service load conditions.

Summary

ASD vs. LRFD

	ASD (Allowable Stress Design)	**LRFD** (Load & Resistance Factor Design)

Alias	Working Stress Design	Strength Design Ultimate Strength Design
Design Criterion	Working Stress ≤ Allowable Stress	**Resistance** of Member ≤ **Load** Effects of Loads
Load Factors	Not Used	Probability-Based **Load** and **Resistance Factors** (uniform reliability, more realistic and economic)
Failure Mode	Not Considered	Based on Ultimate Load-Carrying Capacity (more realistic and rational approach)
Economy	Less Economic Results	More Economic Results

FLEXURAL ANALYSIS OF BEAMS

Case Study 3-1b Transformed Area Method –singly reinforced beam

Calculate the bending stresses in the beam shown below for a bending moment of 65 kips-ft. by using the **transformed area method**. Use **n** = 9 and check the bending stresses against the allowable stresses, F_s = 20 ksi. and F_c = 1350 psi.

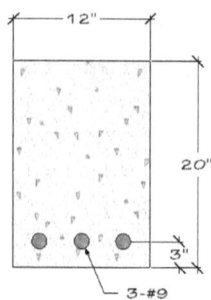

Solution)
a) Get the **Transformed Section**.

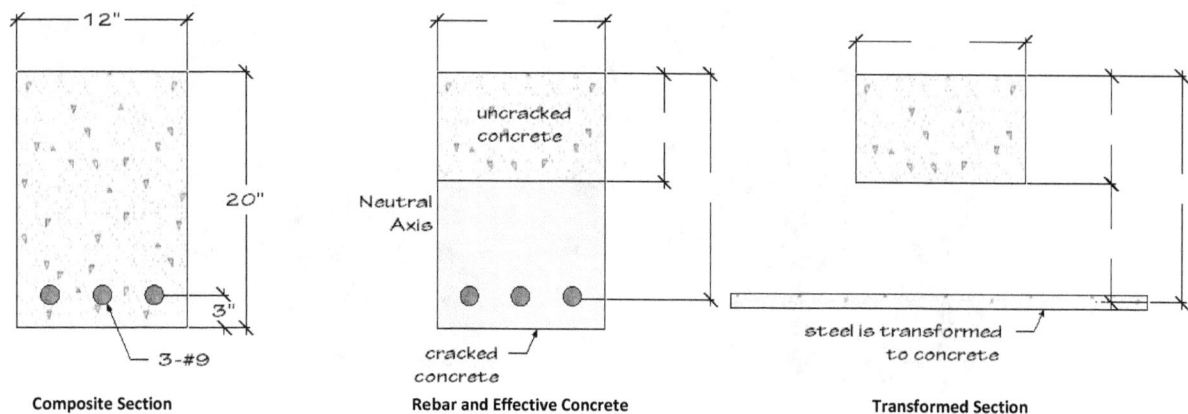

b) Locate the **Neutral Axis** using the area moment. (*Note : The area moment w.r.t. the N.A. is ZERO!!*)

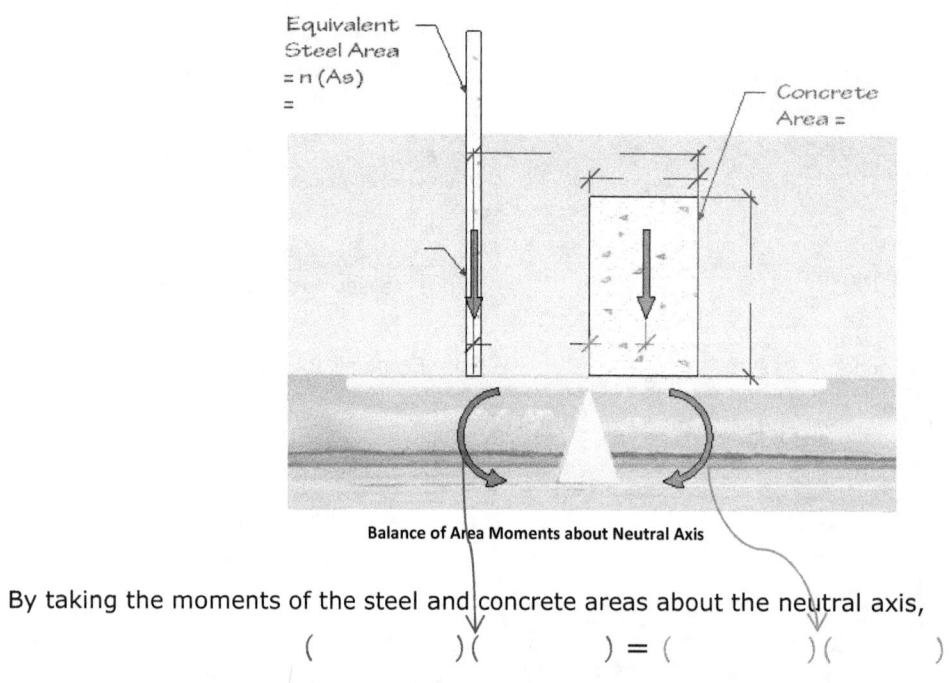

Balance of Area Moments about Neutral Axis

By taking the moments of the steel and concrete areas about the neutral axis,

$$(\quad\quad)(\quad\quad) = (\quad\quad)(\quad\quad)$$

This, when rearranged, results in the quadratic equation.

FLEXURAL ANALYSIS OF BEAMS

Solving the quadratic equation gives:

$$x = \frac{-(\quad) \pm \sqrt{(\quad)^2 - 4(\quad)(\quad)}}{2(\quad)}$$

$x = $ \hspace{2cm} (Note : Discard the negative root since x is a distance.)

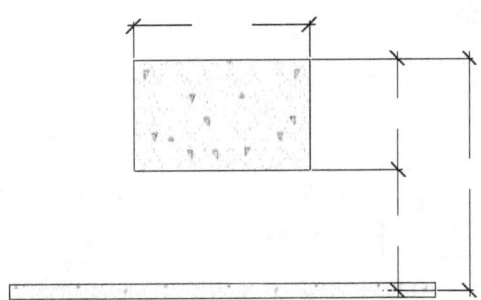

c) Calculate the **Moment of Inertia** of the transformed section with respect to the neutral axis.

$$I_c = \frac{(\quad)(\quad)^3}{3} = \quad in^4$$

$$I_s = (\quad)(\quad)^2 = \quad in^4$$

$$I_{total} = \quad in^4$$

d) Calculate the **Compressive** Bending Stress in the concrete.

$$f_c = \frac{M}{I}y = \frac{(\quad)(12)(1000)}{(\quad)}(\quad) = \quad psi$$

$f_c = (\quad)$ psi $<$ $F_c = (\quad)$ psi. (**O.K.** or **N.G.**)

e) Calculate the **Tensile** Bending Stresses in the reinforcements.

(Note : The stress in steel is **n** (modular ratio) times the concrete stress at the same strain level.)

$$f_s = (n)\frac{M}{I}y = (\quad)\frac{(\quad)(12)}{(\quad)}(\quad) = \quad ksi$$

$f_s = (\quad)$ ksi $<$ $F_s = (\quad)$ ksi. (**O.K.** or **N.G.**)

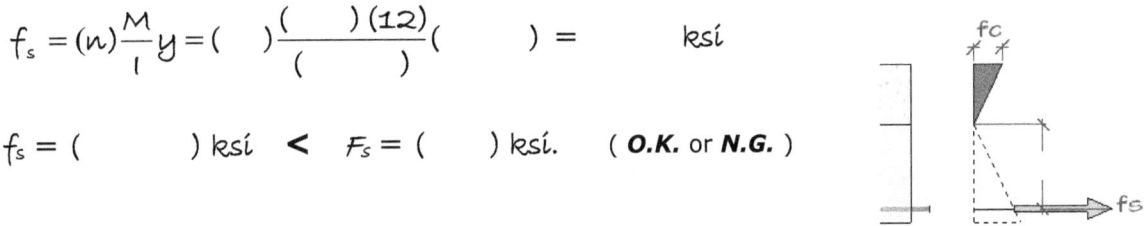

FLEXURAL ANALYSIS OF BEAMS

Workshop 3-1a Transformed Area Method –singly reinforced beam

Calculate the bending stresses in the beam shown below for a bending moment of 60 kips-ft. by using the **transformed area method**. Use **n** = 10 and check the bending stresses against the allowable stresses, F_s = 20 ksi. and F_c = 1350 psi.

Solution)

a) Get the **Transformed Section**.

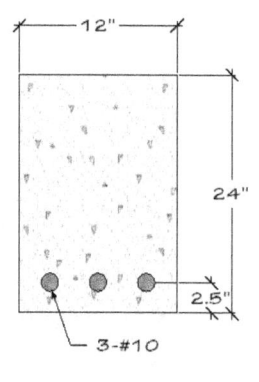
Composite Section

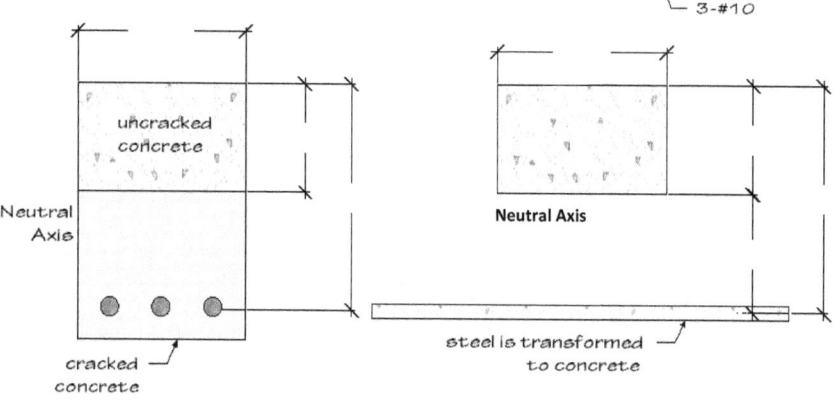

b) Locate the **Neutral Axis** using the area moment. (*Note : The area moment w.r.t. the N.A. is ZERO!!*)

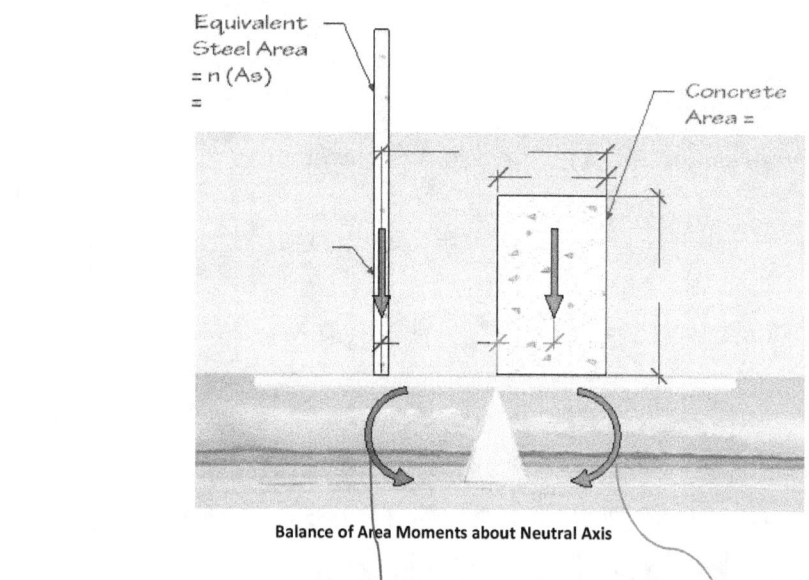

Balance of Area Moments about Neutral Axis

By taking the moments of the steel and concrete areas about the neutral axis,

$$(\quad\quad)(\quad\quad) = (\quad\quad)(\quad\quad)$$

This, when rearranged, results in the quadratic equation.

FLEXURAL ANALYSIS OF BEAMS

Solving the quadratic equation gives:

$$x = \frac{-() \pm \sqrt{()^2 - 4()()}}{2()}$$

$x =$ \hspace{4cm} (Note : Discard the negative root since x is a distance.)

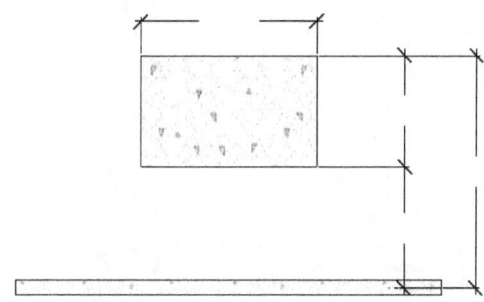

c) Calculate the **Moment of Inertia** of the transformed section with respect to the neutral axis.

$$I_c = \frac{()()^3}{3} = in^4$$

$$I_s = ()()^2 = in^4$$

$$I_{total} = in^4$$

d) Calculate the **Compressive** Bending Stress in the concrete.

$$f_c = \frac{M}{I}y = \frac{()(12)(1000)}{()}() = psi$$

$f_c = ()$ psi $<$ $F_c = ()$ psi. (**O.K.** or **N.G.**)

e) Calculate the **Tensile** Bending Stresses in the reinforcements.

(Note : The stress in steel is **n** (modular ratio) times the concrete stress at the same strain level.)

$$f_s = (n)\frac{M}{I}y = ()\frac{()(12)}{()}() = ksi$$

$f_s = ()$ ksi $<$ $F_s = ()$ ksi. (**O.K.** or **N.G.**)

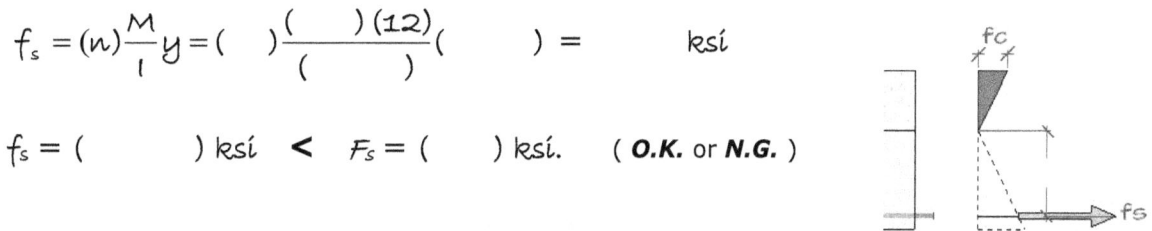

FLEXURAL ANALYSIS OF BEAMS

Workshop 3-1b Transformed Area Method –singly reinforced beam

Calculate the bending stresses in the beam shown below for a bending moment of 55 kips-ft. by using the **transformed area method**. Use **n** = 10 and check the bending stresses against the allowable stresses, F_s = 20 ksi. and F_c = 1450 psi.

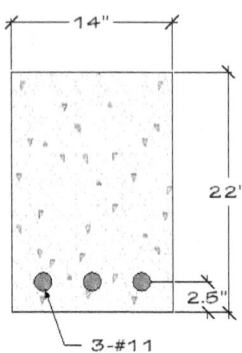

Solution)

a) Get the **Transformed Section**.

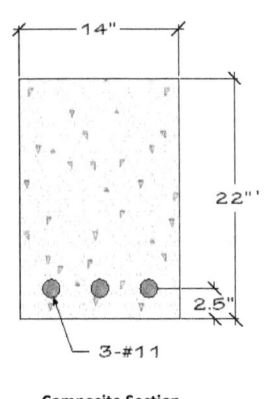
Composite Section

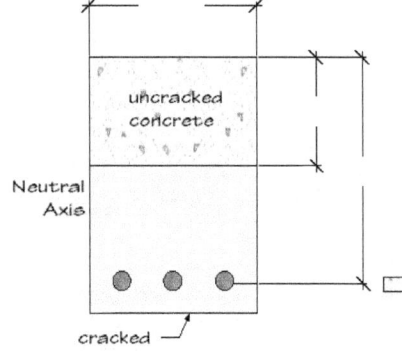
Rebar and Effective Concrete

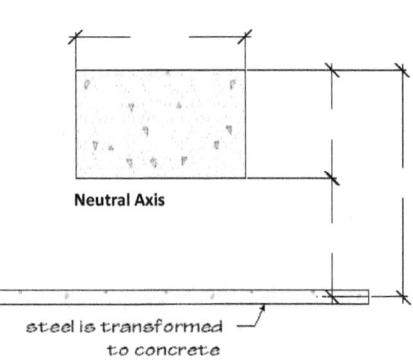
Transformed Section

b) Locate the **Neutral Axis** using the area moment. (*Note : The area moment w.r.t. the N.A. is ZERO!!*)

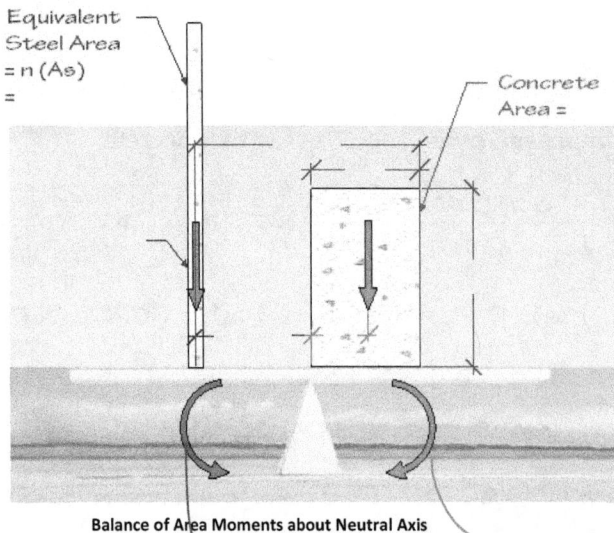
Balance of Area Moments about Neutral Axis

By taking the moments of the steel and concrete areas about the neutral axis,

$$(\quad\quad)(\quad\quad) = (\quad\quad)(\quad\quad)$$

This, when rearranged, results in the quadratic equation.

FLEXURAL ANALYSIS OF BEAMS

Solving the quadratic equation gives:

$$x = \frac{-(\quad) \pm \sqrt{(\quad)^2 - 4(\quad)(\quad)}}{2(\quad)}$$

x =   (Note: Discard the negative root since x is a distance.)

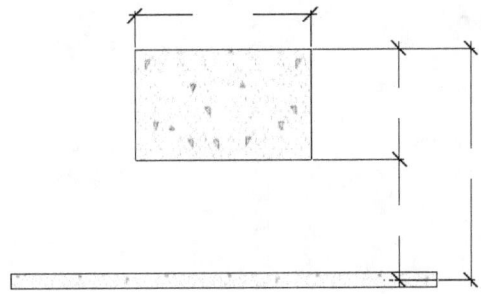

c) Calculate the **Moment of Inertia** of the transformed section with respect to the neutral axis.

$$I_c = \frac{(\quad)(\quad)^3}{3} = \quad in^4$$

$$I_s = (\quad)(\quad)^2 = \quad in^4$$

$$I_{total} = \quad in^4$$

d) Calculate the **Compressive** Bending Stress in the concrete.

$$f_c = \frac{M}{I}y = \frac{(\quad)(12)(1000)}{(\quad)}(\quad) = \quad psi$$

$f_c = (\quad)$ psi $<$ $F_c = (\quad)$ psi.   (**O.K.** or **N.G.**)

e) Calculate the **Tensile** Bending Stresses in the reinforcements.

(Note: The stress in steel is **n** (modular ratio) times the concrete stress at the same strain level.)

$$f_s = (n)\frac{M}{I}y = (\quad)\frac{(\quad)(12)}{(\quad)}(\quad) = \quad ksi$$

$f_s = (\quad)$ ksi $<$ $F_s = (\quad)$ ksi.   (**O.K.** or **N.G.**)

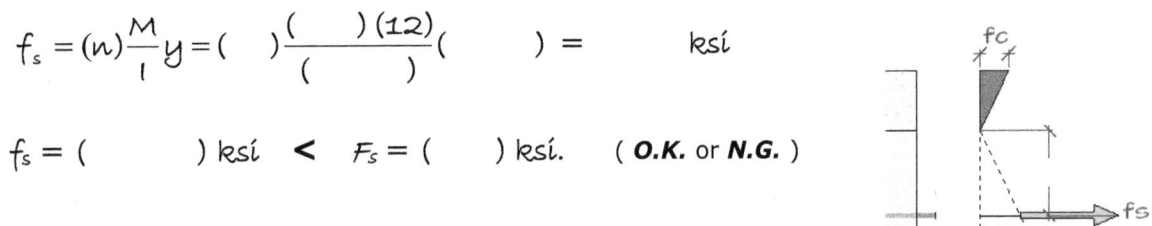

FLEXURAL ANALYSIS OF BEAMS

Workshop 3-1c Transformed Area Method –singly reinforced beam

Calculate the bending stresses in the beam shown below for a bending moment of 55 kips-ft. by using the **transformed area method**.

Use **n** = 10 and check the bending stresses against the allowable stresses, **f_s** = 20 ksi. and **F_c** = 1450 psi.

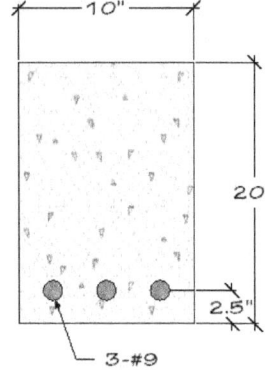

Solution)

a) Get the **Transformed Section**.

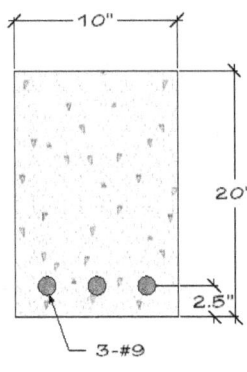

b) Locate the **Neutral Axis** using the area moment.

c) Calculate the **Moment of Inertia** of the transformed section with respect to the neutral axis.

d) Calculate the **Compressive** Bending Stress in the concrete.

e) Calculate the **Tensile** Bending Stresses in the reinforcements.

FLEXURAL ANALYSIS OF BEAMS

Case Study 3-2b Transformed Area Method –doubly reinforced beam

Calculate the bending stresses in the beam shown below for a bending moment of 118 kips-ft. by using the **transformed area method**. Use n = 10 and check the bending stresses against the allowable stresses, f_s = 20 ksi. and F_c = 1450 psi.

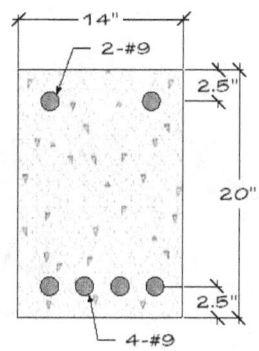

Solution)

a) Get the **Transformed Section**.

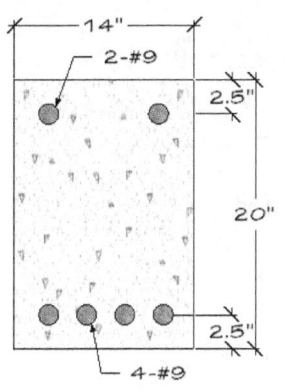 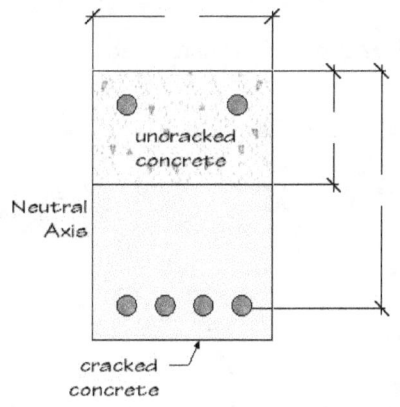 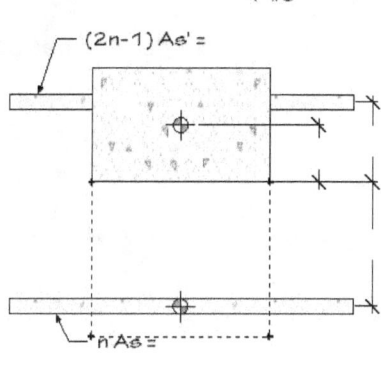

Moment of Transformed Area

	Transformed Area	Moment Lever	Area Moment
Concrete Area			
Compression Steel	$(2n-1) A_s' =$		
Tension Steel	$(n) A_s =$		

b) Locate the **Neutral Axis**. (*Note : The area moment about the N.A. is ZERO!!*)

Solve this quadratic equation using your TI86 calculator to obtain;

$$x = \frac{-(\quad) \pm \sqrt{(\quad)^2 - 4(\quad)(\quad)}}{2(\quad)}$$

x =   (*Note : Discard the negative root since x is a distance.*)

FLEXURAL ANALYSIS OF BEAMS

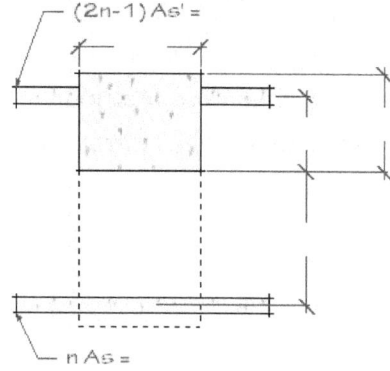

c) Calculate the **Moment of Inertia** of the transformed section with respect to the neutral axis.

$$I_c = \frac{()()^3}{3} = \text{in}^4$$

$$I_s' = ()()^2 = \text{in}^4$$

$$I_s = ()()^2 = \text{in}^4$$

$$I_{total} = \text{in}^4$$

d) Calculate the **Compressive** Bending Stress in the concrete.

$$f_c = \frac{M}{I}y = \frac{()(12)(1000)}{()}() = \text{psi}$$

$fc = ()$ psi $<$ $F_c = ()$ psi. (**O.K.** or **N.G.**)

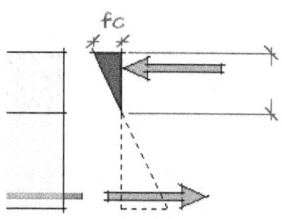

e) Calculate the Bending Stresses in the **Compression** steel.

(Note : The stress in steel is **2n-1** times the concrete stress at the same strain level.)

$$f_s' = (2n-1)\frac{M}{I}y = ()\frac{()(12)}{()}() = \text{ksi}$$

$f_s' = ()$ ksi $<$ $F_s = ()$ ksi. (**O.K.** or **N.G.**)

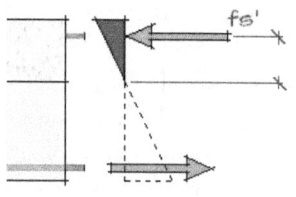

f) Calculate the Bending Stresses in the **Tension** steel.

(Note : The stress in steel is **n** (modular ratio) times the concrete stress at the same strain level.)

$$f_s' = n\frac{M}{I}y = ()\frac{()(12)}{()}() = \text{ksi}$$

$f_s = ()$ ksi $<$ $F_s = ()$ ksi. (**O.K.** or **N.G.**)

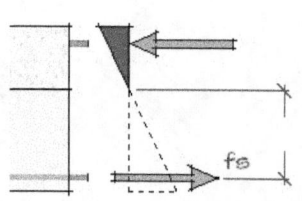

FLEXURAL ANALYSIS OF BEAMS

Workshop 3-2a Transformed Area Method –doubly reinforced beam

Calculate the bending stresses in the beam shown below for a bending moment of 118 kips-ft. by using the **transformed area method**.
Use n = 10 and check the bending stresses against the allowable stresses, f_s = 20 ksi. and F_c = 1450 psi.

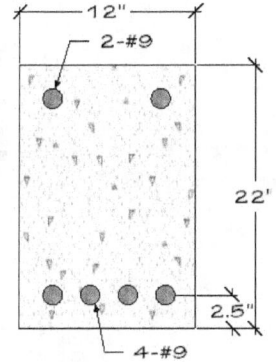

Solution)

a) Get the **Transformed Section**.

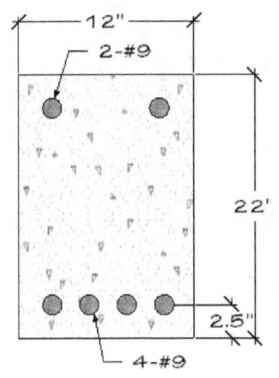 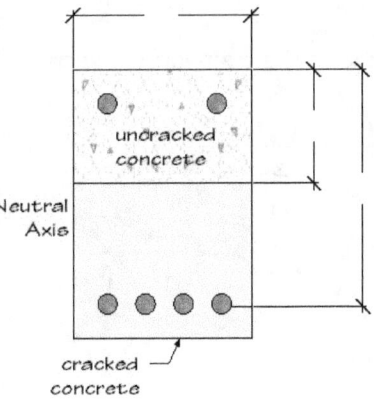 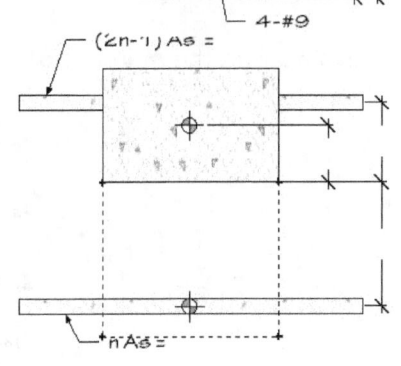

Moment of Transformed Area

	Transformed Area	Moment Lever	Area Moment
Concrete Area			
Compression Steel	$(2n-1)\, A_s' =$		
Tension Steel	$(n)\, A_s =$		

b) Locate the **Neutral Axis**. (Note : The area moment about the N.A. is ZERO!!)

Solve this quadratic equation using your TI86 calculator to obtain;

$$x = \frac{-(\quad) \pm \sqrt{(\quad)^2 - 4(\quad)(\quad)}}{2(\quad)}$$

x =   (Note : Discard the negative root since x is a distance.)

FLEXURAL ANALYSIS OF BEAMS

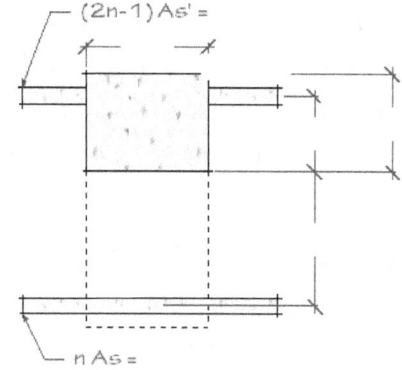

c) Calculate the **Moment of Inertia** of the transformed section with respect to the neutral axis.

$$I_c = \frac{()()^3}{3} = in^4$$

$$I_s' = ()()^2 = in^4$$

$$I_s = ()()^2 = in^4$$

$$I_{total} = in^4$$

d) Calculate the **Compressive** Bending Stress in the concrete.

$$f_c = \frac{M}{I}y = \frac{()(12)(1000)}{()}() = psi$$

$fc = () psi < F_c = () psi.$ (**O.K.** or **N.G.**)

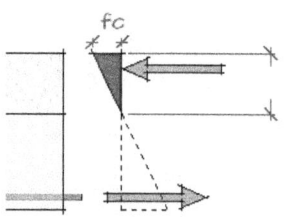

e) Calculate the Bending Stresses in the **Compression** steel.

(Note : The stress in steel is **2n-1** times the concrete stress at the same strain level.)

$$f_s' = (2n-1)\frac{M}{I}y = ()\frac{()(12)}{()}() = ksi$$

$f_s' = () ksi < F_s = () ksi.$ (**O.K.** or **N.G.**)

f) Calculate the Bending Stresses in the **Tension** steel.

(Note : The stress in steel is **n** (modular ratio) times the concrete stress at the same strain level.)

$$f_s' = n\frac{M}{I}y = ()\frac{()(12)}{()}() = ksi$$

$f_s = () ksi < F_s = () ksi.$ (**O.K.** or **N.G.**)

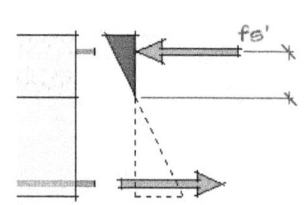

ACI STRENGTH OF BEAMS

CHAPTER 4

4. ACI STRENGTH OF BEAMS

4.1 Introduction

The American Concrete Institute (ACI) is the governing agency for all concrete construction in the U.S. It was established in 1904 to serve and represent user interests in the field of concrete. The ACI publishes many different standards, but the most commonly referenced standard used by architects and engineers is the ACI 318 "Building Code Requirements for Structural Concrete." It is updated every 3 years and the latest version is ACI 318-19 updated in 2019. Almost all Building Codes, including the IBC, refer to ACI 318 as the basis for structural design of concrete members.

4.2 Beam Strength according to ACI Code

The ACI nominal bending strength of a reinforced concrete beam is based on the Whitney stress block as studied in the previous chapter.

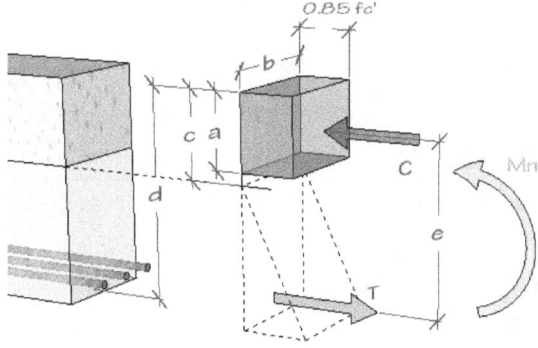

$$M_n = T \times e = T\left(d - \frac{a}{2}\right)$$

The depth of the Whitney stress block, $a = \beta_1 c$ and the values for β_1 are reduced for high-strength concretes as follows:

f_c' (psi)	3000	4000	5000	6000	7000
β_1	0.85	0.85	0.80	0.75	0.70

4.3 Ductility Considerations

Reinforced concrete beams fail in either one of the two following modes:

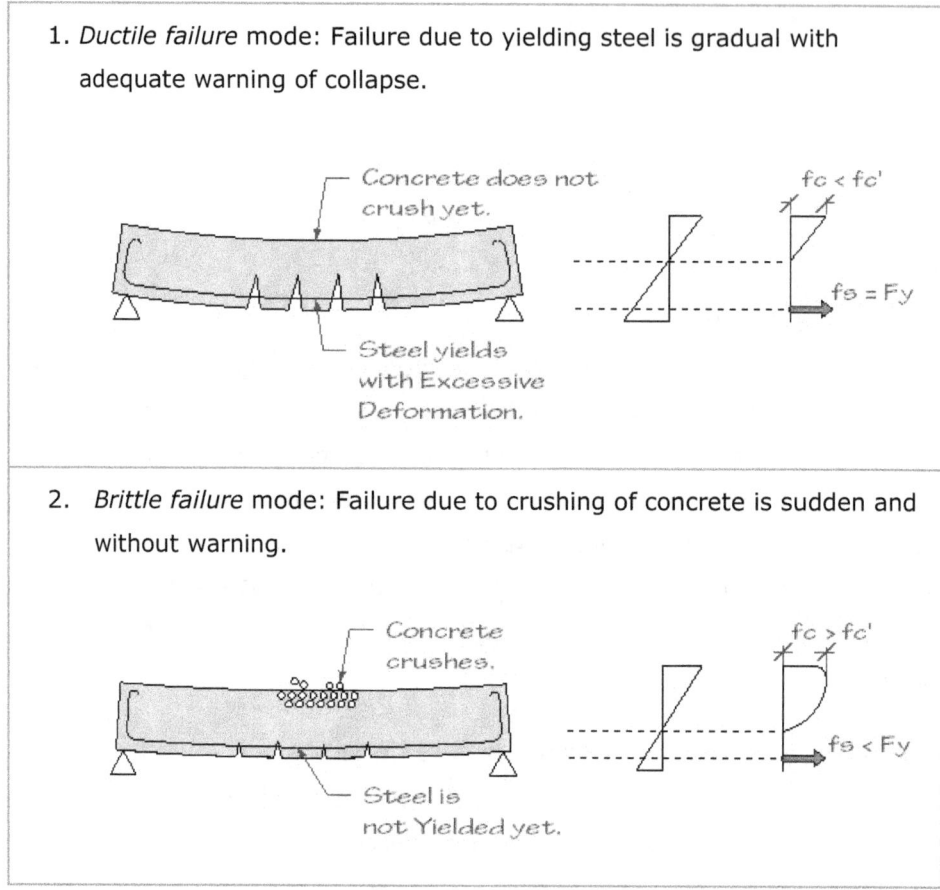

1. *Ductile failure* mode: Failure due to yielding steel is gradual with adequate warning of collapse.

2. *Brittle failure* mode: Failure due to crushing of concrete is sudden and without warning.

If the steel does not yield at all before the concrete crushes ($\varepsilon_c = 0.003$), the failure is brittle. Note that the extreme fiber concrete compressive strain at ultimate is assumed to be 0.003 in all cases. The strength reduction factor is adjusted depending upon the type of failure. The following definitions are used in specifying the factors.

1. **Compression-controlled section** - The definition of "compression controlled" is found in ACI 318 10.3.3. Sections are compression controlled when the net tensile strain in the extreme tensile steel at the ultimate stage is less than or equal to the compression-controlled strain limit (i.e. the reinforcement tensile strain at the balanced condition, or 0.002 for Grade 60 steel).

2. **Tension-controlled section** - The definition of "*tension controlled*" is found in ACI 318 10.3.4. Sections are defined to be *tension controlled* when the strain in the steel is at or in excess of 0.005 when the concrete reaches its maximum usable strain. This is in excess of the yield strain in the reinforcing steel.

ACI STRENGTH OF BEAMS

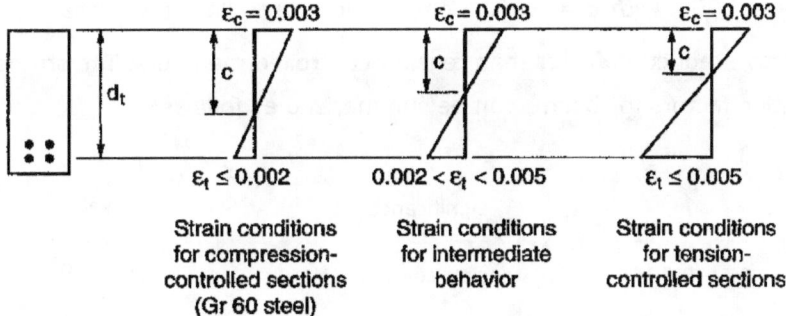

Strain conditions for compression-controlled sections (Gr 60 steel) | Strain conditions for intermediate behavior | Strain conditions for tension-controlled sections

3. Note that the definitions are based on the reinforcement strain in the extreme level of reinforcement, and not at the centroid of the tensile reinforcement. Strain distributions corresponding to tension and compression-controlled sections are shown in the figure below.

These definitions can be related to the type of failure as follows:
   a. Compression-controlled sections are either balanced or over-reinforced
   b. Transition sections are somewhat under-reinforced
   c. Tension-controlled sections are significantly under-reinforced

Strain Limit for Beams (ACI 10.3.5)

ACI 318-19 requires that T-beams (members without a significant axial force) be designed such that the net tensile strain in the extreme tensile steel at the ultimate stage is greater than or equal to 0.004. This ensures that T-beams are designed to be sufficiently under-reinforced. Per ACI 318-19 definitions, beams must be either tension-controlled, or in the transition zone between tension-controlled and compression-controlled designs. Beams cannot be designed as compression-controlled.

4.4 Strength Reduction Factors (ACI 9.3.2)

The ACI Code requires a lower strength reduction factor (higher factor of safety) for compression-controlled members because they exhibit brittle failures. The ϕ factor for tension is 0.9 and the one for compression-controlled sections is 0.65 for members with other than spiral transverse reinforcement. Most T-beams fall into this category. A linear transition is assumed between the tension- and compression-controlled limits as shown in the figure below.

ACI 318-19 limits the design of beams such that the strain in the extreme layer of tension reinforcement is at least 0.004. At a strain $\varepsilon_t = 0.004$, the corresponding strength reduction factor (for other than spiral reinforced members) is 0.81. Thus, it can be stated that the strength reduction factor for extreme layer of tension reinforcement. *It is generally most economical to* *design beams such that the strain in the extreme layer of tension reinforcement exceeds 0.005, with $\phi = 0.90$.* "Compression controlled" beams have a more restrictive reduction factor than tension-controlled members. The strength reduction factors for beams can be summarized as follows;

	significance	ϕ -value
$\varepsilon_t > 0.005$	tension-controlled	$\phi = 0.9$
$0.004 < \varepsilon_t < 0.005$	in the transition zone	$\Phi = 0.65 + (\varepsilon_t - 0.002)\dfrac{0.25}{0.003}$
$\varepsilon_t < 0.004$	beyond minimum limit	increase beam dimensions

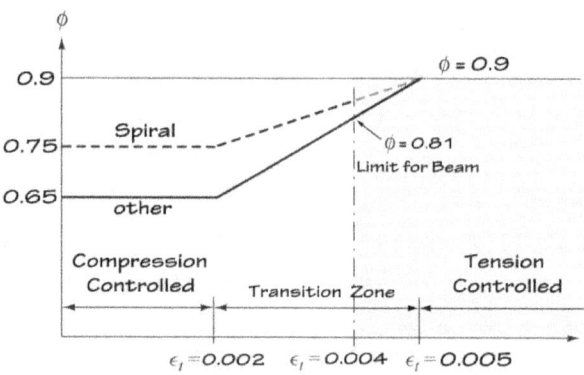

4.5 Balanced Section (Under-Reinforced and Over-Reinforced Beams)

A balanced-reinforced beam is one in which both the compressive and tensile zones reach yielding at the same imposed load on the beam, and the concrete will crush and the tensile steel will yield at the same time. This design criterion is however as risky as over-reinforced concrete, because failure is sudden as the concrete crushes at the same time of the tensile steel yields, which gives a very little warning of distress in tension failure.

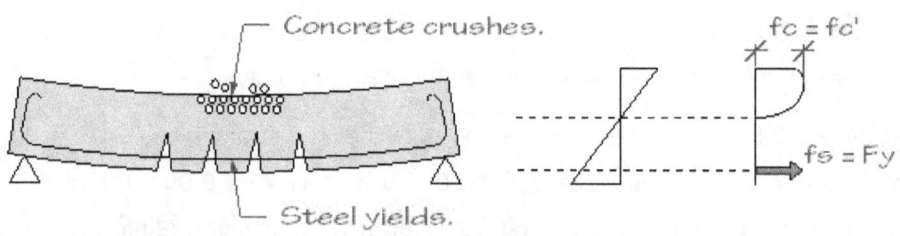

ACI STRENGTH OF BEAMS

The bending moment strength increases almost linearly with increasing amounts of reinforcement. But this applies to steel ratios not exceeding 2%. The steel ratio, at times called reinforcement ratio, is defined by:

$$\rho = \frac{A_s}{b\,d}$$

The idea that moment capacity increases with increasing steel ratio is fairly straightforward. The expression implies so succinctly.

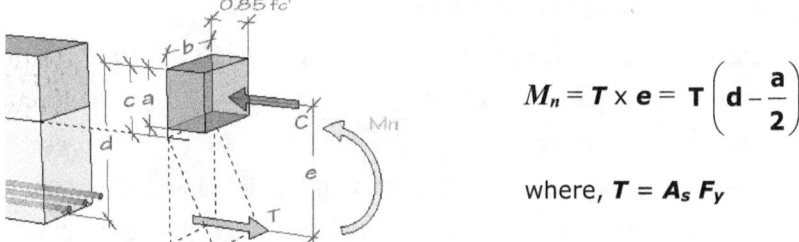

$$M_n = T \times e = T\left(d - \frac{a}{2}\right)$$

where, $T = A_s F_y$

Increasing the amount of reinforcement in tension is not always beneficial. The amount of reinforcement needs to be limited to approximately 2% of $b \times d$ for several practical and safety reasons. The first practical reason is that steel ratios exceeding 2% lead to congestion and problems during concrete casting. Another reason is that, as increases, crushing of the concrete is reached before the steel reinforcement yields. There is a threshold, a definite amount of reinforcement, for which the limiting strain of concrete and the nominal yield strain of the reinforcement are reached at the same time. The state in which the limiting strain in concrete and the strain at yield of steel are reached simultaneously is called "balanced failure." The steel ratio in the balanced section is called the balanced steel ratio, ρ_b. When this condition occurs the reduction factor ϕ is either 0.65 or 0.70 depending on the nature of the lateral confinement steel. For properly designed beams, this condition rarely occurs.

1. If the balanced steel ratio, ρ_b, exceeded, the reinforcement would not yield before the concrete reaches its limiting strain, 0.003. Beams, in which the steel yields before the concrete develop the full compressive strength at the ultimate load, are called "under-reinforced beams". Failures of under-reinforced beams are ductile and require deformations before failure that are large and serve as warning.

2. Beams, which fail by crushing of the concrete before the steel yields due to an excess of steel, are called "over-reinforced beams". Failures of over-reinforced beams, on the other hand, are brittle, and thus occur so suddenly without warning signs.

Under-reinforced beams are preferred over over-reinforced beams for ductility considerations. The balanced strain condition for a rectangular beam with tension reinforcement only is:

$$\rho_b = \frac{0.85 f_c}{f_y} \beta_1 \left(\frac{x_b}{d}\right) \qquad (3.5.3)$$

$$\rho_b = \frac{0.85 f_c}{f_y} \beta_1 \left(\frac{87000}{87000 + f_y}\right) \qquad (3.5.4)$$

4.6 Maximum Reinforcement Ratio

In order to assure a ductile failure, the ACI limits (ACI 10.3.3) the amount of tension steel to not more than 75 % of the amount in the balanced strain condition, ρ_{max} = 0.75 ρ_b. A more direct way of controlling ductility is to prescribe a maximum value for the neutral axis distance x at the imminent failure, x_{max} = 0.75 x_b. To ensure some degree of ductility in beams, codes limit the maximum steel ratio, ρ_{max} of a beam to approximately 54% of ρ_b. ACI encourages the designer to use reinforcement ratios lower than ρ_{max} by allowing the use of a larger strength reduction factor for sections with reinforcement ratios not exceeding 5/8 of ρ_b. For these reasons and to prevent practical problems during construction, it is desirable that reinforced concrete beams should not contain reinforcement exceeding a ratio of 2%.

Steel strain (ε_t)	Strength Reduction Factor (ϕ)	Note
0.005	0.9	Tension-controlled
0.002	0.65	Compression-controlled (tied)
0.002	0.7	Compression-controlled (spiral)
0.004	0.81667	Maximum limit for singly reinforced (tied)
0.003667	0.78889	balanced condition (tied)

4.7 Minimum reinforcement limits for beams (ACI 10.5)

ACI 318-19 requires a minimum amount of reinforcement in beams so that T-beams are prevented from failing immediately after cracking. The minimum amount of reinforcement is given as:

$$A_{s,min} = \frac{3\sqrt{f'_c}}{f_y} b_w d \geq \frac{200}{f_y} b_w d$$

Note that ACI 10.5.3 stipulates that the above limit need not be applied if the area of tensile reinforcement provided is at least 33% greater than required by analysis.

ACI STRENGTH OF BEAMS

Case Study 4.1a

Determine the ACI design moment strength, ϕM_n, of a beam with b = 15", h = 27" (3" cover) and 4-#9 tension reinforcement. $f_c' = 4$ ksi, and $f_y = 60$ ksi.

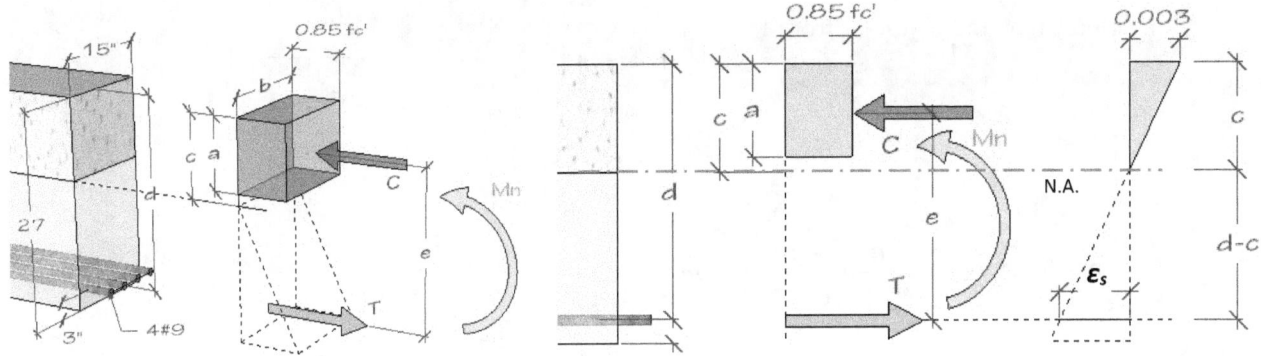

Solution)

Calculation of the **Nominal Strength, M_n**

1) **Tensile force** in the reinforcing *steel*

$$T = A_s f_y = (4.0 \text{ in}^2)(60 \frac{k}{\text{in}^2}) = 240 \text{ k}$$

(Note: All steel bars yielded so the steel stress is Fy.)

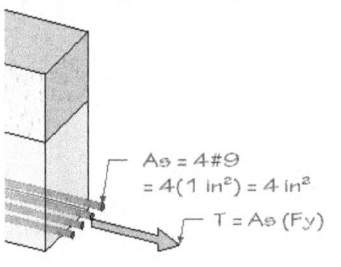

2) **Compressive force** in the *concrete*

$$C = (a \times b)(0.85 f_c') = (15 a)(0.85 \times 4 \text{ ksi}) = 51a$$

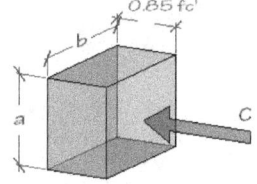

3) Depth of stress block, *a*, using *horizontal equilibrium*

$$C = T \quad \therefore 51a = 240 \quad \text{or,} \quad a = \frac{240}{51} = 4.71 \text{ in}$$

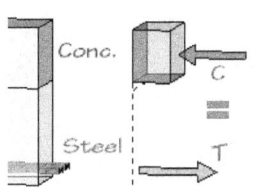

4) Nominal moment strength, M_n

$$M_n = T\left(d - \frac{a}{2}\right) = (240)\left(24 - \frac{4.71}{2}\right) = 5194.8 \text{ k-in}$$
$$= 432.9 \text{ k-ft.}$$

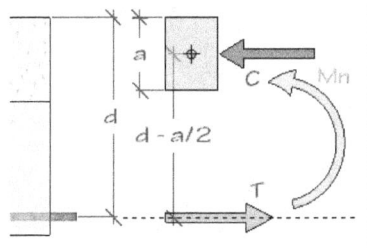

ACI STRENGTH OF BEAMS

Determine the **Strength Reduction Factor, ϕ**

1) Neutral Axis Distance, c

i. Determine the β_1-factor from :

f_c' (psi)	3000	4000	5000	6000	7000
β_1	0.85	(0.85)	0.80	0.75	0.70

ii. Calculate c by $c = \dfrac{a}{\beta_1} = \dfrac{4.71}{0.85} = 5.54"$

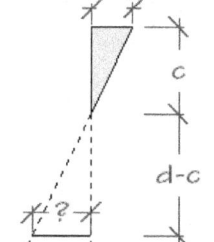

2) Tensile Strain in Steel, ε_s

From the similarity of the triangles,

$$\varepsilon_s = \dfrac{d-c}{c}(0.003) = \dfrac{24 - 5.54}{5.54}(0.003) = 0.010$$

3) Strength Reduction Factor, ϕ

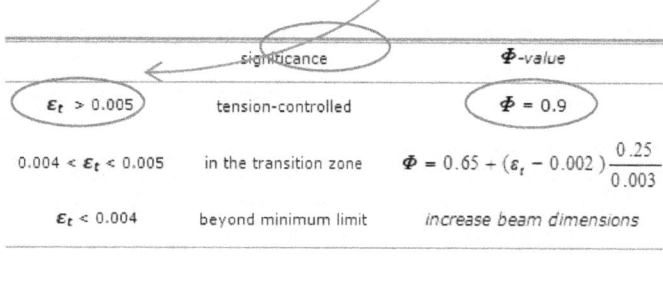
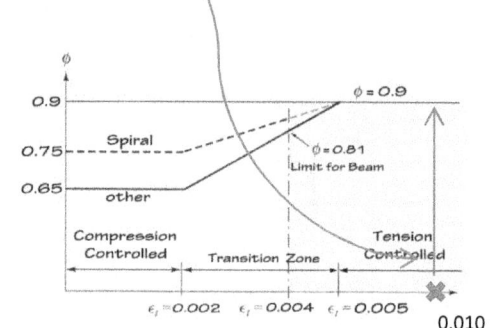

significance	Φ-value
$\varepsilon_t > 0.005$ — tension-controlled	$\Phi = 0.9$
$0.004 < \varepsilon_t < 0.005$ — in the transition zone	$\Phi = 0.65 + (\varepsilon_t - 0.002)\dfrac{0.25}{0.003}$
$\varepsilon_t < 0.004$ — beyond minimum limit	increase beam dimensions

Therefore, the strength reduction factor, $\phi = 0.9$

Finally,

ACI Design Moment Strength, ϕM_n

$$\phi M_n = (0.9)(432.9 \text{ k-ft}) = \boxed{389.6 \text{ k-ft.}}$$

4.8 ACI Singly Reinforced Concrete Beam Design Process

Design Objective : $\phi M_n > M_u$

Reduced Nominal Strength > *Amplified* Load Effects

Or,

Provided Design Strength > *Required* Strength

When designing a singly reinforced concrete beam, the flexural limit state ϕM_n is used to determine when the beam will fail. For singly reinforced beams that fail in tension, the strength reduction factor (ϕ) will always be 0.9. This reduction factor is to account for variability in material strength and uncertainties involved in construction procedures. As defined by the American Concrete Institute (ACI), the nominal moment strength is reached when the extreme concrete fiber crushes. This is when the strain equals 0.003. It must be noted that designing a beam is not a linear process but a trial-and-error process and thus it may take several tries to satisfy the design requirement. It is not uncommon to cycle this process 2-3 times before satisfying the strength requirements.

1. Structural Analysis of the Beam

    The first step for designing a beam is to analyze the load which the beam will be carrying. Beam loads are typically simplified as a uniformed distributed load. Determine the shear forces and moments. Concrete beams are designed to fail in flexure (not in shear), so the design moment (M_u) can be found from the moment diagram. Then, the required value of $M_n = M_u/\phi$.

2. Specify the Compression Strength of the Concrete.

    The engineer must make educated assumptions based on what the beam is supporting in order to specify the concrete's strength. Most beams are designed using normal concrete. Normal concrete compression strength ranges from 3,000–7,000 psi. High strength concrete has compression strengths from 7,000–15,000 psi.

3. Specify the Tensile Strength of the Steel Reinforcement.

    For a typical concrete beam, the engineer will specify ASTM A615 steel which has a yield strength (F_y) of 60,000 psi. The tensile strength of steel ranges from 40 ksi to 120 ksi.

4. Determine the Cross-Sectional Dimensions of the Beam.

    In a building, a beam depth is usually limited by ceiling height limitations due to architectural consideration. The dimension of the beam's cross-section must accommodate the constraints of the structure.

5. Calculate the Area of Steel Required.

   With given values of M_n, b and d, the area of steel (A_s) required in a singly reinforced concrete beam is calculated with the Table 7.1 – 7.6.

6. Select the Area of Steel to be Provided.

   The area of steel provided must be greater than the area of steel required that is calculated in the previous step. Using the steel reinforcement table in the Appendix, try to select a steel area that will require 3 to 6 bars. If you select a bar size that requires more than 6 bars for the required area, reselect a larger bar size. It is difficult in construction to fit more than 6 bars in a narrow beam. The area of steel provided must be slightly larger than the area of steel required.

8. Calculate the Nominal Moment Strength

   Use the following equation to calculate the nominal moment strength:

   $$M_n = T \times e = T\left(d - \frac{a}{2}\right) \quad \text{where, } T = A_s F_y$$

9. Verify that $\phi M_n > M_u$

   Now that the nominal moment strength (M_n) of the beam has been calculated, it must be verified that it is greater than the design moment strength (M_u) that was found from structural analysis.

   Note: If this inequality is not satisfied, return to step 2 to increase the strength of the concrete, step 3 to increase the tensile strength of the steel, or step 4 to make the beam's cross-section larger.

10. Sketch the Beam

    Draw the outline of the beam to a scale of your choice. Be sure to label the height and width of the cross-section, length of the beam, and call out the number of bars used and bar#. The steel reinforcement will be 2.5 inches from the bottom of the beam when using this method of design.

4.9 Summary of Design of Singly Reinforced Beam

The problem is to determine **b**, **d**, and **As** with a given required moment capacity of **Mu** and material properties **fc'** and **Fy**. Since there are only two applicable equations of equilibrium, but three unknowns, many possible solutions exist.

1. Assume ϕ = 0.9 and check at the end.
2. Determine **Mn** using:

    Mn = Mu/ ϕ

3. Assume a preliminary Steel Ratio.

    $$\rho = 0.18 \frac{f'_c}{f_y}$$

4. Use Tables 4-1 and 4-6 to determine the required **Rn** with the assumed value of **ρ**.
5. Determine the required **bd²** from **Rn** with the known (required) value of **Mn** using:

    $$R_n = \frac{M_n}{bd^2}$$

6. Choose values for **b** and **d**, according to the architectural limitations, with a reasonable proportion of **d/b**=1.5 to 2.0.
7. Determine revised **ρ** for the new **Rn** using Tables 7-1 thru 7-6.

    $$R_n = \frac{M_n}{bd^2}$$

8. Compute **As** from **As = ρ (b x d)**.
9. Select reinforcement and calculate strength to check if

    ϕ Mn > Mu

10. Remember to check ϕ = 0.9.

Design Table for Singly Reinforced Rectangular Beams

The design tables, Table 4.1 – 4.6, are to find **As** with given **b** and **d** as follows:

$$R_n = \frac{M_n}{bd^2}$$

Enter Table 4.1 – 4.4 with **Rn** to find the steel ratio, **ρ**. A linear interpolation may be required. Then, the steel area, **As** is calculated:

As = ρ (b x d)

ACI STRENGTH OF BEAMS

4.10 Summary

LOAD FACTORS *(representative and typical, not constant)*

Dead Load	1.2
Live Load	1.6

STRENGTH REDUCTION FACTORS (Resistance Factors)

0.90	Tension-Controlled Beams and Slabs
0.75	Shear and Torsion in Beam
0.65 or 0.70	Columns
0.65 or 0.7 to 0.9	Columns supporting very small axial loads
0.65	Bearing

STEEL RATIO

Ratio between Cross-sectional area of Reinforcing steel bar and that of Concrete

$$\rho = \frac{A_s}{bd} \qquad \text{or,} \qquad A_s = \rho(bd)$$

In design,

$$\rho = \frac{0.85 f_c'}{F_y}\left(1 - \sqrt{1 - \frac{2R_n}{0.85 f_c'}}\right) \qquad \text{where, } R_n = \frac{M_u}{\phi \, bd^2} \qquad \text{(or, use Tables 4-1 to 4-6)}$$

MINIMUM CLEAR COVER FOR REINFORCEMENTS

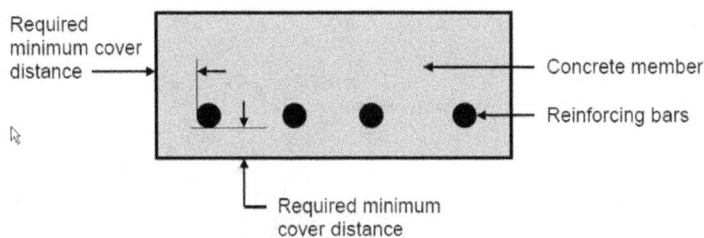

Minimum Concrete Cover Over Reinforcing Bars			
Condition:			Minimum cover:
Concrete cast against and permanently exposed to earth			3"
Concrete exposed to earth or weather	No. 6 through No. 18 bars		2"
	No. 5 and smaller bars		1.5"
Concrete NOT exposed to earth or weather	Slabs, walls & joists	No. 14 & No. 18	1.5"
		No. 11 and smaller	0.75"
	Beams, columns	Main reinf., stirrups, ties, spirals	1.5"
	Shells, folded plates	No. 6 and larger	0.75"
		No. 5 and smaller	0.5"

ACI STRENGTH OF BEAMS

$\rho < \rho_b$		**Under-reinforced Section** A beam with a steel ratio (ρ) smaller than a balanced ratio (ρ_b). For this beam, at the ultimate load, the tension steel reaches its yield strength first while the compression concrete is still under-stressed. Because the steel is a ductile material, appreciable deflections results after yielding. (*We want this type of failure – ductile type of failure!*)
$\rho = \rho_b$		**Balanced Section** and **Balanced Steel Ratio** (ρ_b) For a beam with a balanced steel ratio (ρ_b), at the ultimate load, the compression concrete begins to be crushed and, at the same time, the tensile steel begins to yield.
$\rho > \rho_b$		**Over-reinforced Section** A beam with a steel ratio (ρ) greater than a balanced ratio (ρ_b). For this beam, at the ultimate load, the compression concrete reaches its ultimate strength first while the tension stress in the reinforcing bar is still below the yield strength. Because the concrete is a brittle material, the failure occurs suddenly without warning.

DESIGN OF RECTANGULAR BEAMS

Estimate of Beam Weight	0.5 kips/ft is a good start point in a preliminary analysis.
Beam Proportion	**d/b** ratio of 1.5 - 2 is economical for the 20 – 25 ft. span. Use the whole inches. (for construction purposes) Use multiples of 2 or 3 inches for beam width.
Selection of Re-Bars	Use one size only in a beam. (for construction purposes) Use #11 or smaller. (for bond between concrete and steel)
Clear Cover	Protection from fire and corrosion. *Minimum distance from the surface of the concrete.* (1.5") Use Table A.5 for minimum Beam Width.
Spacing of Re-Bars	Clear distance between bars ≥ 1 in. *and* bar diameter

ACI STRENGTH OF BEAMS

Case Study 4.1a

Determine the ACI design moment strength, ϕM_n, of a beam with b = 15", h = 27" (3" cover) and 4-#9 tension reinforcement. $f_c' = 4$ ksi, and $f_y = 60$ ksi.

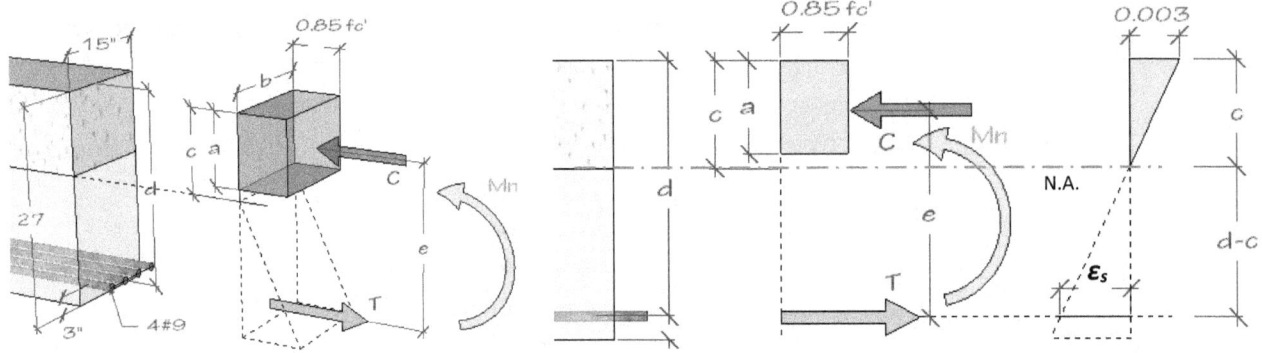

Solution)

Calculation of the **Nominal Strength, M_n**

1) Tensile force in the reinforcing steel $T = A_s f_y = ($ $)($ $) =$ (Note : All steel bars yielded so the steel stress is Fy.)	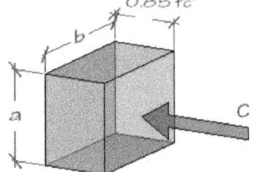
2) Compressive force in the concrete $C = (a \times b)(0.85 f_c') = ($ $)($ $) =$	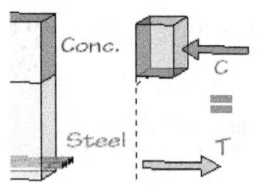
3) Depth of stress block, a, using *horizontal equilibrium* $C = T \quad \therefore$	
4) Nominal moment strength, M_n $M_n = T\left(d - \dfrac{a}{2}\right) = ($ $)\left($ $- \dfrac{()}{2}\right) =$	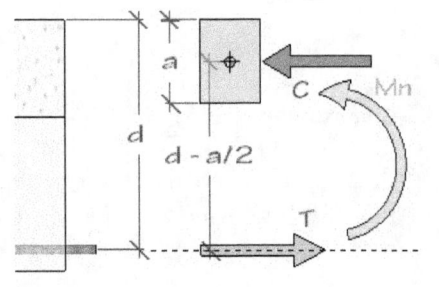

ACI STRENGTH OF BEAMS

Determine the **Strength Reduction Factor, ϕ**

5) Neutral Axis Distance, c

i. Determine the β_1-factor from :

f_c' (psi)	3000	4000	5000	6000	7000
β_1	0.85	0.85	0.80	0.75	0.70

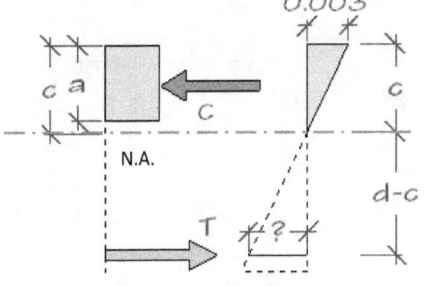

ii. Calculate c by $\quad c = \dfrac{a}{\beta_1} =$

6) Tensile Strain in Steel, ε_s

From the similarity of the triangles,

$$\varepsilon_s = \dfrac{d-c}{c}(0.003) =$$

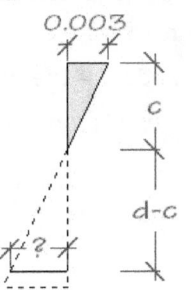

7) Strength Reduction Factor, ϕ

	significance	ϕ-value
$\varepsilon_t > 0.005$	tension-controlled	$\phi = 0.9$
$0.004 < \varepsilon_t < 0.005$	in the transition zone	$\phi = 0.65 + (\varepsilon_t - 0.002)\dfrac{0.25}{0.003}$
$\varepsilon_t < 0.004$	beyond minimum limit	increase beam dimensions

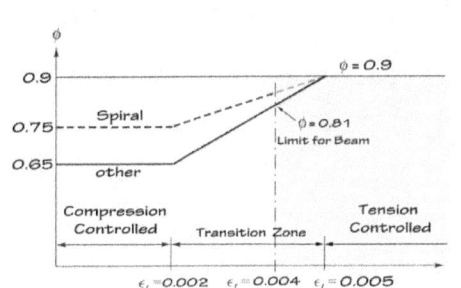

Therefore, the strength reduction factor, $\phi =$

Finally,

ACI Design Moment Strength, ϕM_n

$\phi M_n = ($ $\quad$ $)($ $\quad$ $) = $ ☐

ACI STRENGTH OF BEAMS

Workshop 4.1a
Determine the ACI design moment strength, ϕM_n, of a beam with b = 14", h = 26" and 3-#9 tension reinforcement. $f_c' = 4$ ksi, and $f_y = 60$ ksi.

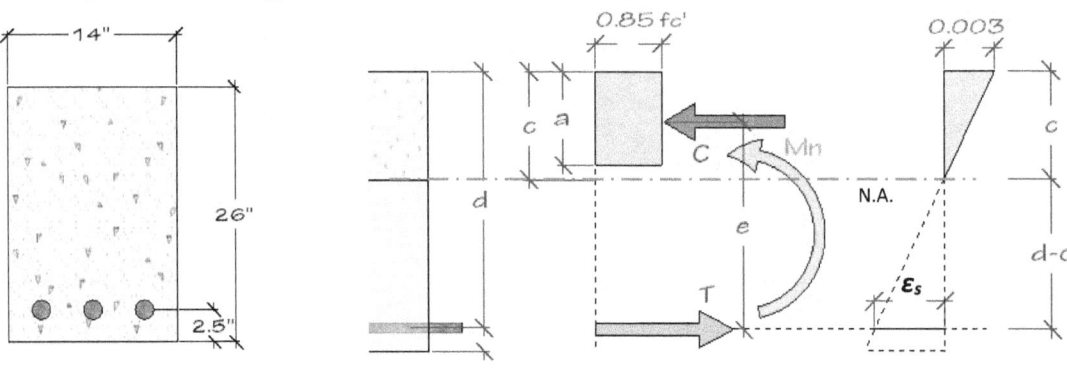

Solution)

Calculation of the **Nominal Strength, M_n**

1) Tensile force in the reinforcing steel

   $T = A_s f_y = ($ $)($ $) = $

   (Note : All steel bars yielded so the steel stress is Fy.)

   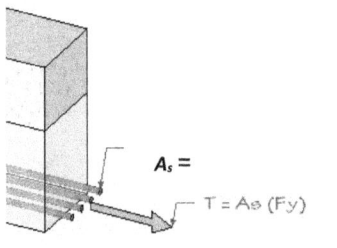

   $A_s = $

2) Compressive force in the concrete

   $C = (a \times b)(0.85 f_c') = ($ $)($ $) = $

   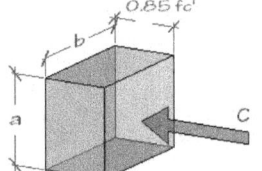

3) Depth of stress block, a, using horizontal equilibrium

   $C = T$ $\therefore$

   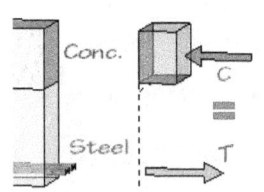

4) Nominal moment strength, M_n

   $M_n = T\left(d - \dfrac{a}{2}\right) = ($ $)\left(- \dfrac{()}{2} \right) =$

   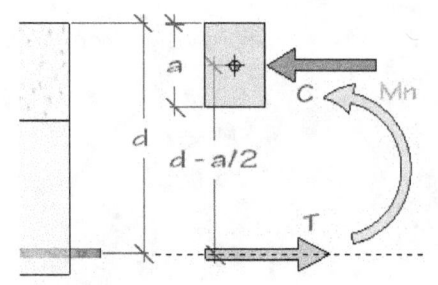

ACI STRENGTH OF BEAMS

Determine the **Strength Reduction Factor**, ϕ

5) Neutral Axis Distance, c

i. Determine the β_1-factor from :

f_c' (psi)	3000	4000	5000	6000	7000
β_1	0.85	0.85	0.80	0.75	0.70

ii. Calculate c by $c = \dfrac{a}{\beta_1} =$

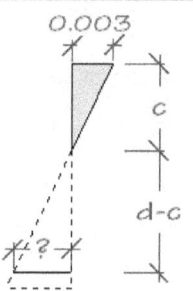

6) Tensile Strain in Steel, ε_s

From the similarity of the triangles,

$$\varepsilon_s = \dfrac{d-c}{c}(0.003) =$$

7) Strength Reduction Factor, ϕ

	significance	ϕ-value
$\varepsilon_t > 0.005$	tension-controlled	$\phi = 0.9$
$0.004 < \varepsilon_t < 0.005$	in the transition zone	$\phi = 0.65 + (\varepsilon_t - 0.002)\dfrac{0.25}{0.003}$
$\varepsilon_t < 0.004$	beyond minimum limit	increase beam dimensions

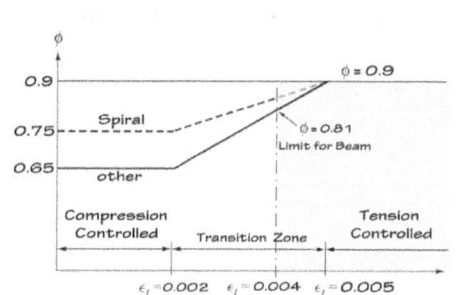

Therefore, the strength reduction factor, $\phi =$

Finally,

ACI Design Moment Strength, ϕM_n

$\phi M_n = (\quad)(\quad) = \boxed{}$

ACI STRENGTH OF BEAMS

Workshop 4.1b

Determine the ACI design moment strength, ϕM_n, of a beam with b = 12", h = 24" and 3-#10 tension reinforcement. $f_c' = 4$ ksi, and $f_y = 60$ ksi.

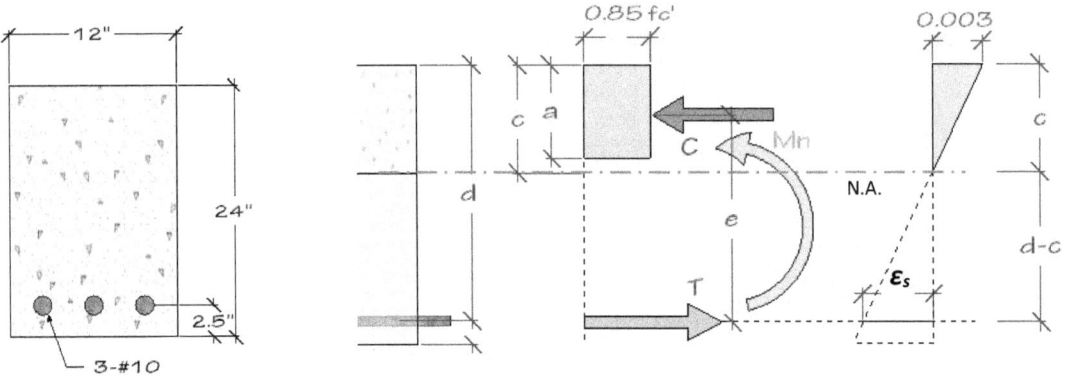

Solution)

Calculation of the **Nominal Strength, M_n**

1) Tensile force in the reinforcing steel
$T = A_s f_y = ($ $)($ $) =$ 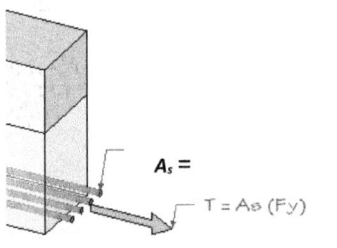   (Note : All steel bars yielded so the steel stress is Fy.)

2) Compressive force in the concrete
$C = (a \times b)(0.85 f_c') = ($ $)($ $) =$ 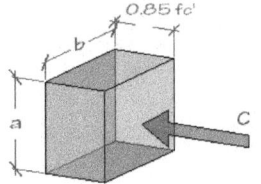

3) Depth of stress block, a, using horizontal equilibrium
$C = T$ $\therefore$ 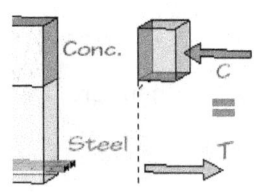

4) Nominal moment strength, M_n
$M_n = T\left(d - \dfrac{a}{2}\right) = ($ $)\left($ $- \dfrac{(\quad)}{2}\right) =$ 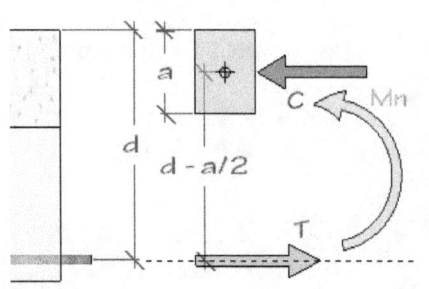

ACI STRENGTH OF BEAMS

Determine the **Strength Reduction Factor, ϕ**

5) Neutral Axis Distance, c

i. Determine the β_1-factor from :

f_c' (psi)	3000	4000	5000	6000	7000
β_1	0.85	0.85	0.80	0.75	0.70

ii. Calculate c by $c = \dfrac{a}{\beta_1} =$

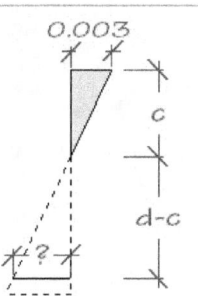

6) Tensile Strain in Steel, ε_s

From the similarity of the triangles,

$$\varepsilon_s = \frac{d-c}{c}(0.003) =$$

7) Strength Reduction Factor, ϕ

	significance	ϕ-value
$\varepsilon_t > 0.005$	tension-controlled	$\phi = 0.9$
$0.004 < \varepsilon_t < 0.005$	in the transition zone	$\phi = 0.65 + (\varepsilon_t - 0.002)\dfrac{0.25}{0.003}$
$\varepsilon_t < 0.004$	beyond minimum limit	increase beam dimensions

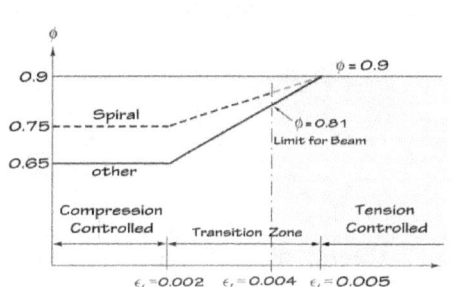

Therefore, the strength reduction factor, $\phi =$

Finally,

ACI Design Moment Strength, ϕM_n

$\phi M_n = ($ $)($ $) = $ ⬜

Workshop 4.1c

Determine the ACI design moment strength, ϕM_n, of a beam with b = 12", h = 24" and 3-#10 tension reinforcement. $f_c' = 3$ ksi, and $f_y = 50$ ksi.

Solution)

Calculation of the **Nominal Strength, M_n**

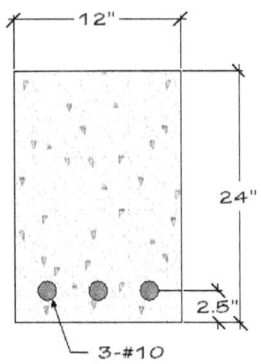

1) *Tensile force* in the reinforcing *steel*

2) *Compressive force* in the *concrete*

3) Depth of stress block, *a*, using *horizontal equilibrium*

4) Nominal moment strength, M_n

ACI STRENGTH OF BEAMS

Determine the **Strength Reduction Factor, ϕ**

5) Neutral Axis Distance, c

i. Determine the β_1-factor from:

f_c' (psi)	3000	4000	5000	6000	7000
β_1	0.85	0.85	0.80	0.75	0.70

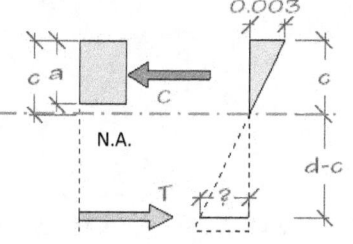

ii. Calculate c by $c = \dfrac{a}{\beta_1} =$

6) Tensile Strain in Steel, ε_s

From the similarity of the triangles,

$$\varepsilon_s = \dfrac{d-c}{c}(0.003) =$$

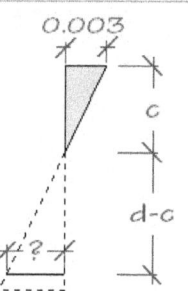

7) Strength Reduction Factor, ϕ

	significance	ϕ-value
$\varepsilon_t > 0.005$	tension-controlled	$\phi = 0.9$
$0.004 < \varepsilon_t < 0.005$	in the transition zone	$\phi = 0.65 + (\varepsilon_t - 0.002)\dfrac{0.25}{0.003}$
$\varepsilon_t < 0.004$	beyond minimum limit	increase beam dimensions

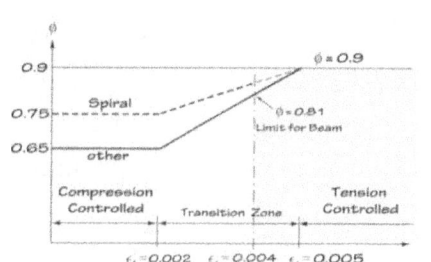

Therefore, the strength reduction factor, $\phi =$

Finally,

ACI Design Moment Strength, ϕM_n

$\phi M_n = ($ $)($ $) =$ ⬚

CHAPTER 5

5. T-BEAMS & ONE-WAY SLAB

1.1 T-beams

In reinforced concrete floor systems, slabs and attached beams are normally constructed at the same time monolithically. Consequently, the beam and a certain portion of the slab will act as a unit and it is difficult to separate the actions of the beams from the action of the slab. But in design, our assumptions do not have to be consistent with all the facts. As long as the product of design is functional, safe, and pleasant to the eye, the process followed in design is of relatively little importance. To design beams cast monolithically with a slab it is assumed that the beams have T-shaped cross sections. The top of the T-beam serves as a flange or compression member in resisting compressive stresses. The thickness of the flange (t_f) of this pseudo beam is set equal to the thickness of the slab. The web of the beam below the compression flange serves to resist shear stress and to provide greater separation for the coupled forces of bending. A concrete T-beam has a similar design (or analysis) procedure as a rectangular beam, although the effective width, b_e, of the flange must be determined first.

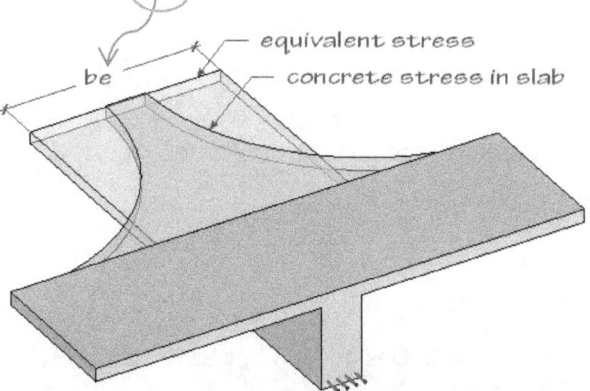

Should the flanges of a T-beam be rather stocky and compact in cross section, bending stresses will be fairly uniformly distributed across the compression zone. If, however, the flanges are wide and thin, bending stresses will vary quite a bit across the flange due to shear deformations. The farther a particular part of the slab or flange is away from the stem, the smaller will be its bending stress. Instead

T-BEAMS & ONE-WAY SLAB

of considering a varying stress distribution across the full width of the flange, the ACI Code (8.12.2) calls for a smaller width with an assumed uniform stress distribution for design purposes. The objective is to have the same total compression force in the reduced width that actually occurs in the full width with its varying stresses. **b_e** in the above picture shows the effective size of a T-beam. For T-beams with flanges on both sides of the web, the code states that the effective flange width may not exceed one-fourth of the beam span, and the overhanging width on each side may not exceed eight times the slab thickness or one-half the clear distance to the next web. An isolated T-beam must have a flange thickness no less than one-half the web width, and its effective flange width may not be larger than four times the web width (ACI 8.12.4).

If there is a flange on only one side of the web, the width of the overhanging flange cannot exceed one-twelfth the span, 6 **h_f**, or half the clear distance to the next web (ACI 8.12.3). It can be summarized as follows:

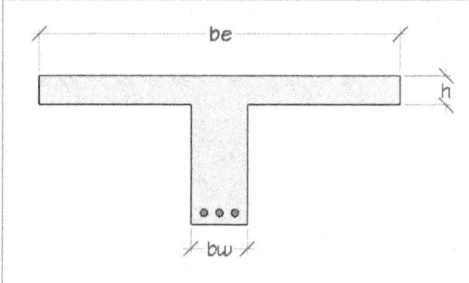

Smallest value of:	Smallest value of:
a. $b_E = \dfrac{\text{Beam Span}}{4}$	a. $b_E = \dfrac{\text{Beam Span}}{12}$
b. $b_E = b_w + 16h$	b. $b_E = b_w + 6h$
c. b_E = center-to-center spacing of beams	c. b_E = ½ clear distance to the next web

The analysis of T-beams is quite similar to the analysis of rectangular beams in that the specifications relating to the strains in the reinforcing are identical. To repeat briefly, it is desirable to have ε_t values $\geq$ 0.005, and they may not be less than 0.004 unless the member is subjected to an axial load $\geq$ 0.10 **f_c' A_g**. In practical design situations, ε_t values are almost always much larger than 0.005 in T-beams because of their very large compression flanges. For such members, the neutral axis distance, **c** is normally very small, and calculated ε_t values very large. If a beam has an unsymmetrical cross-section, the beam bends vertically and horizontally. If an L beam (i.e., edge T-beam with a flange on one side only) deflects both vertically and horizontally, it will be necessary to analyze it as an unsymmetrical section with bending about both the horizontal and vertical axes. However, it may be safely assumed that L beams are not free to bend laterally. Thus, they bend vertically only and may be handled as symmetrical sections, exactly as with T beams. The neutral axis (N.A.) for T-beams can fall either in the flange or in the stem, depending on the proportions of the slabs and stems. It should be noted that the design/analysis of a T-beam will change dependent on whether or not the compression zone is completely in the flange, or if the compression zone extends down into the web.

1. If the neutral axis falls in the flange in a T-section (subjected to for a positive moment), the section above the neutral axis is rectangular. Because the concrete below the neutral axis is assumed to be cracked, the T-shape has no effect on the flexure calculations (except for the self-weight). Thus, this T-beam is analyzed as a rectangular beam.

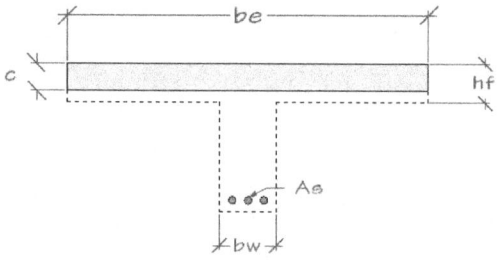

2. If the neutral axis falls in the web in a T-section, the compression concrete above the neutral axis no longer consists of a single rectangle (but a T-shape), and thus the normal rectangular beam expressions do not apply. The neutral distance, c must be determined by including the flange and the stem of the web in the moment area calculation.

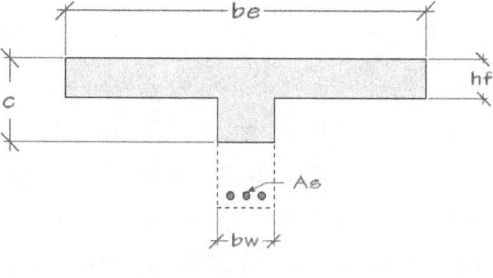

Continuous Beam

For a continuous T-beam subjected to both positive and negative moments, as shown in the figure below, the effective moment of inertia used for calculating deflections varies along the member length. For example, at the center of the span where the positive moment is largest, the web is cracked and the effective section consists of the hatched section plus the tensile reinforcing in the bottom of the web.

At the interior support location where the largest negative moment occurs, the flange is cracked and the effective section consists of the certain part of the web

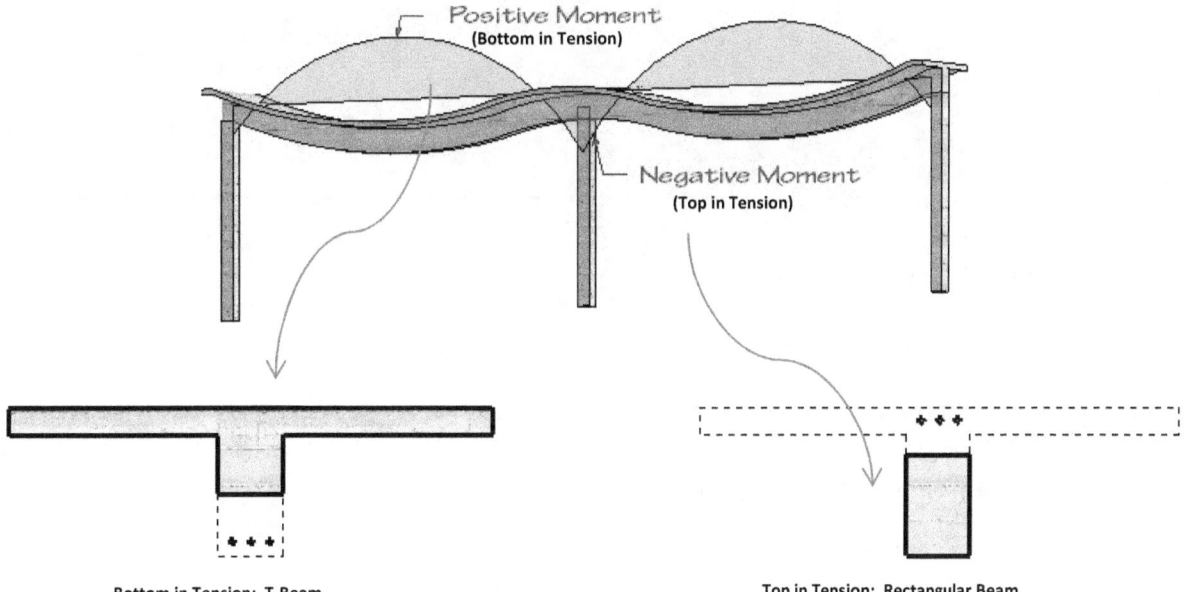

Bottom in Tension: T-Beam   Top in Tension: Rectangular Beam

plus the tensile bars in the top. Finally, near the points of inflection, the moment will be so low that the beam will probably be uncracked, and thus the whole cross section is effective. In order to calculate the deflection in a continuous beam, it is necessary to account the varying moment of inertia along the span. However, this procedure is extremely lengthy. For this reason, the ACI Code (9.5.2.4) permits the use of a constant moment of inertia throughout the member equal to the average of the I_e values computed at the critical positive- and negative-moment sections. The I_e values at the critical negative-moment sections are averaged with each other, and then that average is averaged with I_e at the critical positive-moment section. It should also be noted that the multipliers for long-term deflection at these sections should be averaged, as were the I_e values. This approximate deflection calculation method is commonly used for continuous spans.

T-BEAMS & ONE-WAY SLAB

Case Study 5-1a

Determine the ACI design moment strength, M_n, of the T-beam shown below. The span length of the beam is 20 ft. and beams are centered 9 ft. apart. F_y = 60 ksi and f_c' = 4 ksi.

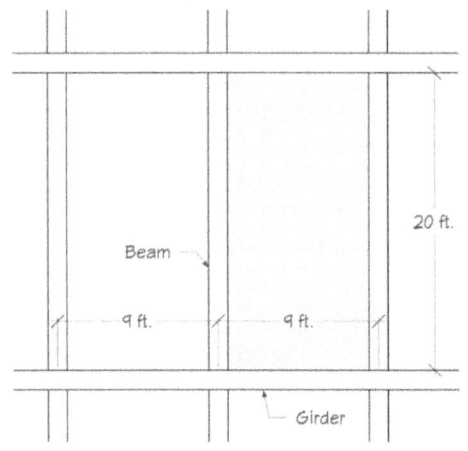
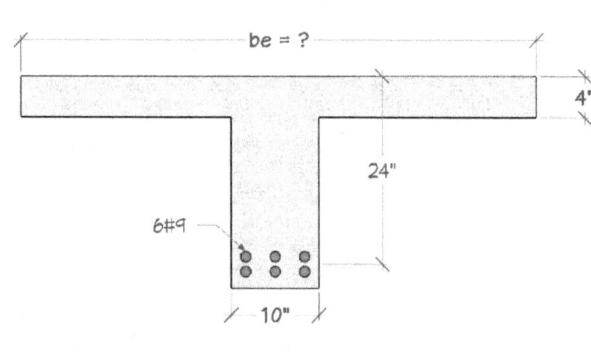

Solution)

1. **Effective flange width** of the T-beam

   Smallest value of:

   a. $b_E = \dfrac{L}{4} = \dfrac{20}{4} = 5\,ft = 60\,in$

   b. $b_E = b_w + 16h = 10" + 16(4") = 74\,in$

   c. b_E = center-to-center spacing of beams $= 9\,ft = 108\,in$

   Thus, the effective flange width, $b_E = 60\,in$

2. **Tensile force** in the reinforcing **steel**

   $T = A_s F_y = (6.0)(60) = 360\,k$

   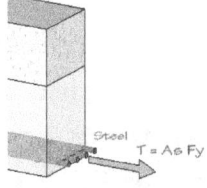

3. **Compressive force** in the **concrete**

   $C = (a \times b)(0.85 f_c') = A_c\,(0.85 \times 4\,ksi)$

   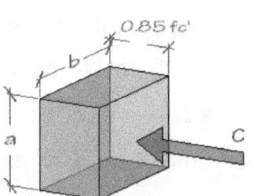

4. Distance to N.A. using **horizontal equilibrium** condition

   $C = T$ or, $A_c\,(0.85 \times 4\,ksi) = 360\,k$

   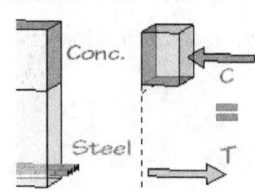

T-BEAMS & ONE-WAY SLAB

or, $A_c = \dfrac{360}{(0.85 \times 4)} = 105.88 \text{ in}^2$

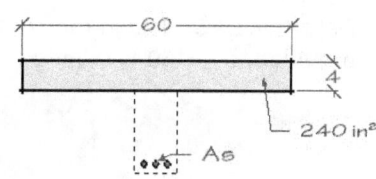

$105.88 \text{ in}^2 <$ flange area $= 60 \times 4 = 240 \text{ in}^2$

⇒ 1. The N.A. is within the flange. → Rectangular Beam with $b = b_E$.
~~2. The N.A. is within the web. → T-beam with $b_f = b_E$.~~

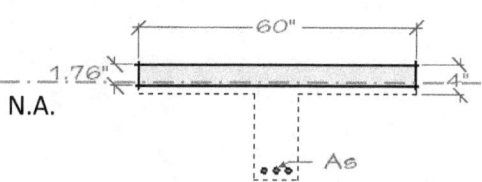

$a = \dfrac{A_c}{b} = \dfrac{105.88}{60} = 1.76 \text{ in}$

5. Noting that **C** and **T** form a couple moment which resists to the applied moment.

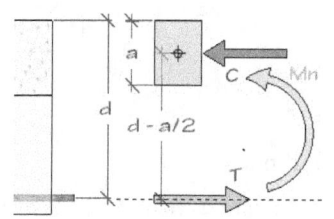

$M_n = (T)(d - a/2) = (360 \text{ k})\left(24 - \dfrac{1.76}{2} \text{ in}\right)$

$= 8323 \text{ k-in} = 693.6 \text{ k-ft}$ ← **Ans.**

6. Checking Strain in Tensile Steel (*to calculate the resistance factor, ϕ*)

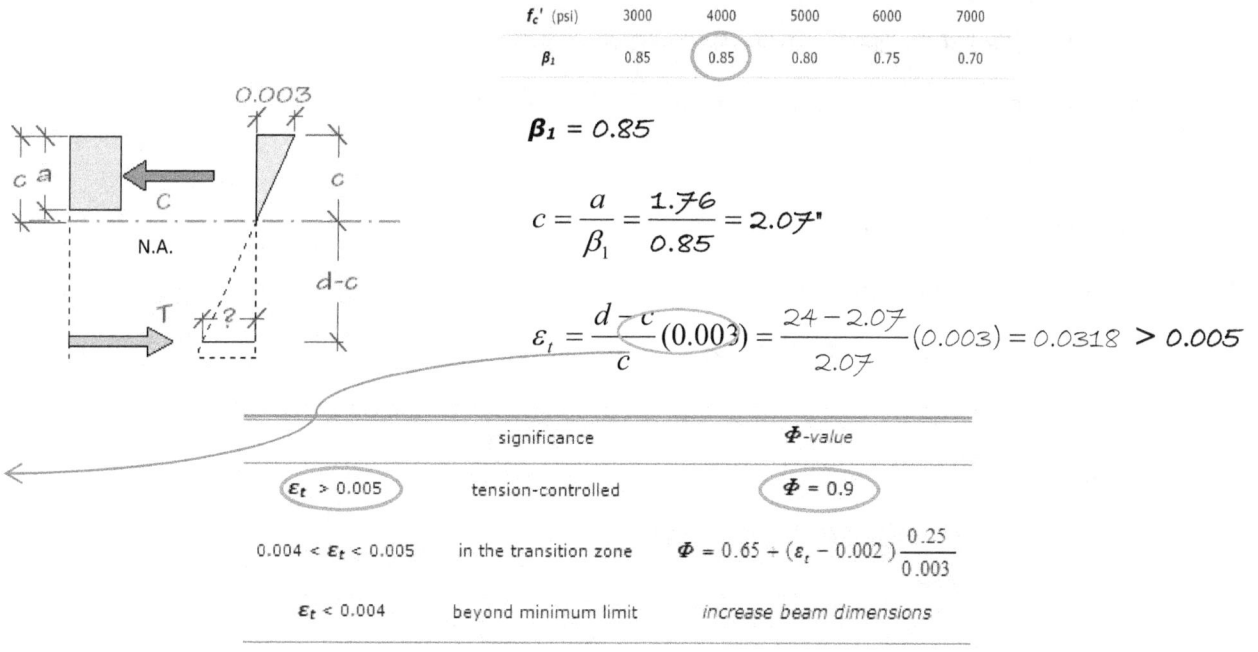

f_c' (psi)	3000	4000	5000	6000	7000
β_1	0.85	0.85	0.80	0.75	0.70

$\beta_1 = 0.85$

$c = \dfrac{a}{\beta_1} = \dfrac{1.76}{0.85} = 2.07"$

$\varepsilon_t = \dfrac{d-c}{c}(0.003) = \dfrac{24 - 2.07}{2.07}(0.003) = 0.0318 > 0.005$

	significance	ϕ-value
$\varepsilon_t > 0.005$	tension-controlled	$\phi = 0.9$
$0.004 < \varepsilon_t < 0.005$	in the transition zone	$\phi = 0.65 + (\varepsilon_t - 0.002)\dfrac{0.25}{0.003}$
$\varepsilon_t < 0.004$	beyond minimum limit	increase beam dimensions

7. **ACI Design Moment Strength, ϕM_n**

$M_u = \phi M_n = (0.9)(693.6 \text{ k-ft}) = \boxed{624.2 \text{ k-ft.}}$

Case Study 5-2a

Determine ACI design moment strength, M_n, of the T-beam shown below when 8-#10 steel bar is provided. $F_y = 60$ ksi, and $f_c' = 4$ ksi

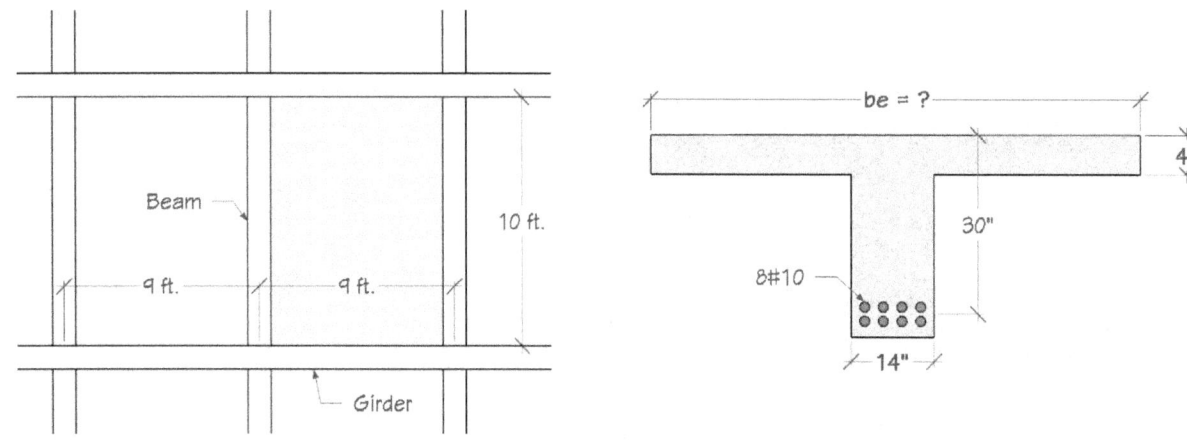

Solution)

1. **Effective flange width** of the T-beam

   Smallest value of:

   a. $b_E = \dfrac{L}{4} = \dfrac{10}{4} = 2.5 \text{ ft} = 30 \text{ in}$

   b. $b_E = b_w + 16h = 14" + 16(4") = 78 \text{ in}$

   c. $b_E = $ center-to-center spacing of beams $= 9 \text{ ft} = 108 \text{ in}$

   Thus, the effective flange width, $b_E = 30$ in

2. **Tensile force** in the reinforcing **steel**

   $$T = A_s F_y = (10.12)(60) = 607.2 \text{ k}$$

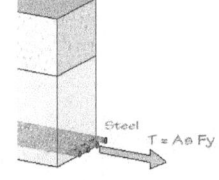

3. **Compressive force** in the **concrete**

   $$C = (a \times b)(0.85 f_c') = Ac\,(0.85 \times 4 \text{ ksi})$$

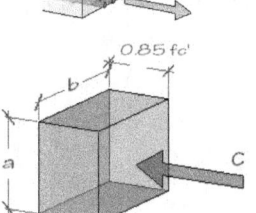

4. Distance to N.A. using **horizontal equilibrium** condition

   $$C = T \quad \text{or,} \quad Ac\,(0.85 \times 4 \text{ ksi}) = 607.2$$

   or, $\quad A_c = \dfrac{607.2}{(0.85 \times 4)} = 178.6 \text{ in}^2$

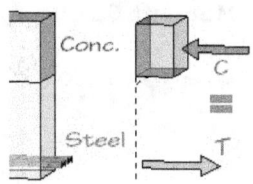

T-BEAMS & ONE-WAY SLAB

5. Location of the neutral axis.

   $A_c = 178.6 \text{ in}^2 >$ flange area $= 30 \times 4 = 120 \text{ in}^2$

   Area in web $= 178.6 \text{ in}^2 - 120 \text{ in}^2 = 58.6 \text{ in}^2$

   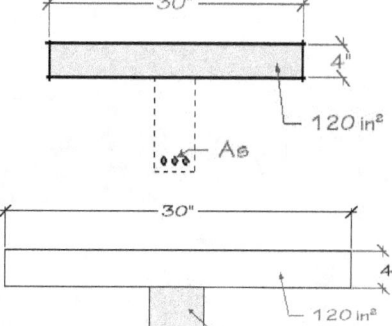

   ~~1. The N.A. is within the flange. → Rectangular Beam with b = b_E.~~

   ⇒ 2. The N.A. is within the web. → T-beam with $b_f = b_E$.

6. Depth of the compressive stress block.
   (note : $A_c \neq a \times b$)

   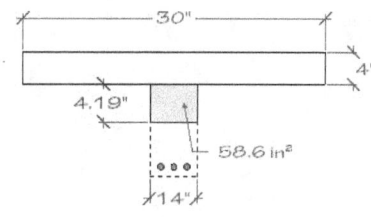

   $\dfrac{58.6}{14} = 4.19$ gives the depth of the effective web.

7. **Moment of Compression Force in Flange**

   $C_f = (30" \times 4")(0.85 \times 4 \text{ ksi}) = 408 \text{ k}$

   $M_f = (408 \text{ k})(30" - 4"/2)$

   $\quad\;\; = 11424 \text{ k-in} = 952 \text{ k-ft}$

   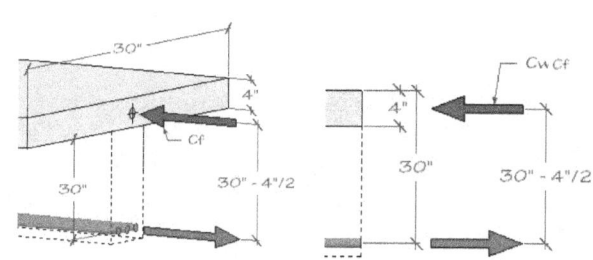

8. **Moment of Compression Force in Web**

   $C_w = (58.6 \text{ in}2)(0.85 \times 4 \text{ ksi}) = 199.24 \text{ k}$

   $M_w = (199.24 \text{ k})(30" - 4 - 4.19"/2))$

   $\quad\;\; = 4762.83 = 396.9 \text{ k-ft}$

   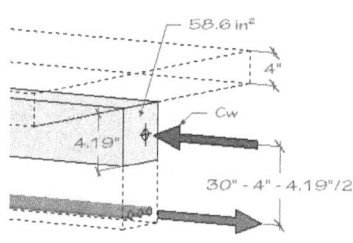

9. **Total Nominal Moment Strength**

   $M_n = M_f + M_w = 952 \text{ k-ft} + 396.9 \text{ k-ft} = 1348.9 \text{ k-ft}$

10. **Strength Reduction Factor, ϕ**

T-BEAMS & ONE-WAY SLAB

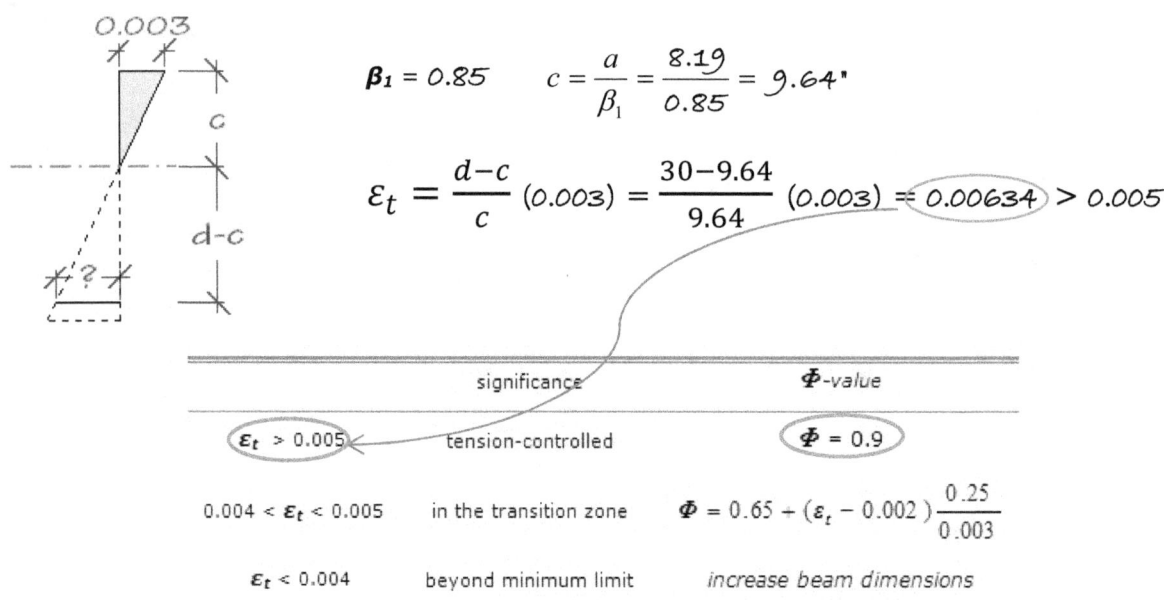

f_c' (psi)	3000	4000	5000	6000	7000
β_1	0.85	0.85	0.80	0.75	0.70

$$\beta_1 = 0.85 \qquad c = \frac{a}{\beta_1} = \frac{8.19}{0.85} = 9.64"$$

$$\varepsilon_t = \frac{d-c}{c}(0.003) = \frac{30-9.64}{9.64}(0.003) = 0.00634 > 0.005$$

	significance	Φ-value
$\varepsilon_t > 0.005$	tension-controlled	$\Phi = 0.9$
$0.004 < \varepsilon_t < 0.005$	in the transition zone	$\Phi = 0.65 + (\varepsilon_t - 0.002)\dfrac{0.25}{0.003}$
$\varepsilon_t < 0.004$	beyond minimum limit	increase beam dimensions

11. **ACI Design Moment Strength, ϕM_n**

$$M_u = \phi M_n = (0.9)(1348.9 \text{ k-ft}) = \boxed{1214 \text{ k-ft}}$$

T-BEAMS & ONE-WAY SLAB

Workshop 5-1a
Determine ACI design moment strength, M_n, of the T-beam when 4-#9 steel bar is provided. The span length of the beam is 28 ft. and beams are centered 12 ft. apart. $f_c' = 4$ ksi, and $F_y = 50$ ksi

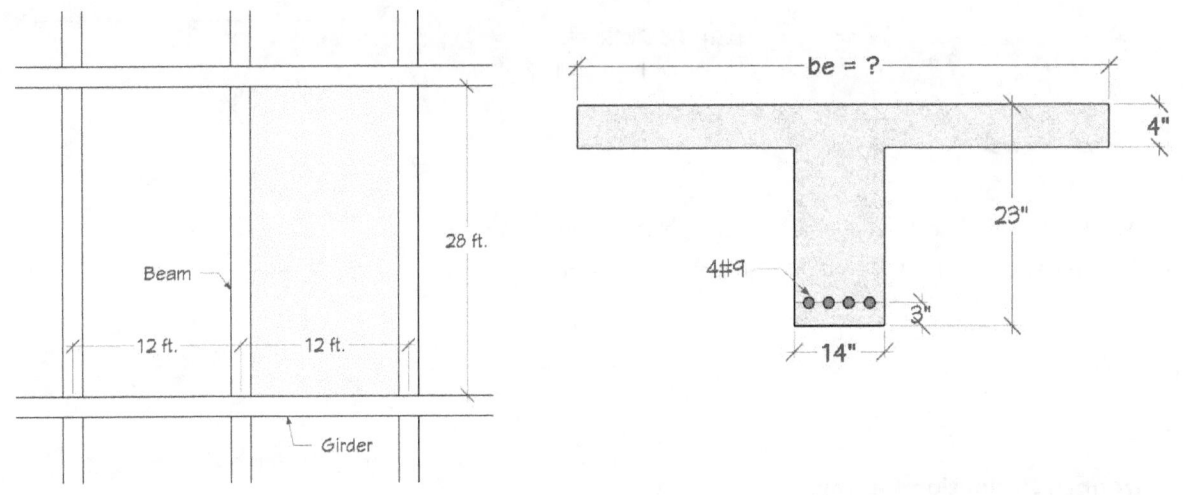

Solution)

1. **Effective flange width** of the T-beam

   Smallest value of:

   a. $b_E = \dfrac{L}{4} =$

   b. $b_E = b_w + 16h =$

   c. $b_E =$ center-to-center spacing of beams $=$

   Thus, the effective flange width, $b_E =$

2. **Tensile force** in the reinforcing **steel**

   $T = A_s F_y =$

3. **Compressive force** in the **concrete**

   $C = (a \times b)(0.85 f_c') =$

   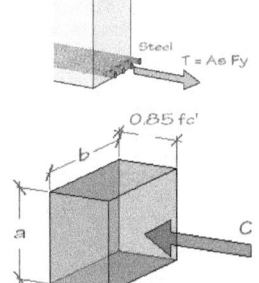

4. Distance to N.A. using **horizontal equilibrium** condition

   $C = T$ or,

   or, $A_c =$

   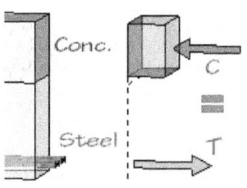

T-BEAMS & ONE-WAY SLAB

5. Location of the neutral axis.

$A_c = ($ $) in^2$ $\genfrac{}{}{0pt}{}{>}{<}$ flange area =

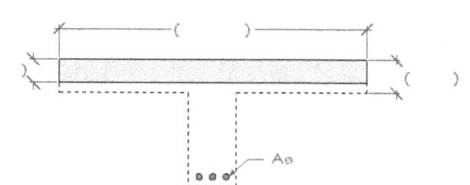

Area in web =

1. The N.A. is within the flange. → Rectangular Beam with b = b_E.
2. The N.A. is within the web. → T-beam with $b_f = b_E$.

$$a = \frac{A_c}{b} =$$

6. **Strength Reduction Factor, ϕ**

f_c' (psi)	3000	4000	5000	6000	7000
β_1	0.85	0.85	0.80	0.75	0.70

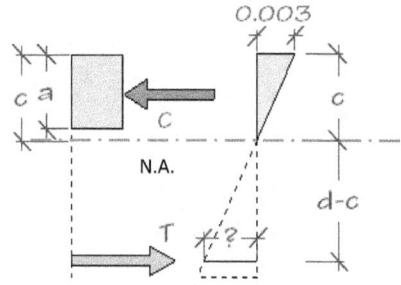

$\beta_1 = ($ $)$

$$c = \frac{a}{\beta_1} =$$

$$\varepsilon_t = \frac{d-c}{c}(0.003) =$$

	significance	ϕ-value
$\varepsilon_t > 0.005$	tension-controlled	$\phi = 0.9$
$0.004 < \varepsilon_t < 0.005$	in the transition zone	$\phi = 0.65 + (\varepsilon_t - 0.002)\dfrac{0.25}{0.003}$
$\varepsilon_t < 0.004$	beyond minimum limit	increase beam dimensions

7. **ACI Design Moment Strength, ϕM_n**

$M_u = \phi M_n =$

T-BEAMS & ONE-WAY SLAB

Workshop 5-2a
Determine ACI design moment strength, M_n, of the T-beam shown below when 8-#10 steel bar is provided. F_y = 60 ksi, and f_c' = 4 ksi.

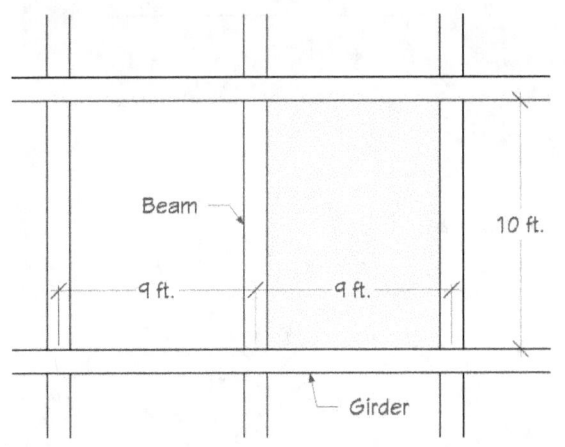
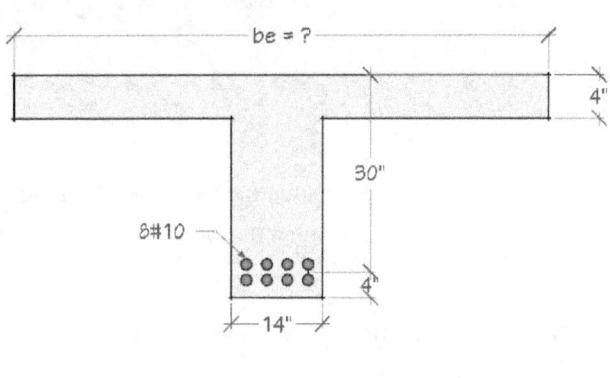

Solution)
1. **Effective flange width** of the T-beam

    Smallest value of:

    a. $b_E = \dfrac{L}{4} =$

    b. $b_E = b_w + 16h =$

    c. $b_E =$ center-to-center spacing of beams $=$

    Thus, the effective flange width, $b_E =$

2. **Tensile force** in the reinforcing **steel**

    $T = A_s F_y =$

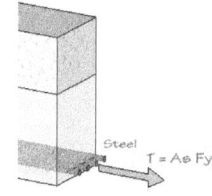

3. **Compressive force** in the **concrete**

    $C = (a \times b)(0.85 f'_c) =$

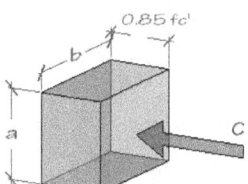

4. Distance to N.A. using **horizontal equilibrium** condition

    $C = T$ or,

    or, $A_c =$

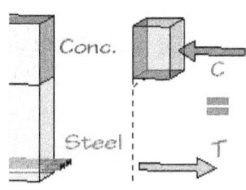

T-BEAMS & ONE-WAY SLAB

5. Location of the neutral axis.

    A_c = (   ) in² $>\atop<$ flange area =

    Area in web =

    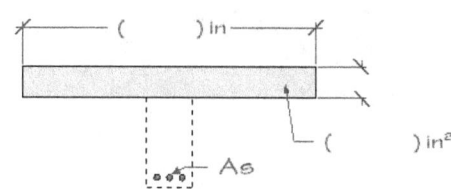

    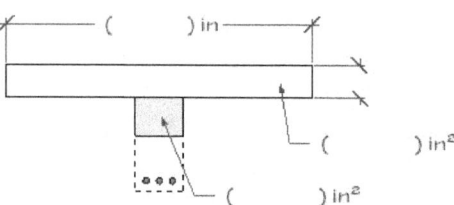

    1. The N.A. is within the flange. → Rectangular Beam with b = b_E.
    2. The N.A. is within the web. → T-beam with b_f = b_E.

6. Depth of the compressive stress block.
   (note : $A_c \neq a \times b$)

    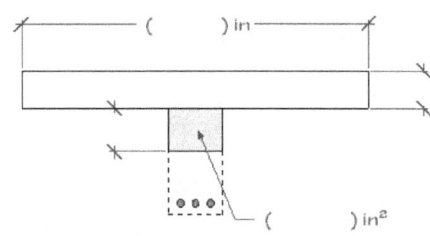

7. **gMoment of Compression Force in Flange**

    C_f =

    M_f =

    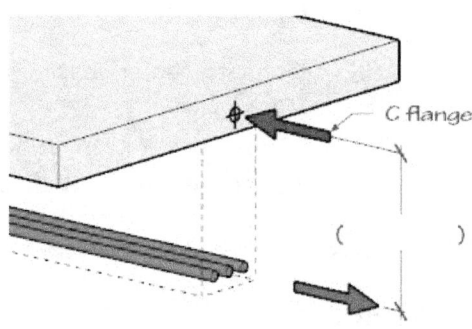

8. **Moment of Compression Force in Web**

    C_w =

    M_w =

    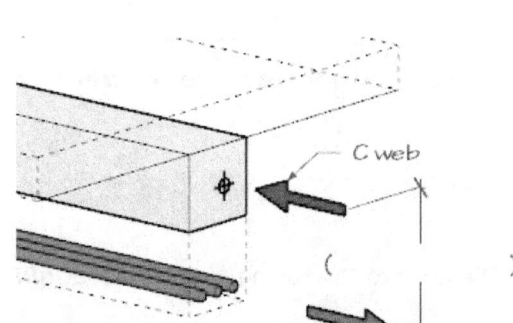

9. **Total Nominal Moment Strength**

    $M_n = M_f + M_w$ =

T-BEAMS & ONE-WAY SLAB

10. **Strength Reduction Factor, ϕ**

f_c' (psi)	3000	4000	5000	6000	7000
β_1	0.85	0.85	0.80	0.75	0.70

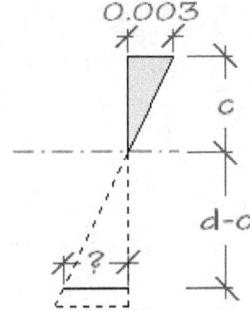

$\beta_1 = (\quad)$ $\qquad c = \dfrac{a}{\beta_1} =$

$\varepsilon_t = \dfrac{d-c}{c}(0.003) =$

	significance	Φ-value
$\varepsilon_t > 0.005$	tension-controlled	$\Phi = 0.9$
$0.004 < \varepsilon_t < 0.005$	in the transition zone	$\Phi = 0.65 + (\varepsilon_t - 0.002)\dfrac{0.25}{0.003}$
$\varepsilon_t < 0.004$	beyond minimum limit	increase beam dimensions

11. **ACI Design Moment Strength, ϕM_n**

$M_u = \phi M_n =$

T-BEAMS & ONE-WAY SLAB

Workshop 5-2b
Determine ACI design moment strength, M_n, of the T-beam shown below. The span length of the beam is 18 ft. and beams are centered 9 ft. apart. $f_c' = 3$ ksi, and $F_y = 60$ ksi

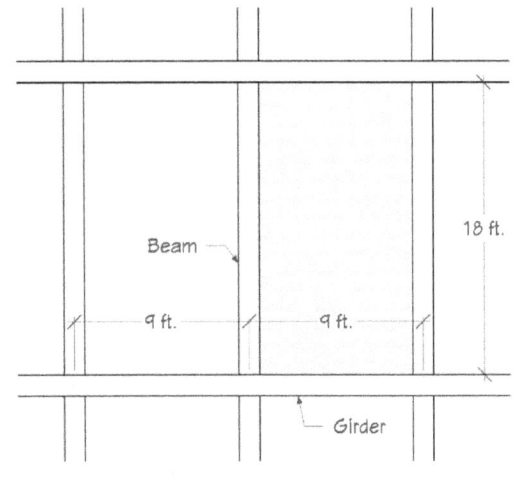

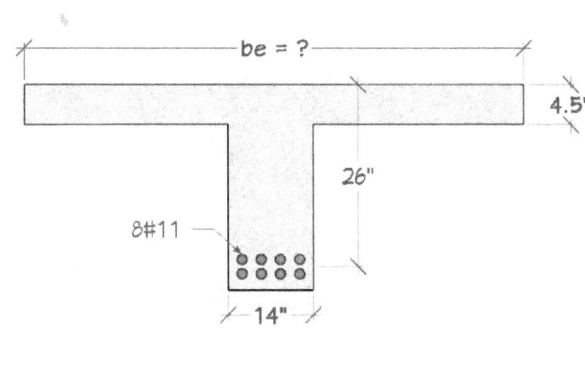

Solution)

1. **Effective flange width** of the T-beam

   Smallest value of:

   a. $b_E = \dfrac{L}{4} =$

   b. $b_E = b_w + 16h =$

   c. $b_E =$ center-to-center spacing of beams $=$

   Thus, the effective flange width, $b_E =$

2. **Tensile force** in the reinforcing **steel**

   $T = A_s F_y =$

   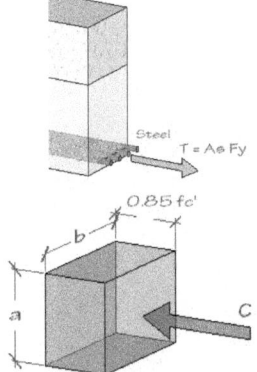

3. **Compressive force** in the **concrete**

   $C = (a \times b)(0.85 f_c') =$

4. Distance to N.A. using **horizontal equilibrium** condition

   $C = T$ or,

   or, $A_c =$

   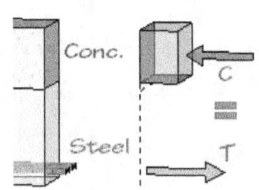

T-BEAMS & ONE-WAY SLAB

5. Location of the neutral axis.

    $A_c = ($ $) \text{ in}^2 \genfrac{}{}{0pt}{}{>}{<}$ flange area =

    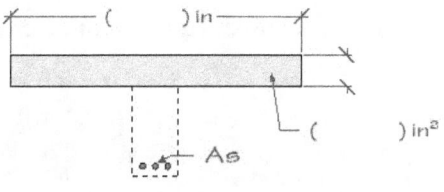

    Area in web =

    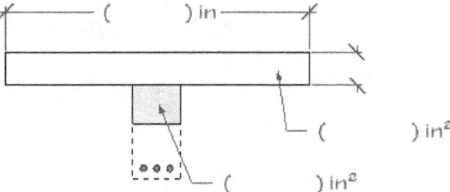

    1. The N.A. is within the flange. → Rectangular Beam with $b = b_E$.
    2. The N.A. is within the web. → T-beam with $b_f = b_E$.

6. Depth of the compressive stress block.
    (note : $A_c \neq a \times b$)

    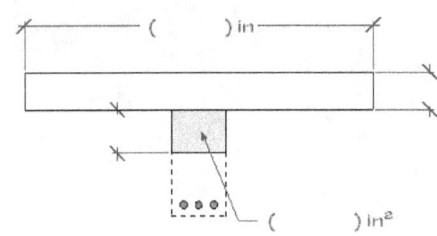

7. **Moment of Compression Force in Flange**

    $C_f =$

    $M_f =$

    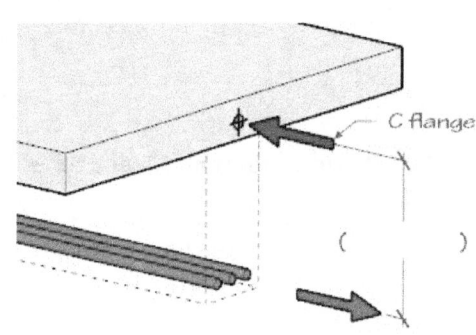

8. **Moment of Compression Force in Web**

    $C_w =$

    $M_w =$

    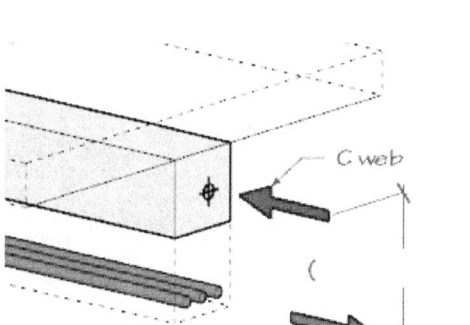

9. **Total Nominal Moment Strength**

    $M_n = M_f + M_w =$

T-BEAMS & ONE-WAY SLAB

10. Strength Reduction Factor, ϕ

f_c' (psi)	3000	4000	5000	6000	7000
β_1	0.85	0.85	0.80	0.75	0.70

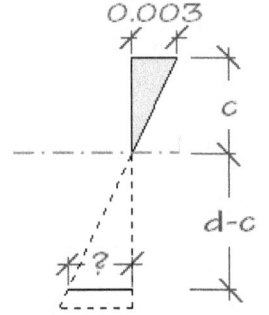

$\beta_1 = (\quad)$ $c = \dfrac{a}{\beta_1} =$

$\varepsilon_t = \dfrac{d-c}{c}(0.003) =$

	significance	Φ-value
$\varepsilon_t > 0.005$	tension-controlled	$\Phi = 0.9$
$0.004 < \varepsilon_t < 0.005$	in the transition zone	$\Phi = 0.65 + (\varepsilon_t - 0.002)\dfrac{0.25}{0.003}$
$\varepsilon_t < 0.004$	beyond minimum limit	increase beam dimensions

11. ACI Design Moment Strength, ϕM_n

$M_u = \phi M_n =$

5.1 Floor Systems

Selecting the most effective floor system can be vital to achieving overall economy, especially for low- and mid-rise buildings and for buildings subjected to relatively low lateral forces where the cost of the lateral-force-resisting system is minimal. Concrete, reinforcement, and formwork are the three primary expenses in cast-in-place concrete floor construction to consider throughout the design process, but especially during the initial planning stages. Of these three, formwork comprises about 55 percent of the total cost and has the greatest influence on the overall cost of the floor system. The cost of the concrete, including placing and finishing, typically accounts for about 30 percent of the overall cost. The reinforcing steel has the lowest influence on overall cost (15%). To achieve overall economy, designers should satisfy the following three basic principles of formwork economy:

a. Specify readily available standard form sizes. Rarely will custom forms be economical, unless they are required in a quantity that allows for mass production.
b. Repeat sizes and shapes of the concrete members wherever possible. Repetition allows reuse of forms from bay-to-bay and from floor-to-floor.
c. Strive for simple formwork. In cast-in-place concrete construction, economy is rarely achieved by reducing quantities of materials.

Regardless of the geometry, standardized floor and roof systems are available that provide cost-effective solutions in typical situations. The most common types are classified as one-way systems and two-way systems. Examined later are the structural members that make up these types of systems. It is common for one type of floor or roof system to be specified on one entire level of building; this is primarily done for cost savings. However, there may be cases that warrant a change in framing system. The feasibility of using more than one type of floor or roof system at any given level needs to be investigated carefully.

5.2 One-Way Systems

A one-way reinforced concrete floor or roof system consists of members that have the main flexural reinforcement running in one direction. In other words, reactions from supported loads are transferred primarily in one direction. Because they are primarily subjected to the effects from bending (and the accompanying shear), members in one-way systems are commonly referred to as flexural members. Members in a one-way system are usually horizontal but can be provided at a slope if needed. Sloped members are commonly used at the roof level to accommodate drainage requirements.

T-BEAMS & ONE-WAY SLAB

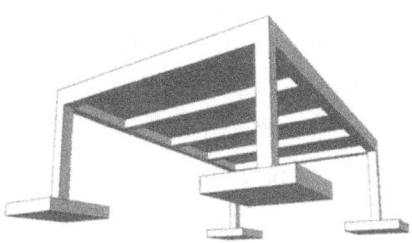

In a typical **one-way slab**, the load is transferred to the beams that span perpendicular to the slabs. The beams, in turn, transfer the loads to the girders, and the girders transfer the loads to the columns. Individual spread footings may carry the column loads to the soil below. It is evident that load transfer between the members of this system occurs in one direction. Main flexural reinforcement for the one-way slabs is placed in the direction parallel to load transfer, which is the short direction. Similarly, the main flexural reinforcement for the beams and girders is placed parallel to the length of these members. Concrete for the slabs, beams, and girders is cast at the same time after the forms have been set and the reinforcement has been placed in the formwork. This concrete is also integrated with columns. In addition, reinforcing bars are extended into adjoining members. Like all cast-in-place systems, this clearly illustrates the monolithic nature of reinforced concrete structural members.

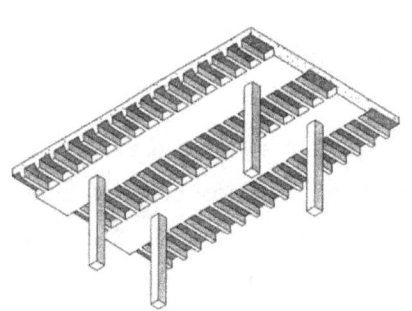

In a standard **one-way joist system**, the one-way slab transfers the load to the joists, which transfer the loads to the column-line beams (or, girders). This system utilizes standard forms where the clear spacing between the ribs is 30 in. or less. Because of its relatively heavy weight and associated costs, this system is not used as often as it was in the past.

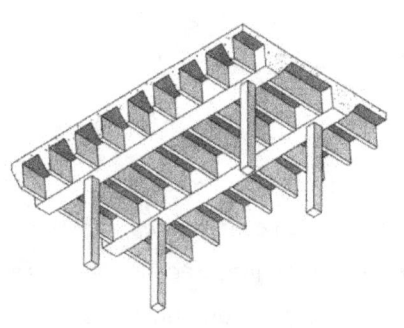

Similar to the standard one-way joist system is the **wide-module joist system**. The clear spacing of the ribs is typically 53 or 66 in., which, according to the Code, technically makes these members beams instead of joists. Load transfer follows the same path as that of the standard joist system. Stair systems are typically designed as one-way systems.

5.3 Two-Way Systems

As the name suggests, two-way floor and roof systems transfer the supported loads in two directions. Flexural reinforcement must be provided in both directions.

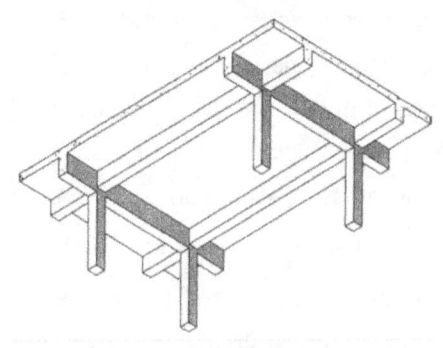

A typical **two-way slab system** is illustrated on the left. The slab transfers the load in two orthogonal directions to the column-line beams, which, in turn, transfer the loads to the columns. Like a standard one-way joist system, this system is not utilized as often as it once was because of cost.

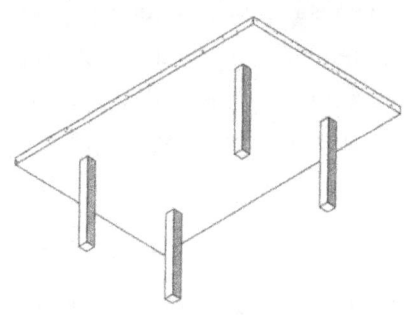

A typical **flat plate system** is shown on the left. This popular system, which is frequently used in residential buildings, consists of a slab supported by columns. The formwork that is required is the simplest of all floor and roof systems. Because the underside of the slab is flat, it is commonly used as the ceiling of the space below; this results in significant cost savings.

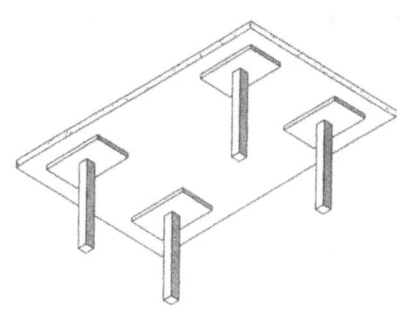

Similar to the flat plate system is the **flat slab system**. Drop panels are provided around the columns to increase moment and shear capacity of the slab. They also help to decrease slab deflection. Column capitals or brackets are sometimes provided at the top of columns.

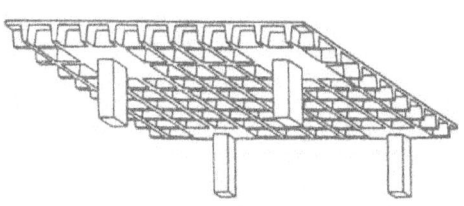

The two-way system depicted in the figure is referred to as a two-way joist system or a waffle slab system. This system consists of rows of concrete joists at right angles to each other, which are formed by standard metal domes. Solid concrete heads are provided at the columns for shear strength. Such systems provide a viable solution in cases where heavy loads need to be supported on long spans.

Preliminary sizing of the slab.

Before analyzing the floor system, designers must assume preliminary member sizes. Typically, the slab and/or beam thickness is determined first to ensure that the deflection requirements of ACI 318-19, Section 9.5 are satisfied. For solid, one-way slabs and beams that are not supporting or attached to partitions or other construction likely to be damaged by large deflections, Table 5.1 may be used to determine minimum thickness **h**. For continuous one-way slabs and beams, determine **h** based on one-end continuous, since this thickness will satisfy deflection criteria for all spans. The preliminary thickness of a *solid one-way slab* with normal weight concrete and Grade 60 reinforcement is $l / 24$, where l is the span length in inches. Similarly, for *beams*, minimum **h** is $l / 18.5$. Deflections need not be computed when a thickness at least equal to the minimum is provided. For non-prestressed, two-way slabs, minimum thickness requirements are given in Section 9.5.3. By satisfying these minimum requirements, which are illustrated in the figure on the next slide for Grade 60 reinforcement, deflections need not be computed. Deflection calculations for two-way slabs are complex, even when linear elastic behavior is assumed.

Continuous (Multi-span) Slabs

Concrete structural members are typically poured integrally together. Beams and slabs often span multiple supports and are not "simply supported" as steel and wood framed beams are. These concrete beams and slabs are continuous and have both positive moments and negative moments. The location of tension bars in the members is related to the location of moment: Tension bars are located in the BOTTOM for M_{pos} and in the TOP for M_{neg}

2- Equal Span Condition:

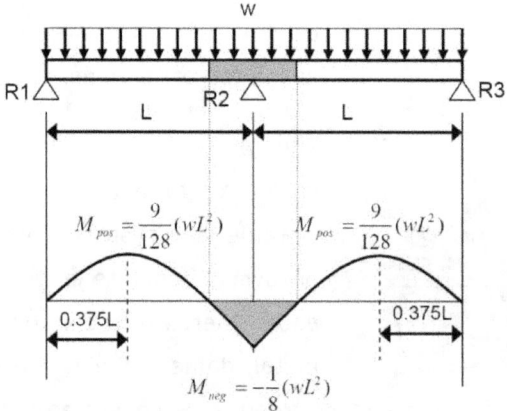

3- Equal Span Condition:

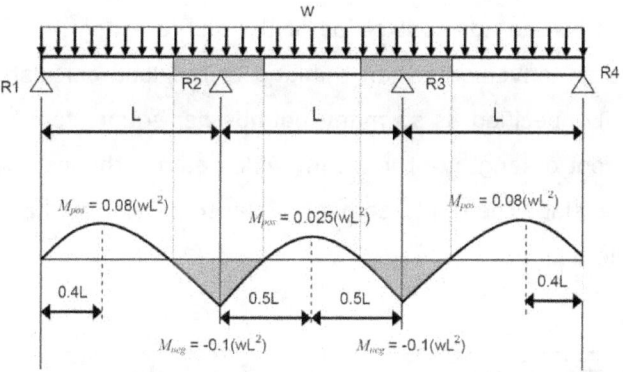

At the transition between the **M_{pos}** and **M_{neg}** zones, a minimum overlap of bars is required per ACI 318. These overlaps are required for developing the full bar strength in tension. The friction developed between the concrete and the ribs of the rebar must equal the tensile strength of the bar. The necessary length of the bar embedment to achieve this friction force is called the "Development Length", **L_d**, and is specified as a multiple of bar diameters. For example, the **L_d** for a Grade 60 rebar and concrete **f_c'** = 4000 psi is 38 x bar diameter.

5.4 Analysis and Design of One-way Slab

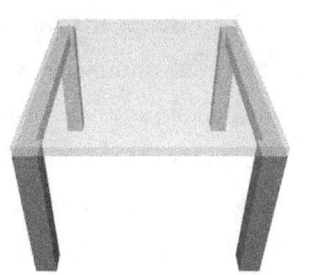

One-way Slab

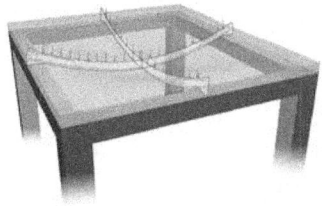

Two-way Slab

Reinforced concrete slabs are large flat plates supported by beams, walls, or columns. If they are supported on two opposite sides only, they are referred to as **one-way slabs** because the bending is in one direction only - that is, perpendicular to the supported edges. If the slab is supported by beams on all four edges, it is referred to as a **two-way slab** because the bending is in both directions. Actually, if a rectangular slab is supported on all four sides, but the long side is two or more times as long as the short side, the slab will, for all practical purposes, act as a one-way slab, with bending primarily occurring in the short direction. Such slabs are designed as one-way slabs. This workbook is concerned with one-way slabs and two-way slabs are not covered because a large majority of reinforced concrete slabs fall into the one-way class. Conventionally, a 12-in.-wide strip of a one-way slab is designed as a beam. The slab is assumed to consist of a series of such beams side by side. The method of analysis is somewhat conservative because the system effects due to lateral restraint provided by the adjacent strips of the slab are neglected. The 12-in.-wide beam is quite convenient when thinking of the load calculations because loads are normally specified as so many pounds per square foot, and thus the load carried per foot of length of the 12-in.-wide beam is the load supported per square foot by the slab. The reinforcement is placed parallel to the long direction of the 12-in.-wide beams.

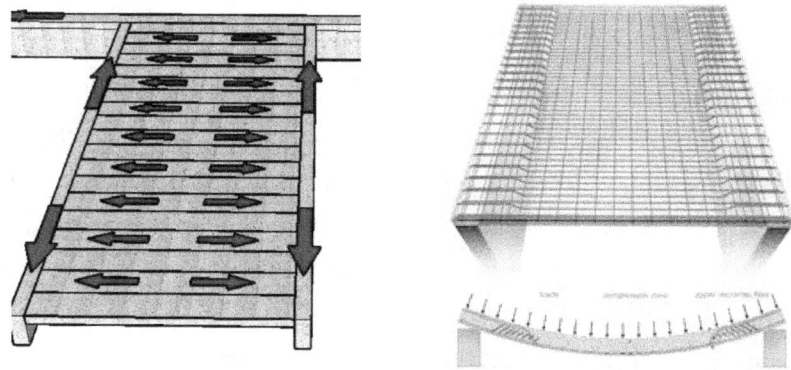

Load Transfer and Behavior of One-way Slab

The maximum spacing of the main reinforcement may not exceed three times the slab thickness, or 18 in., according to the ACI Code (7.6.5). Also, there will be some reinforcing placed in the perpendicular direction to resist shrinkage and temperature stresses. The thickness required for a particular one-way slab depends on the bending, the deflection, and shear requirements. The ACI Code (9.5.2.1) provides certain span/depth limitations for concrete flexural members where deflections are not calculated. Because of the quantities of concrete involved in floor slabs, their depths are rounded off to closer values than are used for beam depths. Slab thicknesses are usually rounded off to the nearest 1/4 in. on the high side for slabs of 6 in. or less in thickness and to the nearest 1/2 in. on the high side for slabs thicker than 6 in. As concrete hardens, it shrinks. In addition, temperature changes occur that cause expansion and contraction of the concrete. When cooling occurs, the shrinkage effect and the shortening due to cooling add together. The code (7.12) states that shrinkage and temperature reinforcement must be provided in a direction perpendicular to the main reinforcement for one-way slabs. For two-way slabs, reinforcement is provided in both directions for bending. The code states that for Grade 40 or 50 deformed bars, the minimum percentage of this steel is 0.002 times the gross cross-sectional area of the slab. Notice that the gross cross-sectional area is **b** x **h** (where **h** is the slab thickness).

T-BEAMS & ONE-WAY SLAB

Summary

12 in.-width Beam

What is a **One-Way Slab**? (∵ one-way bending)	Supported on two opposite sides only. (cf. *Two-Way Slab – 4 side supported*) Long side/short side ratio ≥ 2.0 Large percentage of slabs falls into this category.
Analysis and Design	***A 12 in. wide strip of a slab*** *is considered* **as a rectangular beam.**
Thickness of Slab	Use Table 4 Round off to the nearest 1/4 in. for up to 6"-thick slabs Round off to the nearest 1/2 in. for thicker than 6"
Bar Spacing	Max. bar spacing ≤ lesser of ($3h$, 18 in.) (where, h = thickness of slab)
Temperature Steel	Must be provided in the direction perpendicular to the main bar. Min. steel area, A_s = 0.002 (12 in)(h). - for Grades **40** or **50** Min. steel area, A_s = 0.0018 (12 in)(h). - for Grade **60** Max. Spacing ≤ lesser of ($5h$, 18 in.) (where, h = thickness of slab)

Table 5.4 Minimum Thickness of Beams or One-way Slabs
(unless deflections are computed)

	Members not supporting partitions to be damaged by large deflection			
	Simply Supported	One End continuous	Both Ends continuous	Cantilever
Solid one-way slab	$l/20$	$l/24$	$l/28$	$l/10$
Beams Ribbed one-way slab	$l/16$	$l/18.5$	$l/21$	$l/8$

(Note : Span Length l is in inches.)

Case Study 5-1

Determine the ultimate moment capacity, M_u, of the slab shown on the right. Use f_c' = 4000 psi and F_y = 60 ksi. (Use Φ = 0.9)

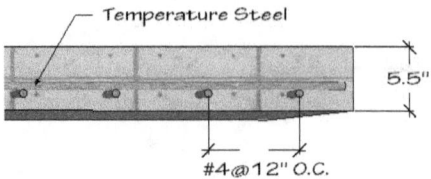

Workshop 5-1a

Determine the ultimate moment capacity, M_u, of the slab shown on the right. Use f_c' = 3500 psi and F_y = 50 ksi. (Use Φ = 0.9)

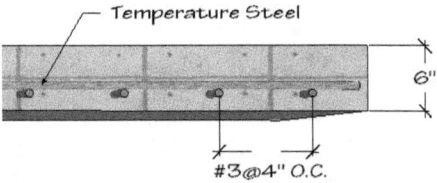

Workshop 5-1b
Determine the ultimate moment capacity, M_u, of the slab shown on the right. Use $f_c' = 4000$ psi and $F_y = 50$ ksi. (Use $\Phi = 0.9$)

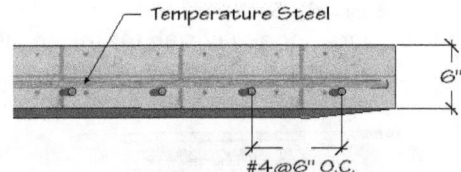

Workshop 5-1c
Determine the ultimate moment capacity, M_u, of the slab shown on the right. Use $f_c' = 4000$ psi and $F_y = 60$ ksi. (Use $\Phi = 0.9$)

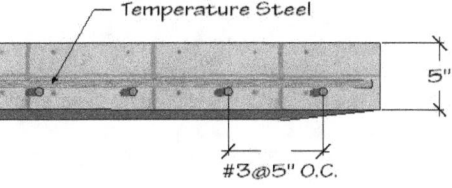

T-BEAMS & ONE-WAY SLAB

Case Study 5-2
Design a one-way slab for inside of a building using the data given below.
Span = 10 ft, Live Load = 200 psf, F_y = 60 ksi and f_c' = 4 ksi

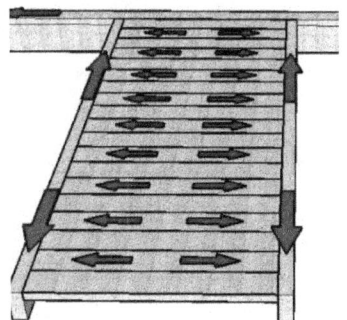

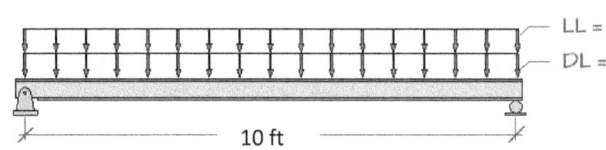

Solution)

Minimum Slab Thickness, h
From Table 5.4, $h = l/20 =$ *(round up to next 1/4")*

Design Moment Calculation
DL = slab wt. =

LL =

$w_u = 1.2D + 1.6L = 1.2($ $) + 1.6($ $) =$

For a simple beam with a distributed load,

$$M_u = \frac{wl^2}{8} =$$

Slab Depth, d
d = h − cover − half bar diameter = (   ) in − ¾ in − ¼ in (assumed) = (   ) in.

Steel Ratio

$$R_n = \frac{M_u}{\phi bd^2} =$$

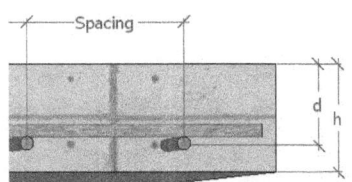

$$\rho = \frac{0.85 f_c'}{f_y}\left(1 - \sqrt{1 - \frac{2R_n}{0.85 f_c'}}\right) =$$

T-BEAMS & ONE-WAY SLAB

Minimum/Maximum Steel Ratio Checking

From **Table(**   **)** with F_y = (   ) ksi, and f_c' = (   ) ksi,

ρ_{max} =   >   (**O.K.** or **N.G.**)

ρ_{min} =   <   (**O.K.** or **N.G.**)

Reinforcing Bars

A_s =

From **Table(**   **)**, use   -→ A_s =

Max. Spacing = lesser of **[**(3h =   ), or (18 in)**]** =

Spacing (   ) in ≤ Max. Spacing = (   ) in.

Temperature Rebars

For grades 60 bars, ρ_{min} =   ∴ A_s = ρ (12 h) =

From **Table(**   **)**, use #   , A_s =

Max. Spacing = lesser of **[**(5h =   ), or (18 in)**]** =

Spacing (   ) in ≤ Max. Spacing = (   ) in.

T-BEAMS & ONE-WAY SLAB

Workshop 5-2a

Design a one-way slab for inside of a building using the data given below.
LL = 250 psf, F_y = 50 ksi, f_c' = 4 ksi and Beam Span = 10 ft.

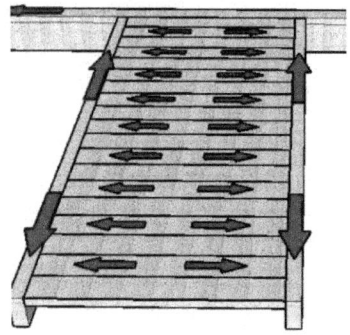
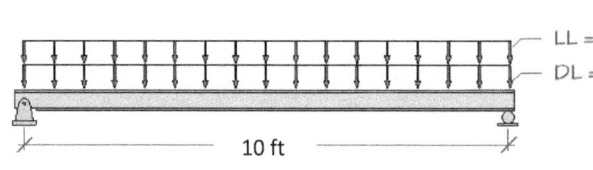

Solution)

Minimum Slab Thickness, h

From Table 4.1, $h = l/20 =$ (round up to next 1/4")

Design Moment Calculation

DL = slab wt. =

LL =

$w_u = 1.2D + 1.6L = 1.2($ $) + 1.6($ $) =$

For a simple beam with a distributed load,

$$M_u = \frac{wl^2}{8} =$$

Slab Depth, d

$d = h$ − cover − half bar diameter = (   ) in − ¾ in − ¼ in (assumed) = (   ) in.

Steel Ratio

$$R_n = \frac{M_u}{\phi b d^2} =$$

$$\rho = \frac{0.85 f_c'}{f_y}\left(1 - \sqrt{1 - \frac{2 R_n}{0.85 f_c'}}\right) =$$

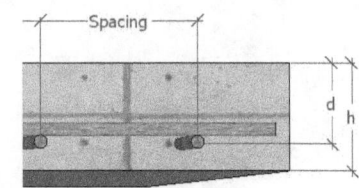

T-BEAMS & ONE-WAY SLAB

Minimum/Maximum Steel Ratio Checking

From **Table(   )** with F_y = (   ) ksi, and f_c' = (   ) ksi,

ρ_{max} =   >   (**O.K.** or **N.G.**)

ρ_{min} =   <   (**O.K.** or **N.G.**)

Reinforcing Bars

A_s =

From **Table(   )**, use   → A_s =

Max. Spacing = lesser of **[(3h** =   ), or (18 in)**]** =

Spacing (   ) in ≤ Max. Spacing = (   ) in.

Temperature ReBars

For grades 60 bars, ρ_{min} =   ∴ A_s = ρ (*12 h*) =

From **Table(   )**, use #   , A_s =

Max. Spacing = lesser of **[(5h** =   ), or (18 in)**]** =

Spacing (   ) in ≤ Max. Spacing = (   ) in.

Workshop 5-2b

Design a one-way slab for inside of a building using the data given below.
LL = 250 psf, F_y = 60 ksi, f_c' = 4 ksi and Beam Span = 12 ft.

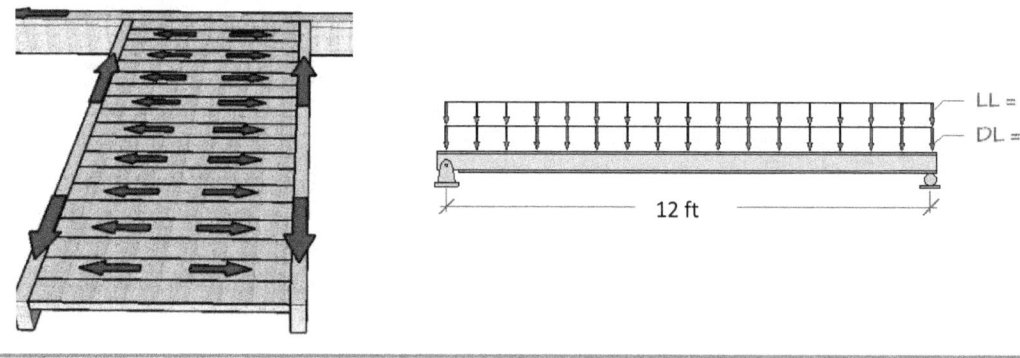

Solution)

6. SHEAR FORCE AND DIAGONAL TENSION

6.1 Introduction

Beams subjected to transverse loads generally experience bending moments and shearing forces. Beams are usually designed for bending moment first and then, sections are checked for shear to determine whether shear reinforcement is required or not. This practice by no means indicates that shear is less significant than bending. On the contrary, shear failure is usually initiated by diagonal tension and is far more dangerous than flexural failure due to its brittle nature. The shear force acting on a vertical section in a reinforced concrete beam does not cause direct rupture of that section. Shear by itself or in combination with flexure may cause failure indirectly by producing tensile stresses on inclined planes. If these tensile stresses exceed the relatively low tensile strength of concrete, diagonal cracks develop. The shear cracking takes place on a plane perpendicular to the plane on which principal tensile stresses occur. If these cracks are not checked, splitting of the beam or what is known as diagonal tension failure will take place.

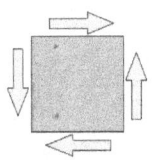
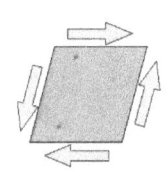
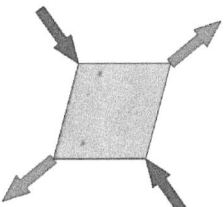
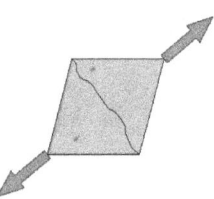

Pure Shear **Shear + Bending** **Principal Stresses** **Diagonal Tension**

6.2 Types of Shear Cracks

Cracking in reinforce concrete beams is often regarded as normal and indicates that the tension bars are actually working. However, excessive cracking needs to be controlled by additional bars called stirrups placed perpendicular to the cracks. Two types of inclined cracking occur in beams: flexure-shear cracking and web-shear cracking.

A. Flexure-Shear Cracks

The most common type, develops from the tip of a flexural crack at the tension side of the beam and propagates towards mid depth until it is checked on the compression side of the beam. For these cracks to form, the bending moment must exceed the cracking moment of the cross section and a significant shear must exist.

B. Web Shear Cracks

Web shear cracking begins from an interior point in a member at the level of the centroid of uncracked section and moves on a diagonal path to the tension face when the diagonal tensile stresses produced by shear exceed the tensile strength of concrete. This type of cracking is common on beams with thin webs and in regions of high shear and small moment. This combination exists adjacent to simple supports or at points of inflection in continuous beams.

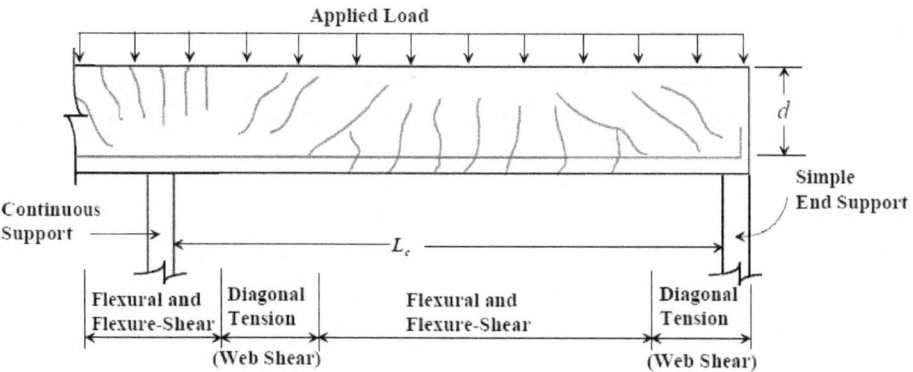

6.3 Nominal Shear Stress

The only equation available to relate shear stress to shearing force is derived for a beam of constant cross section constructed of a homogeneous elastic material.

$$f_v = \frac{VQ}{Ib}$$

However, this equation cannot be applied to reinforced concrete beams for the following reasons:

1. Reinforced concrete is non-homogeneous material.

SHEAR FORCE & DIAGONAL TENSION

2. Concrete is not elastic.
3. Variable extent of cracking along the length of a beam, making it impossible to determine cross-sectional properties.

Therefore, the ACI Code has adopted a simple procedure for establishing the magnitude of shear stress, f_v on a cross section.

$$f_v = \frac{V}{b_w d}$$

where

f_v = nominal shear stress
V = shearing force at specified section
b_w = width of web of cross section
d = effective depth of the section.

6.4 Current Shear Design Philosophy

The current ACI Code shear design procedure is based on the assumption that for beams with no shear reinforcement, failure takes place on a vertical plane when the factored shear force on this plane exceeds the fictitious shear strength of concrete. The fictitious shear strength of concrete is evaluated from empirical expressions specified within the ACI Code. This simplification is done due to the following reasons:

1. Strength of concrete in tension is highly variable, making it hard to evaluate a sustainable diagonal tension.
2. Non-homogeneity of reinforced concrete which makes accurate computation of shear stresses on a particular section a tough task.
3. Shear failures occur on diagonal planes as they are usually initiated by diagonal tension.

According to ACI Code 11.1.1, design of cross sections subject to shear should be based on the following equation.

$$\phi V_n \geq V_u$$

where

ϕ = strength reduction factor for shear = 0.75
V_n = nominal shear strength
V_u = factored shear force at section considered

A smaller strength reduction factor for shear, ϕ_{shear} = 0.75, is used than the typical one for bending, $\phi_{bending}$ = 0.9. As a result, beams are designed to fail in bending, not in shear. Because beams are under-reinforced, they will fail in ductile modes.

The nominal shear force is generally resisted by concrete and shear reinforcement or,

$$V_n = V_c + V_s$$

where
V_c = nominal shear strength of concrete
V_s = nominal shear strength of shear reinforcement

6.5 Shear Strength of Concrete

Shear strength of concrete V_c is evaluated by loading a plain concrete beam to failure. Shear stresses are computed by dividing the shearing force resisted by concrete V_c by ($b_w \times d$). Strength of concrete in shear is directly proportional to the strength of concrete in tension, inversely proportional to the magnitude of bending moment at the section under consideration, and directly proportional to the reinforcement ratio of flexural reinforcement. For the sake of simplicity, V_c is assumed to be the same for beams with or without shear reinforcement. The average shear strength of concrete is $2\sqrt{f_c'}$. It must be noted that the value of f_c' in this equation is in psi, e.g., 3000 or 4000 psi. For members subject to shear and bending only, ACI Code 11.2.1.1 gives the following equation for evaluating V_c:

$$V_c = 2\sqrt{f_c'}\,(b_w \cdot d)$$

6.6 Strength of Shear Reinforcement

When the maximum shear force V_u exceeds the shear force that can be resisted by concrete alone ϕV_c, shear reinforcement must be used. When shear reinforcement is required, the following types of shear reinforcement are permitted by ACI Code 11.4.1, as shown in Figure 5.5.

    a.   Vertical Stirrups;
    b.   Inclined stirrups making an angle of 45 degree or more with longitudinal tension reinforcement;
    c.   Longitudinal reinforcement with bent portion making an angle of 30 degree or more with the tension reinforcement;
    d.   Spirals, circular ties, or hoops;
    e.   Combination of stirrups and bent longitudinal reinforcement.
    f.   Welded wire reinforcement with wires located perpendicular to axis of member.

SHEAR FORCE & DIAGONAL TENSION

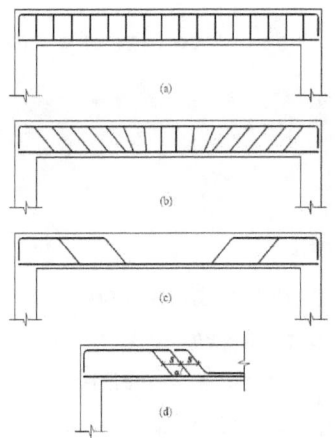

(a) vertical stirrups

(b) inclined stirrups

(c) bent-up bars (two groups)

(d) bent-up bars (three groups)

Before diagonal cracking occurs, the stirrups remain unstressed. After cracking, the stress in the stirrups increases as they pick up a portion of the load formerly carried by the uncracked concrete. The shear force resisted by shear reinforcing bars across the crack V_s is given by diagonal web reinforcements would be the most effective in resisting

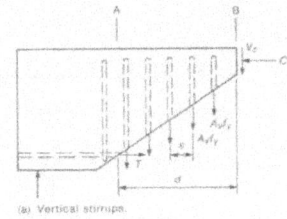

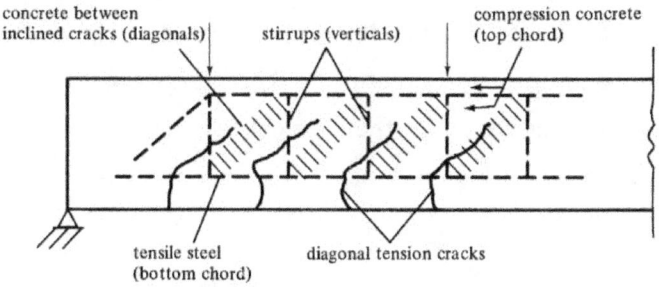

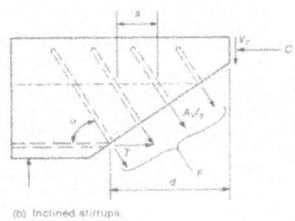

the diagonal tension but is not practical because high labor cost is required to positioning and to keep them during concrete casting.

6.7 Spacing of Vertical Stirrups

It is conservatively assumed that the horizontal projection of the crack equals the effective length **d** of the beam (A 45° crack is assumed.), the number of stirrups crossing the crack can be determined from the following equation, in which S is the center-to-center spacing of the stirrups:

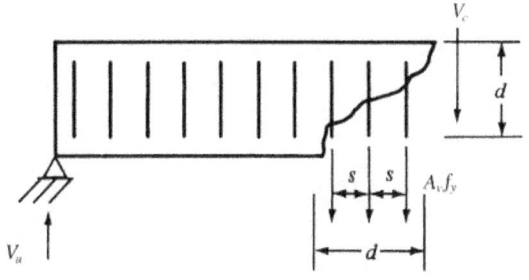

$$n = \text{number of bars} = \frac{d}{S}$$

Then the shear strength of stirrups is

$$V_s = (A_v F_y) n$$ (note: **A_v** = Area of **two legs** of a stirrup)

where,

d = Depth of Beam

s = Spacing of Stirrups

Minimum Amount of Shear Reinforcement

The instant diagonal crack forms, the tension carried by the concrete must be transferred to the stirrups if the beam is not to split into two sections. To ensure that the stirrups will have sufficient strength to absorb the diagonal tension in the concrete, ACI Code 11.4.6 states that a minimum area of shear reinforcement is to be provided in concrete members where the factored shear force V_u, exceeds half the shear strength provided by concrete 0.5 V_c.

Ensuring Ductile Behavior

To prevent a shear-compression failure caused by diagonal compression stresses in the compression zone above the tip of a diagonal crack, ACI Code 11.4.7.9 requires that the maximum force resisted by shear reinforcement Vs is not to exceed 4 times $2\sqrt{f_c'}$ b_w d. Since diagonal tensile stresses develop in the direction perpendicular to the compressive stresses, the compressive strength of the concrete will be less than that based on the Uniaxial test. This is done to ensure a ductile mode of failure by forcing the shear reinforcement to yield before the concrete starts to crush.

Critical Section for Shear

According to ACI Code 11.1.3.1, sections located less than a distance d from face of support are permitted to be designed for the same shear as that calculated at a distance d. Conditions for the validity of ACI Code 11.1.3.1 are listed in ACI Code 11.1.3 and given here:

- Loads applied near the top of the member.
- No concentrated loads are applied between the face of support and a distance d from it. Otherwise the critical section for shear is taken at the face of the support.
- Support reaction in direction of applied shear, introducing compression into the end region of the member. If tension is introduced, the critical section is taken at the face of the support.

Summary of ACI Shear Design Procedure for Beams

Once the beam is designed for moment, thus establishing the concrete dimensions and the required longitudinal reinforcement, the beam is designed for shear as explained in the next steps.

1. Draw the shearing force diagram and establish the critical section for shear.
2. Calculate the nominal capacity of concrete in shear, **V_c**.
3. Check whether the chosen concrete dimensions are adequate for ensuring a ductile mode of failure. If not satisfied, the concrete dimensions should be increased.
4. Classify the factored shearing forces acting on the beam according to the following categories:

    a. For **$V_u \leq 0.5 \phi V_c$**, no shear reinforcement is required.

    b. For **$\phi V_c > V_u > 0.5 \phi V_c$**, the min. shear reinforcement is required.

    c. For **$V_u > \phi V_c$**, shear reinforcement is required.

    When more than one type of shear reinforcement is used to reinforce the same portion of a beam, shear strength **V_s** is calculated as the sum of the **V_s** values evaluated from each type.

5. Check the spacing between shear reinforcement according to ACI Code limits.
6. Sketch the shear reinforcement along the length of the beam.

	ACI 318 Stirrup Spacing Requirements		
	$V_u \leq 0.5 \phi V_c$	$\phi V_c > V_u > 0.5 \phi V_c$	$V_u > \phi V_c$
Required	None	$\dfrac{A_v f_y}{0.75\sqrt{f_c'} b_w} \leq \dfrac{A_v f_y}{50 b_w}$	If $V_s \leq 8\sqrt{f_c'} b_w d$, $\dfrac{\phi(A_v f_y d)}{V_u - \phi V}$ If $V_s > 8\sqrt{f_c'} b_w d$, N.G. Increase the cross-section!
Maximum	None	$d/2 \leq 24$ in.	If $V_s \leq 4\sqrt{f_c'} b_w d$, $d/2 \leq 24$ in. If $V_s > 4\sqrt{f_c'} b_w d$, $d/4 \leq 12$ in.

Case Study 6.1a

Determine the spacing of #3 U-stirrups for the beam subjected to the shear, **V_u = 50,000 lb**. Use F_y = 60 ksi, and **f_c'** = 3 ksi.

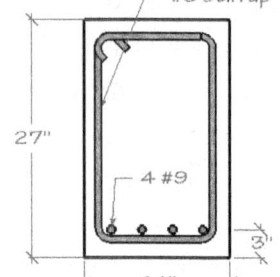

Solution)

1) Shear capacity of concrete

$$\phi V_c = 0.75(2\sqrt{f_c'}\, b_w d) = 0.75(2\sqrt{3000})(14)(24) = 27,605 \text{ lb}$$

If $\frac{1}{2}\phi V_c \geq V_u$, stirrups are not required.

$\frac{1}{2}\phi V_c = \frac{1}{2}(27605\text{ lb}) = 13,803 \text{ lb} < 50,000 \text{ lb}$ ∴ Stirrup is (**required**, or **not required**)

2) Design of Stirrup

Go to Step 2 to design stirrup   Go to Step 4 to use code max.

The V_u, is resisted by both concrete, V_c and stirrup, V_s.

$$V_u = \phi V_c + \phi V_s \quad \text{or,} \quad V_s = \frac{V_u - \phi V_c}{\phi}$$

The shear force to be carried by stirrups, V_s, is :

$$V_s = \frac{V_u - \phi V_c}{\phi} = \frac{50,000 - 27605}{0.75} = 29,860 \text{ lb}$$

If $8\sqrt{f_c'}\, b_w d < V_s$, the beam cross-section must be increased. (stirrups won't work)

$$8\sqrt{f_c'}\, b_w d = (8)(\sqrt{3000})(14)(24) = 147,228 \text{ lb} > 29,860 \text{ lb} \quad (\textbf{O.K.} \text{ or } \textbf{N.G.})$$

Continue to Step 3 to design stirrup   Stop here to increase beam section

3) Stirrup Spacing [A_v = area of 2 legs of a stirrup = 2(#3 area) = 2(0.11)]

$$s = \frac{A_v f_y d}{V_s} = \frac{(2)(0.11)(60,000)(24)}{29860} = 10.61 \text{ in.}$$

---

4) ACI Maximum Spacing Check

1. $s = \dfrac{A_v f_y}{0.75\sqrt{f_c'}\, b_w} = \dfrac{(2)(0.11)(60,000)}{0.75(\sqrt{3000})(14)} = 22.95 \text{ in.}$

2. $s = \dfrac{A_v f_y}{50 b_w} = \dfrac{(2)(0.11)(60,000)}{(50)(14)} = 18.86 \text{ in.}$

3. Case 1. If $V_s \leq 4\sqrt{f_c'}\, b_w d$, the max spacing $\leq$ (**d/2** and **24"**)

   Case 2. If $V_s > 4\sqrt{f_c'}\, b_w d$, the max spacing $\leq$ (**d/4** and **12"**)

   $4\sqrt{f_c'}\, b_w d = (4)(\sqrt{3000})(14)(24) = 73,614 \text{ lb} > V_s = 29,860 \text{ lb}$ → (**Case 1** or Case 2)

   The max spacing = the smaller of [**d/2** = (24")/2 = 12" and **24"**] → 12 in.

ACI Maximum spacing = **smallest** of [10.61", 22.95", 18.86", 12"] = 10.61"

ANSWER : (use multiples of 3 or 4 in. for construction conveniences)   10.61 in. → 9 in.

$$\boxed{\text{Use \#3 stirrup @ 9 in.}}$$

| SHEAR FORCE & DIAGONAL TENSION

Case Study 6.1b

Determine the spacing of #3 U-stirrups for the beam subjected to the shear, **Vu = 50,000 lb**. Use F_y = 60 ksi, and **f_c'** = 3 ksi.

Solution)

1) Shear capacity of concrete

$\phi V_c = 0.75(2\sqrt{f_c'} b_w d) = $

If $\frac{1}{2}\phi V_c \geq V_u$, stirrups are not required.

½ ϕV_c =   ∴ Stirrup is (**required,** or **not required**)

2) Design of Stirrup

Go to Step 2 to design stirrup   *Go to Step 4 to use code max.*

The **Vu**, is resisted by both concrete, **Vc** and stirrup, **Vs**.

$V_u = \phi V_c + \phi V_s$ or, $V_s = \dfrac{V_u - \phi V_c}{\phi}$

The shear force to be carried by stirrups, **Vs**, is :

$V_s = \dfrac{V_u - \phi V_c}{\phi} = $

If $8\sqrt{f_c'} b_w d < V_s$, the beam cross-section must be increased. (stirrups won't work)

$8\sqrt{f_c'} b_w d = $ >   (**O.K.**   or   **N.G.**)

Continue to Step 3 to design stirrup   *Stop here to increase beam section*

3) Stirrup Spacing [Av = area of 2 legs of a stirrup =   ]

$s = \dfrac{A_v f_y d}{V_s} = $

---

4) ACI Maximum Spacing Check

1. $s = \dfrac{A_v f_y}{0.75\sqrt{f_c'} b_w} = $

2. $s = \dfrac{A_v f_y}{50 b_w} = $

4. Case 1. If $V_s \leq 4\sqrt{f_c'} b_w d$, the max spacing ≤ (**d/2 and 24"**)

   Case 2. If $V_s > 4\sqrt{f_c'} b_w d$, the max spacing ≤ (**d/4 and 12"**)

$4\sqrt{f_c'} b_w d) = $ **Vs** =   → (Case 1 or Case 2)

The max spacing = the smaller of [   ] →

ACI Maximum spacing = smallest of [,   ,   ] =

ANSWER : (*use multiples of 3 or 4 in. for construction conveniences*)

SHEAR FORCE & DIAGONAL TENSION

Workshop 6.1a

Determine the spacing of #4 U-stirrups for the beam subjected to the shear, V_u = **125 k**. Use F_y = 60 ksi, and f_c' = 4 ksi.

Solution)

1) Shear capacity of concrete

$$\phi V_c = 0.75(2\sqrt{f_c'}\, b_w d) =$$

If $\frac{1}{2}\phi V_c \geq V_u$, stirrups are not required.

$\frac{1}{2}\phi V_c =$ ∴ Stirrup is (**required**, or **not required**)

2) Design of Stirrup

Go to Step 2 to design stirrup *Go to Step 4 to use code max.*

The V_u, is resisted by both concrete, V_c and stirrup, V_s.

$$V_u = \phi V_c + \phi V_s \quad \text{or,} \quad V_s = \frac{V_u - \phi V_c}{\phi}$$

The shear force to be carried by stirrups, V_s, is :

$$V_s = \frac{V_u - \phi V_c}{\phi} =$$

If $8\sqrt{f_c'}\, b_w d < V_s$, the beam cross-section must be increased. (stirrups won't work)

$8\sqrt{f_c'}\, b_w d =$ >   (**O.K.** or **N.G.**)

Continue to Step 3 to design stirrup *Stop here to increase beam section*

3) Stirrup Spacing [A_v = area of 2 legs of a stirrup =   ]

$$s = \frac{A_v f_y d}{V_s} =$$

4) ACI Maximum Spacing Check

1. $s = \dfrac{A_v f_y}{0.75\sqrt{f_c'}\, b_w} =$

2. $s = \dfrac{A_v f_y}{50\, b_w} =$

5. Case 1. If $V_s \leq 4\sqrt{f_c'}\, b_w d$, the max spacing ≤ (**d/2 and 24"**)

   Case 2. If $V_s > 4\sqrt{f_c'}\, b_w d$, the max spacing ≤ (**d/4 and 12"**)

$4\sqrt{f_c'}\, b_w d) =$ **Vs** =   → (Case 1 or Case 2)

The max spacing = the smaller of [   ] →

ACI Maximum spacing = smallest of [,   ,   ] =

ANSWER : (use multiples of 3 or 4 in. for construction conveniences)

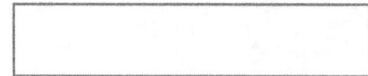

SHEAR FORCE & DIAGONAL TENSION

Workshop 6.1b

Determine the spacing of #4 U-stirrups for the beam subjected to the shear, V_u = **185 k**. Use F_y = 60 ksi, and f_c' = 4 ksi.

Solution)

1) Shear capacity of concrete

$$\phi V_c = 0.75(2\sqrt{f_c'}\,b_w d) =$$

If $\tfrac{1}{2}\phi V_c \geq V_u$, stirrups are not required.

½ ϕV_c =   ∴ Stirrup is (**required**, or **not required**)

Go to Step 2 to design stirrup   *Go to Step 4 to use code max.*

2) Design of Stirrup

The V_u, is resisted by both concrete, V_c and stirrup, V_s.

$$V_u = \phi V_c + \phi V_s \quad \text{or,} \quad V_s = \frac{V_u - \phi V_c}{\phi}$$

The shear force to be carried by stirrups, V_s, is :

$$V_s = \frac{V_u - \phi V_c}{\phi} =$$

If $8\sqrt{f_c'}\,b_w d < V_s$, the beam cross-section must be increased. (stirrups won't work)

$8\sqrt{f_c'}\,b_w d =$ >   (**O.K.**   or   **N.G.**)

Continue to Step 3 to design stirrup   *Stop here to increase beam section*

3) Stirrup Spacing [A_v = area of 2 legs of a stirrup =   ]

$$s = \frac{A_v f_y d}{V_s} =$$

4) ACI Maximum Spacing Check

1. $s = \dfrac{A_v f_y}{0.75\sqrt{f_c'}\,b_w} =$

2. $s = \dfrac{A_v f_y}{50\, b_w} =$

6. Case 1. If $V_s \leq 4\sqrt{f_c'}\,b_w d$, the max spacing ≤ (**d/2 and 24"**)

   Case 2. If $V_s > 4\sqrt{f_c'}\,b_w d$, the max spacing ≤ (**d/4 and 12"**)

$4\sqrt{f_c'}\,b_w d) =$ V_s =   → (Case 1   or   Case 2)

The max spacing = the smaller of [   ] →

ACI Maximum spacing = **smallest** of [,   ,   ,   ] =

ANSWER : (use multiples of 3 or 4 in. for construction conveniences)

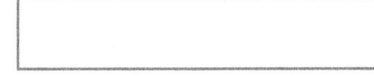

SHEAR FORCE & DIAGONAL TENSION

Workshop 6.1c

Determine the spacing of #4 U-stirrups for the beam subjected to the shear, V_u = **100 k**. Use F_y = 60 ksi, and f_c' = 4 ksi.

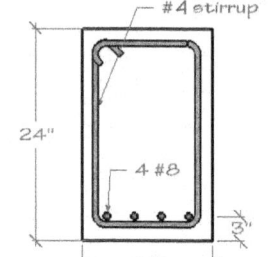

Solution)

1) Shear capacity of concrete

$\phi V_c = 0.75(2\sqrt{f_c'}\, b_w d) =$

If $\frac{1}{2}\phi V_c \geq V_u$, stirrups are not required.

$\frac{1}{2}\, \phi V_c =$ ∴ Stirrup is (**required**, or **not required**)

2) Design of Stirrup

Go to Step 2 to design stirrup   *Go to Step 4 to use code max.*

The V_u, is resisted by both concrete, V_c and stirrup, V_s.

$V_u = \phi V_c + \phi V_s$ or, $V_s = \dfrac{V_u - \phi V_c}{\phi}$

The shear force to be carried by stirrups, V_s, is :

$V_s = \dfrac{V_u - \phi V_c}{\phi} =$

If $8\sqrt{f_c'}\, b_w d < V_s$, the beam cross-section must be increased. (stirrups won't work)

$8\sqrt{f_c'}\, b_w d =$ $\qquad$ > $\qquad$ (**O.K.** or **N.G.**)

Continue to Step 3 to design stirrup   *Stop here to increase beam section*

3) Stirrup Spacing [A_v = area of 2 legs of a stirrup = $\qquad$]

$s = \dfrac{A_v f_y d}{V_s} =$

---

4) ACI Maximum Spacing Check

1. $s = \dfrac{A_v f_y}{0.75\sqrt{f_c'}\, b_w} =$

2. $s = \dfrac{A_v f_y}{50\, b_w} =$

7. Case 1. If $V_s \leq 4\sqrt{f_c'}\, b_w d$, the max spacing ≤ (**d/2 and 24"**)

   Case 2. If $V_s > 4\sqrt{f_c'}\, b_w d$, the max spacing ≤ (**d/4 and 12"**)

$4\sqrt{f_c'}\, b_w d) =$ $\qquad$ $V_s =$ $\qquad$ → (Case 1 or Case 2)

The max spacing = the smaller of [$\qquad$] →

ACI Maximum spacing = smallest of [, , ,] =

ANSWER : (use multiples of 3 or 4 in. for construction conveniences)

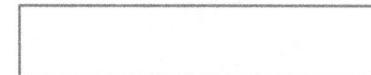

SHEAR FORCE & DIAGONAL TENSION

Workshop 6.1d

Determine the spacing of #4 U-stirrups for the beam subjected to the shear, $V_u = 11$ k. Use $F_y = 60$ ksi, and $f_c' = 4$ ksi.

Solution)

1) Shear capacity of concrete

$$\phi V_c = 0.75(2\sqrt{f_c'}\, b_w d) =$$

If $\tfrac{1}{2}\phi V_c \geq V_u$, stirrups are not required.

$\tfrac{1}{2}\,\phi V_c =$ $\qquad\qquad\qquad\qquad\qquad\qquad$ ∴ Stirrup is (**required**, or **not required**)

2) Design of Stirrup

Go to Step 2 to design stirrup $\qquad$ *Go to Step 4 to use code max.*

The V_u, is resisted by both concrete, V_c and stirrup, V_s.

$$V_u = \phi V_c + \phi V_s \quad \text{or,} \quad V_s = \frac{V_u - \phi V_c}{\phi}$$

The shear force to be carried by stirrups, V_s, is :

$$V_s = \frac{V_u - \phi V_c}{\phi} =$$

If $8\sqrt{f_c'}\, b_w d < V_s$, the beam cross-section must be increased. (stirrups won't work)

$8\sqrt{f_c'}\, b_w d =$ $\qquad\qquad\qquad\qquad\qquad >$ $\qquad\qquad$ (**O.K.** or **N.G.**)

Continue to Step 3 to design stirrup $\qquad$ *Stop here to increase beam section*

3) Stirrup Spacing [A_v = area of 2 legs of a stirrup = $\qquad$]

$$s = \frac{A_v\, f_y\, d}{V_s} =$$

---

4) ACI Maximum Spacing Check

1. $s = \dfrac{A_v\, f_y}{0.75\sqrt{f_c'}\, b_w} =$

2. $s = \dfrac{A_v\, f_y}{50\, b_w} =$

8. Case 1. If $V_s \leq 4\sqrt{f_c'}\, b_w d$, the max spacing $\leq$ (**d/2 and 24"**)

   Case 2. If $V_s > 4\sqrt{f_c'}\, b_w d$, the max spacing $\leq$ (**d/4 and 12"**)

   $4\sqrt{f_c'}\, b_w d) =$ $\qquad\qquad$ $V_s =$ $\qquad\qquad$ → (Case 1 or Case 2)

   The max spacing = the smaller of [$\qquad\qquad\qquad\qquad$] →

ACI Maximum spacing = smallest of [$\quad$, $\quad$, $\quad$] =

ANSWER : (use multiples of 3 or 4 in. for construction conveniences)

7. DESIGN OF COLUMNS

7.1 Introduction

A column is a vertical structural member supporting axial compressive loads, with or without moments. A column forms a very important component of a structure. Columns support vertical loads from beams, which in turn support walls and slabs, and transmit these loads to the foundations. It should be realized that the failure of a column may result in the collapse of the entire structure. The design of a column should therefore receive importance. The more general term, 'compression member' is used to refer to columns, walls, and members in concrete trusses that are in compression. These may be vertical, inclined, or horizontal. A column is a special case of a compression member that is vertical. The cross-sectional dimensions of a column are generally considerably less than its height. As a result, the slenderness ratio of a column is considerable and stability effects must be considered in the design of the compression member. In addition, the bending moments from the beam ends are transferred to columns in a reinforced concrete frame through the inherently rigid connections due to monolithic casting of concrete.

7.2 Classification of columns

A reinforced column may be classified based on slenderness ratio into 3 following categories:

(1) Stocky Compression Block (or, Pedestals) – Axial Force only
If the height of an upright column is less than three times its least lateral dimension, it may be considered as a pedestal. ACI permits a pedestal to be designed without reinforcement.

(2) Short Reinforced Concrete Columns - Axial Force & Primary Moment
The majority of reinforced concrete columns are sufficiently short that slenderness effects can be ignored. Such columns are referred to as short columns. Short columns are subjected to primary stresses caused by flexure, axial force, and shear. Secondary stresses associated with

DESIGN OF COLUMNS

deformations are usually very small in most columns used in practice. Material failure, generally crushing of concrete, causes short columns to fail.

(3) Slender Reinforced Concrete Columns - (Buckling) Consideration
If the moments induced by slenderness effects weaken a column appreciably, it is referred to as a slender column or a long column. Long columns generally fail by buckling effects especially if they are not braced laterally. In this case, axial force, primary and secondary moments must be taken into consideration. Consequently, slender columns resist lower axial loads than short columns having the same cross-section.

7.3 Types of Columns

According to the method used for laterally bracing the longitudinal bars, columns may be divided into tied columns and spiral columns.

Tied Column

A tied column is a concrete column reinforced with rectangular reinforcement called "ties" in addition to longitudinal reinforcement. The longitudinal bars are tied together with smaller bars at intervals up the column. The longitudinal (vertical) bars protruding from a column extend through the floor slab into the next-higher column and are lap spliced with the bars in that column. Over 95 percent of all columns in

Tied Column | **Spiral Column**

buildings in non-seismic regions are tied columns. The part of the section enclosed by the ties is called the core. The part of the section outside the core is called the shell.

Spiral Column

The spiral column is a concrete column reinforced with helical (other than ties) in addition to longitudinal reinforcement. It has a circular core confined by helical reinforcement wound at a spacing that is typically not smaller than 1 in. and that rarely exceeds 3 in. Spiral columns are generally circular, although square or polygonal shapes are sometimes used. The spiral acts to restrain the lateral expansion of the column core under high axial loads and, in doing so, delays the failure of the core, making the column more ductile, as discussed in the next section. Spiral columns are used more extensively in seismic regions. Spiral reinforcement is protected by a concrete cover (shell). If the gross section of the column (core plus shell) is rectangular, additional longitudinal reinforcement may be placed in the corner regions if desired.

7.4 Axial Strength of Columns

Ideally, if a column is subjected the pure axial load, concrete and reinforcing steel will have the same amount of shortening or compressive strain. Concrete reaches its maximum strength first. Then, concrete continues to yield until steel reaches its yield strength, when the column fails. The exact stresses in the concrete and the steel bars of a column subjected to a long-term load are almost impossible because the parts of the load carried by the concrete and the steel vary with the magnitude and duration of the loads. So, the stresses cannot be determined by multiplying the strains by the respective moduli of elasticity. This is because the modulus of elasticity of the concrete is varying over time due to creep which is a time-dependent deflection. The creep in the concrete gets greater over time and the percentage of load carried by the reinforcement gets lager. Even though the exact stress cannot be determined in columns, the ultimate strength of columns can be estimated with practical level of accuracy through with numerous experimental data. It has been known that the load duration and other such factors have little effect on the ultimate strength of reinforced concrete columns. It is not important whether the concrete or the steel reaches its ultimate strength first. When one material is approaching to its ultimate strength, the stress in the other material will increase rapidly due to excessive deformations. For these reasons, only the ultimate strength of columns is important to design engineers. At failure, the strength contributed by concrete is 0.85 f_c' (A_g- A_s), in which f_c' is compressive strength of concrete, A_g is the gross concrete area and A_s is the total cross-sectional area of longitudinal reinforcement. The strength provided by reinforcing steel is A_sF_y. Theoretical ultimate strength or nominal strength, P_n, of a short axially loaded column is quite accurately determined by the expression that follows.

$$P_n = 0.85 f_c'(A_c) + f_y A_s$$
$$= 0.85 f_c'(A_g - A_s) + f_y A_s$$

DESIGN OF COLUMNS

The formulation presented here has three implicit assumptions:
1) The peak axial load is not to be sustained for a long period of time,
2) The load is applied with no eccentricity,
3) The column is plumb and straight.

In practice, none of these assumptions is accurate. Axial loads caused by gravity can act on columns for long periods of time, loads are always applied at a certain distance from the axis of the column, and columns are seldom perfectly straight and vertical. In design, we need to consider these differences between our theory and reality:

1) The strength of a cylinder or a column loaded slowly (or for a long period) is lower than the strength of a similar cylinder loaded rapidly. In fact, a plain-concrete column can resist a sustained concentric axial load equal to 90% of its expected short-term strength for hours, sometimes days, but usually not for months. As the magnitude of the sustained load increases the time to failure decreases.

2) Eccentricity between the line of action of the load and the axis of the member results in bending. The resulting bending moment causes additional compression of some of the fibers in the element and thus results in a reduction in resistance to axial compression.

The value of 0.85 in the concrete strength (0.85 f_c') was based on the results of columns tested with and without longitudinal. The value, smaller than unity, is rationalized by recognizing that in a column, considerably taller than the test cylinder, the coarse aggregate tends to "sink" to the lower parts of the column driving the water to the top. The migration of the water to the top increases the water-to-cement ratio in the upper parts of the column leading to strength lower than that in the cylinder. It is to be noted that 0.85 was not the result of a statistical study but of a judgment call. However, the constant has been used universally for reinforced concrete structures, even for horizontally cast beams.

To account for the effects of sustained loads and unexpected eccentricity, the maximum load that can be applied to reinforced columns is limited to

$$P_n = \alpha [0.85 f_c' (A_g - A_s) + f_y A_s]$$

where, α (accidental eccentricity factor)

= 0.8 for tied column

= 0.85 for spiral column

If the column is part of a non-sway frame, slenderness effects can be neglected when *e* = $M_u/P_u \leq 0.1h$ for tied columns and *e* = $M_u/P_u \leq 0.05h$ for spiral columns. The equation can be used as long as the accidental moment is sufficiently small so that *e* is less than 0.10*h* for tied columns or less than 0.05*h* for spiral columns.

DESIGN OF COLUMNS

To provide a margin of safety against possible variations in the strength of the materials, unexpected deviations from our projections and reality, and because the consequences of the failure of a column can be catastrophic, the nominal capacity is reduced further using a strength-reduction factor, ϕ.

The **ACI design strength** of a column is finally:

$$P_n = \alpha \, \Phi \, [0.85 f_c' (A_g - A_s) + f_y A_s]$$

where,

	tied column	spiral column
α (accidental eccentricity factor)	0.8	0.85
ϕ (strength reduction factor)	0.65	0.75

Remember:

1) To account for the effects of sustained loads and unexpected eccentricity, the maximum load that can be applied to reinforced columns is reduced by the α-factor.
2) The nominal strength is reduced further using a strength-reduction factor, ϕ.
3) The axial strength of an actual column is obtained assuming that the concrete strength is 85% of that of test cylinders.
4) The sum of the contribution of steel and concrete gives the axial strength of a column.

7.5 Resistance Factors for Columns

The values of the strength reduction factors to be used for columns are well below those used for flexure and shear (0.90 and 0.75, respectively). A value of 0.65 is specified for tied columns and 0.75 for spiral columns. A slightly larger ϕ is specified for spiral columns because of their greater toughness. This is because the consequences of column failures are more severe compare to beams. Another reason is that the quality of the concrete in columns is not as good as the one in beams or slabs because casting concrete into narrow column forms and between the longitudinal and lateral steel is much more difficult than into beams or slab. The failure of a beam is normally dependent on the yield strength of the tensile steel while the failure of a column is greatly related to the ultimate strength of brittle concrete.

7.6 Code Requirements

	Value	Note
Minimum Steel Ratio	1%	to avoid non-ductile failure
Maximum Steel Ratio	8%	(*practical maximum ratio = 5~6%*) - *honeycomb*
Minimum Number of Bars	4 bars	within rectangular ties
	3 bars	within triangle ties
	6 bars	within spirals
Minimum Size of Ties	#3	for #10 or smaller longitudinal bars
	#4	for larger than #10 longitudinal bars
Tie Spacing (center-to-center)	**Smallest** of	a. 16 × diameter of longitudinal bar, d_b b. 48 × diameter of tie c. least lateral dimension of column
Lateral Support of Longitudinal Bars		Every corner and alternate longitudinal bar must be laterally supported by a tie. Unsupported bars must be within 6 inches clear from the supported bars.
Clear Spacing of Longitudinal Bars	**Larger** of	a. 1 in. b. diameter of longitudinal bar, d_b

DESIGN OF COLUMNS

7.7 Combination of Axial Force and Bending Moment

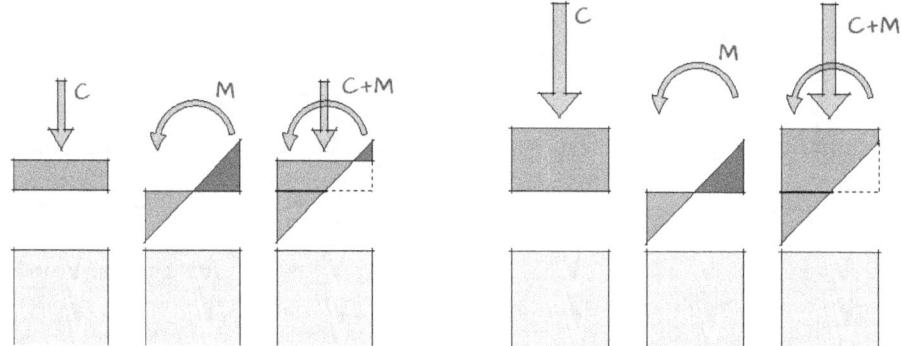

Columns in reinforced concrete frames are generally subjected to combinations of axial force and bending moment. If the limiting combination of axial compression and bending moment are represented using a linear equation, the corresponding diagram is as shown below. The diagram is defined by axial force and bending moment. The diagram that describes these combinations is called an **interaction diagram**.

$$\frac{P_u}{\Phi P_n} + \frac{M_u}{\Phi M_n} \leq 1.0 \quad (=100\%)$$

Of course, this linear interaction diagram is too simplified to be used for practical designs of reinforced concrete columns. Even though this linear interaction diagram will yield too conservative design results, this can be very useful for fundamentally understanding of the strengths of columns with varying proportions of axial loads and bending moments.

1. Any combination of axial force and bending moment that falls inside the curve is safe, whereas any combination falling outside the curve represents failure.
2. If a column is loaded to failure with an axial load only, the failure will occur at point A on the diagram.
3. Moving out from point A on the curve, the axial load capacity decreases as the proportion of bending moment increases.

DESIGN OF COLUMNS

4. At the very bottom of the curve, point C represents the bending strength of the member if it is subjected to moment only with no axial load present.
5. In between the extreme points A and C, the column fails because of a combination of axial load and bending.

Now, we discuss the combined strength of axial force and bending moment that a rectangular reinforced concrete column can resist. The following assumptions are made to simplify the process of calculations.

1. Moment will be considered to act about only one axis.
2. The strain is distributed linearly over the section.
3. The strain at the top fiber is $\varepsilon_{cu} = 0.003$, the limiting strain of concrete in compression, as defined for beams.
4. Instead of the real, non-linear compressive stresses, the Whitney rectangular stress block is used.

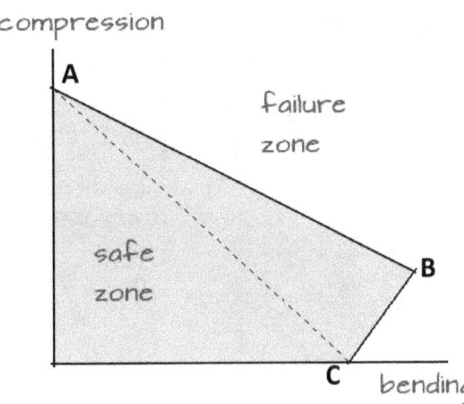

The interaction diagram on the left now has three points A, B, and C corresponding to three limiting states. For most concrete sections used in practice, determining three interconnected points will suffice to obtain a satisfactory understanding of the limiting combinations of axial force and bending moment. Point A represents the compression failure because the bending moment is zero. Point C refers to the bending failure, because the axial force is zero. Point B refers to the so-called **balanced condition** or the state with the limiting compressive strain at one edge of the section and the yield strain for the reinforcement at the centroid of the tensile forces in the bars. The coordinates of points A and B are determined directly from the specified strain conditions. For point C, the bending moment is determined with the limiting concrete strain at one edge of the section and with the neutral axis located so that there is no net axial force on the section. The easiest procedure to determine the moment for point C is to do it by trial and error. If detailed definition of the interaction diagram is desired, more calculations are to be made. All points on the interaction curve may be established by a process of assuming a series of limiting strain conditions, determining the normal stresses on the section for that strain condition, and summing the stresses to determine the axial-force and bending-moment resistances. Increase in the 'safe zone' in the interaction diagram is explained by the fact that compressive axial stresses tend to reduce tensile bending stresses on one side of tension-controlled sections.

Main Points of Column Interaction Diagram

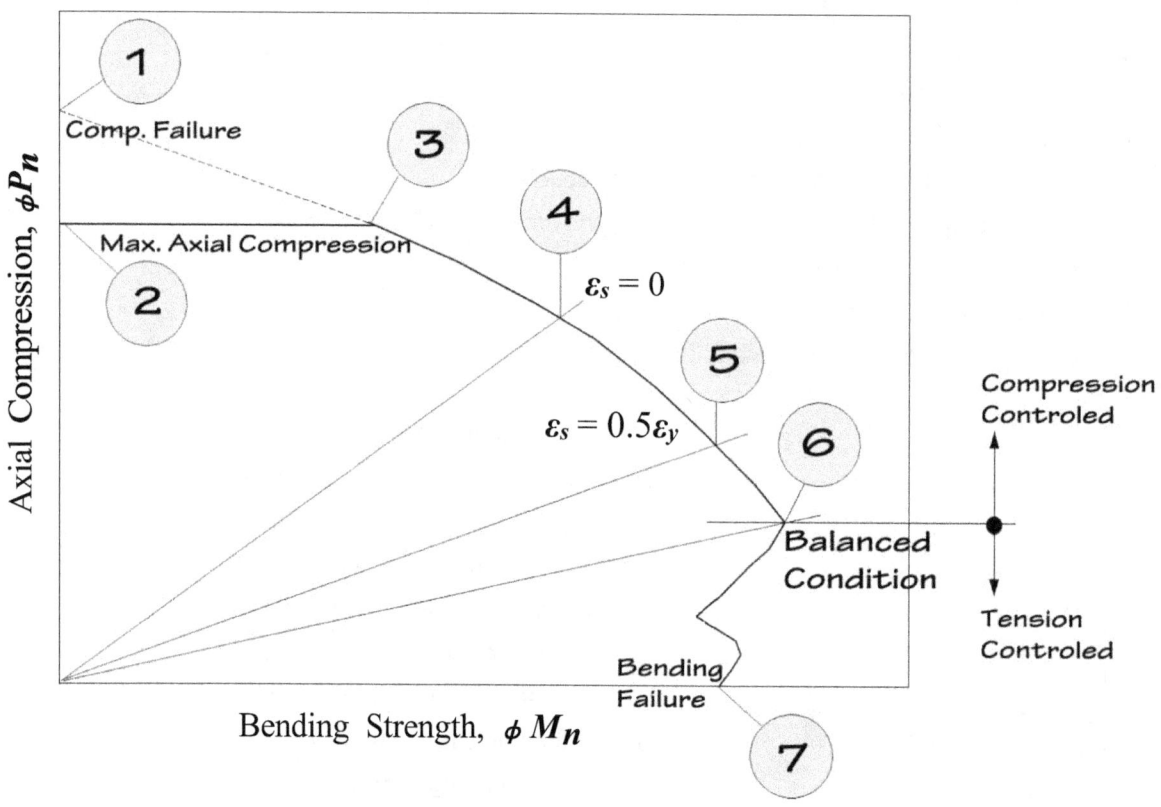

1. Compression Strength with Zero Bending Moment.
2. Maximum Permissible Axial Compression at Zero Eccentricity.
3. Maximum Moment Strength at Maximum Permissible Axial Compression.
4. Zero Strain.
5. 50% Strain.
6. Balanced Conditions.
7. Moment Strength with Zero Axial Force.

DESIGN OF COLUMNS

Case Study 7-1a

Design a square tied column to support an axial dead load DL = 130 kips and an axial live load LL = 180 kips. Consider only accidental eccentricity less than $0.10h$. Initially assume that 2% longitudinal steel is desired. f_c' = 4 ksi, and F_y = 60 ksi.

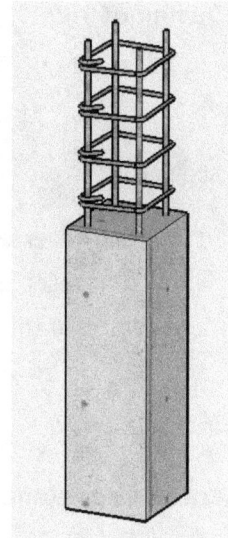

Solution

Factor Loads

P_u = 1.2 DL + 1.6 LL = 1.2 (130 kips) + 1.6 (180 kips) = 444 kips

Select Column Dimension

$$P_u \leq \phi P_n = \phi \alpha [\, 0.85 f_c'(A_g - A_s) + F_y A_s \,]$$

$\rho = 0.02$ (given) ∴ $A_s = 0.02 A_g$

444 ≤ (0.65) (0.8) [0.85 (4) (A_g − 0.002 A_g) + (60)(0.02) A_g]

444 ≤ (0.52) [3.332 A_g + 1.2 A_g]

or, 444 ≤ 2.35664 A_g

$$A_g \geq \frac{444}{2.35664} = 188.40 \, in^2$$

Select a Square $\sqrt{188.40 \, in^2} = 13.72 \, in$ → use 14" (Round up to next inch.)

use 14 × 14   (A_g = 196 in²)

Select Longitudinal Bars

$$P_u \leq \phi P_n = \phi \alpha [\, 0.85 f_c'(A_g - A_s) + F_y A_s \,]$$

444 ≤ (0.65) (0.8) [0.85 (4) (196 − A_s) + (60) A_s]

444 ≤ 0.52 [3.4 (196 − A_s) + 60 A_s]

or, 444 ≤ 346.5 − 1.768 A_s + 31.2 A_s

A_s = 3.31 in²

from Table A.4, use 6-#7 bars   (A_s = 3.61 in²)

DESIGN OF COLUMNS

Design of Ties

    a. Use #3 ties for #10 or smaller longitudinal bars. — *6-#7 bars were used.*

    b. Use #4 ties for larger than #10 longitudinal bars.

Spacing:

16 × diameter of longitudinal bar	(#7 bar) → Dia. = 0.875"	16 × (0.875") = 14"
48 × diameter of tie	(#3 bar) → Dia. = 0.375"	48 × (0.375") = 18"
Least lateral dimension of column	14" × 14" column → 14"	14"

Use #3 ties @ 14 in.

Check Code Requirements

Item	Value	Note	Judgment
Minimum Steel Ratio	1%	$\rho = \dfrac{A_s}{A_g} = \dfrac{3.61\ in^2}{(14 \times 14\ in^2)} = 0.0184 \geq 0.01$	O.K.
Maximum Steel Ratio	8%	$\rho = 0.0184 = 1.84\% \quad < 8\%$	O.K.
Min. Number of Bars	4 bars	6 bars provided > 4 bars	O.K.
Minimum Size of Ties		Checked already.	O.K.
Tie Spacing		Checked already.	O.K.
Lateral Support of Longitudinal Bars		Every corner and alternate longitudinal bar must be laterally supported by a tie. Unsupported bars must be within 6 inches clear from the supported bars.	O.K.
Clear Spacing of Longitudinal Bars	Larger of (1", d_b)	*Larger* of (1", d_b = 0.875 in.) = 1 in. Clear Spacing = 9/2 − 0.875 = 3.625 in > 1 in.	O.K.

Sketch Results

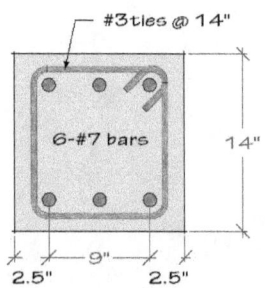

DESIGN OF COLUMNS

Case Study 7-1b

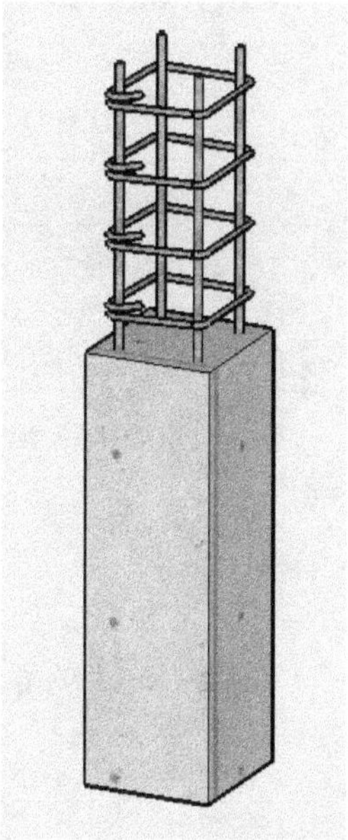

Design a square tied column to support an axial dead load DL = 130 kips and an axial live load LL = 180 kips. Consider only accidental eccentricity less than 0.10h. Initially assume that 2% longitudinal steel is desired. f_c' = 4 ksi, and F_y = 60 ksi.

Solution

Factor Loads

P_u = 1.2 DL + 1.6 LL =

Select Column Dimension

$$P_u \leq \phi P_n = \phi \alpha [\, 0.85 f_c' (A_g - A_s) + F_y A_s \,]$$

$\rho = (\quad\quad)$ $\therefore A_s = (\quad\quad) A_g$

(   ) ≤ (   )(   ) [0.85 (   )(A_g − A_g) + (   )(   ) A_g]

$A_g \geq$

Select a Square $\sqrt{\quad\quad\quad\quad}$ = (   ) in → Use (   )   (Round up to next inch.)

| Use | (A_g =   in²) |

Select Longitudinal Bars

$$P_u \leq \phi P_n = \phi \alpha [\, 0.85 f_c' (A_g - A_s) + F_y A_s \,]$$

(   ) ≤ (   )(   ) [0.85 (   )(− A_s) + (   ) A_s]

A_s = (   )

from Table A.4, | use   - #   bars | (A_s =   in²)

DESIGN OF COLUMNS

Design of Ties

    a. Use #3 ties for #10 or smaller longitudinal bars.

    b. Use #4 ties for larger than #10 longitudinal bars.

Spacing:

16 × diameter of longitudinal bar		
48 × diameter of tie		
Least lateral dimension of column		

Use #   @

Check Code Requirements

Item	Value	Note	Judgment
Minimum Steel Ratio	1%	$\rho = \dfrac{A_s}{A_g} =$	
Maximum Steel Ratio	8%	$\rho =$ < 8%	
Min. Number of Bars	4 bars	> **4 bars**	
Minimum Size of Ties		Checked already.	
Tie Spacing		Checked already.	
Lateral Support of Longitudinal Bars		Every corner and alternate longitudinal bar must be laterally supported by a tie. Unsupported bars must be within 6 inches clear from the supported bars.	
Clear Spacing of Longitudinal Bars	Larger of (1", d_b)	*Larger* of (1", $d_b =$ in.) = in. Clear Spacing = 	

Sketch Results

DESIGN OF COLUMNS

Case Study 7-2a

Using the appropriate interaction curves, determine the value of P_n for the short tied column if e_x = 10 in. Use f_c' = 4 ksi, and F_y = 60 ksi

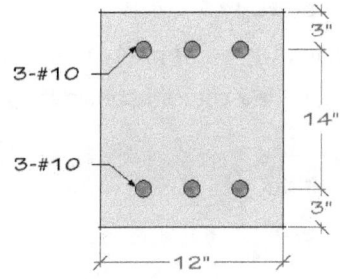

Solution

$$e/h = \frac{10"}{20"} = 0.5$$

$$\rho_g = \frac{A_s}{A_g} = \frac{6(1.27\ in^2)}{12" \times 20"} = 0.0317$$

$$\gamma = 14\ in. / 20\ in. = 0.7$$

Plot a straight line from the origin to the intersection of assumed values of R_n and K_n such that R_n/K_n = the e/h value of 0.5. (say, 0.4 and 0.8, respectively).

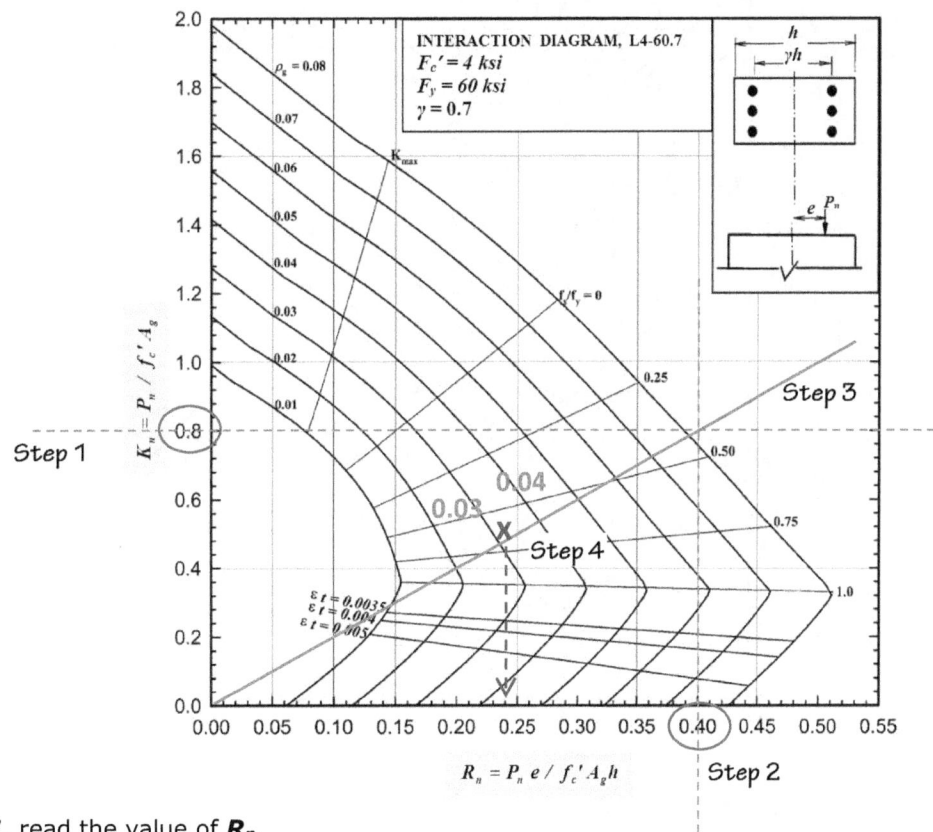

COLUMNS 3.8.2 – Nominal load-moment strength interaction diagram, L4-60.7

For ρ_g = 0.0317, read the value of R_n.

$R_n = 0.24$

$R_n = P_n e / f_c' A_g h = 0.24$ or, $P_n = R_n f_c' A_g h / e$

$P_n = (0.24)(4\ ksi)(12" \times 20")(20")/10" = \boxed{460.8\ k}$

DESIGN OF COLUMNS

Case Study 7-2b

Using the appropriate interaction curves, determine the value of P_n for the short tied column shown if e_x = 10 in.   Use f_c' = 4 ksi, and F_y = 60 ksi

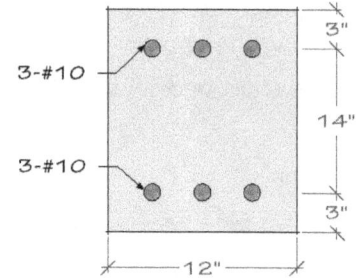

Solution

$e/h =$

$\rho_g = \dfrac{A_s}{A_g} =$

$\gamma =$

Plot a straight line from the origin to the intersection of assumed values of R_n and K_n such that R_n/K_n = the e/h value of (   ). (say,   and   , respectively).

COLUMNS 3.8.2 – Nominal load-moment strength interaction diagram, L4-60.7

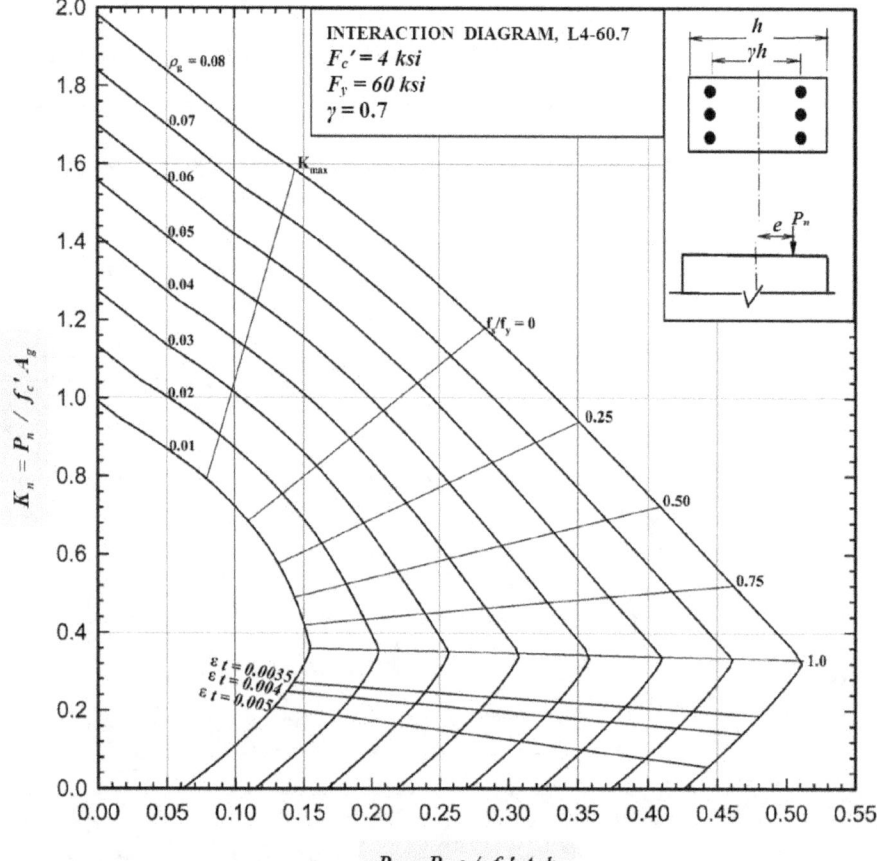

For $\rho_g =$, read the value of R_n.

$R_n =$

$R_n = P_n e / f_c' A_g h =$ or, $P_n = R_n f_c' A_g h / e$

$P_n =$

DESIGN OF COLUMNS

Case Study 7-2c

Using the appropriate interaction curves, determine the value of P_n for the short tied column shown if e_x = 5 in. Use f_c' = 4 ksi, and F_y = 60 ksi

Solution

$e/h =$

$\rho_g = \dfrac{A_s}{A_g} =$

$\gamma =$

Plot a straight line from the origin to the intersection of assumed values of R_n and K_n such that $R_n/K_n =$ the e/h value of (   ). (say,   and   , respectively).

COLUMNS 3.8.2 – Nominal load-moment strength interaction diagram, L4-60.7

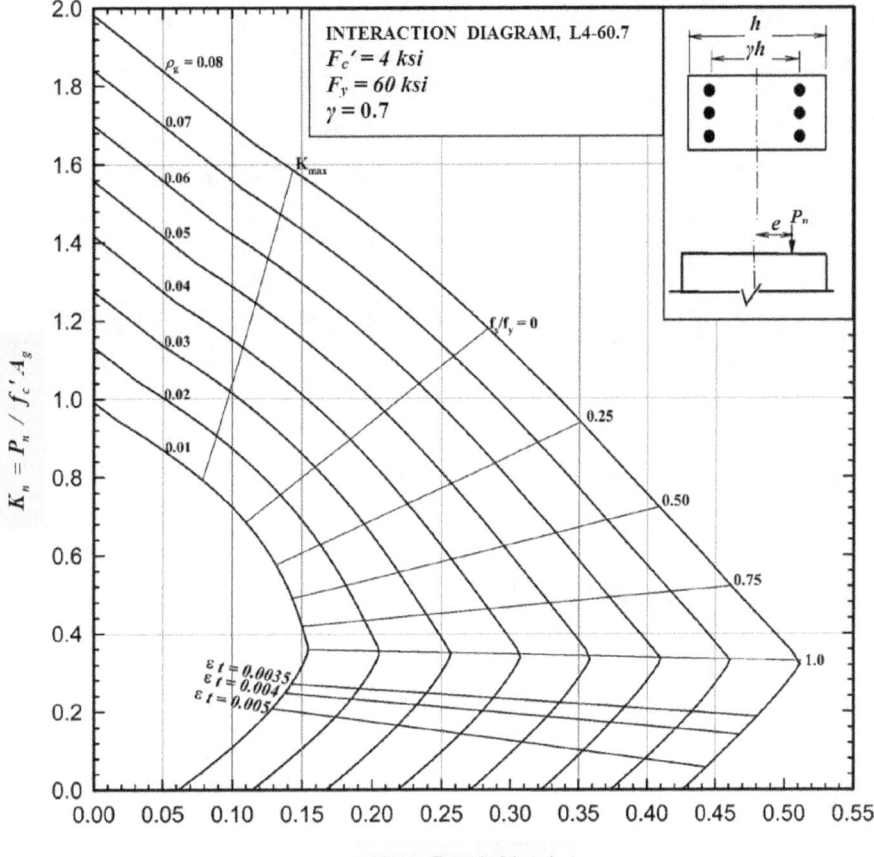

For $\rho_g =$, read the value of R_n.

$R_n =$

$R_n = P_n e / f_c' A_g h =$ or, $P_n = R_n f_c' A_g h / e$

$P_n =$

DESIGN OF COLUMNS

Case Study 7-3a

The short 14"x20" tied column is used to support the following loads and bending moment: P_D = 125k, P_L=140k, M_D=75 k-ft and M_L = 90 k-ft. Select reinforcing bar to be placed in its end faces only using sppropriate ACI column interaction diagrams. Use f_c' = 4 ksi and F_y = 60 ksi

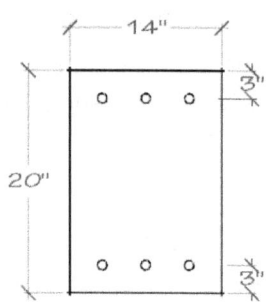

Solution

Factor Loads

$P_u = 1.2\ DL + 1.6\ LL = 1.2\ (125\ k) + 1.6\ (140\ k) = 374\ k$

$P_n = \dfrac{P_u}{\Phi} = \dfrac{374}{0.65} = 575.4\ k$

$M_u = 1.2\ DL + 1.6\ LL = 1.2\ (75\ k\text{-}ft) + 1.6\ (90\ k\text{-}ft) = 234\ k\text{-}ft$

$M_n = \dfrac{M_u}{\Phi} = \dfrac{234}{0.65} = 360\ k\text{-}ft$

Design Parameters

$e = \dfrac{M_n}{P_n} = \dfrac{360\,(12)}{575.4} = 7.51"$ $\qquad \gamma = \dfrac{14}{20} = 0.7$

$K_n = \dfrac{P_n}{f_c'\,A_g} = \dfrac{575.4}{(4)\,14\times20} = 0.513$ $\qquad R_n = \dfrac{P_n\,e}{f_c'\,A_g\,h} = \dfrac{575.4\,(7.51)}{(4)\,(14\times20)\,(20)} = 0.193$

Determine ρ-value from γ-value (using interaction diagrams)

γ-value	ρ-value
x_1 = 0.7	y_1 = 0.0220
x =	y = ?
x_2 =	y_2 =

$y = y_1 + \dfrac{y_2 - y_1}{x_2 - x_1}(x - x_1) = 0.220$

Determine Steel Reinforcement

$A_s = \rho\,(b \times h) = (0.0220)(14)(20) = 6.16\ in^2$ → Use 4-#11 bars ($A_s = 6.25\ in^2$)

DESIGN OF COLUMNS

Case Study 7-3b

The short 14"x20" tied column is used to support the following loads and bending moment: **P_D** = 125k, **P_L**=140k, **M_D**=75 k-ft and **M_L** = 90 k-ft. Select reinforcing bar to be placed in its end faces only using sppropriate ACI column interaction diagrams. Use **f_c'** = 4 ksi and **F_y** = 60 ksi

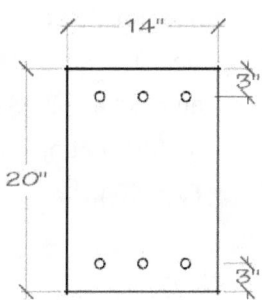

Solution

Factor Loads

$P_u = 1.2\ DL + 1.6\ LL =$

$P_n = \dfrac{P_u}{\Phi} =$

$M_u = 1.2\ DL + 1.6\ LL =$

$M_n = \dfrac{M_u}{\Phi} =$

Design Parameters

$e = \dfrac{M_n}{P_n} =$

$\gamma =$

$K_n = \dfrac{P_n}{f_c' A_g} =$ $R_n = \dfrac{P_n e}{f_c' A_g h} =$

Determine ρ-value from γ-value (using interaction diagrams)

γ-value	ρ-value
$x_1 =$	$y_1 =$
$x =$	$y =$?
$x_2 =$	$y_2 =$

$y = y_1 + \dfrac{y_2 - y_1}{x_2 - x_1}(x - x_1) =$

Determine Steel Reinforcement

$A_s = \rho\ (b \times h) =$

DESIGN OF COLUMNS

Workshop 7-1a

Design a square tied column to support an axial dead load DL = 160 kips and an axial live load LL = 200 kips. Consider only accidental eccentricity less than 0.10h. Initially assume that 2% longitudinal steel is desired. $f_c' $ = 4 ksi, and F_y = 60 ksi.

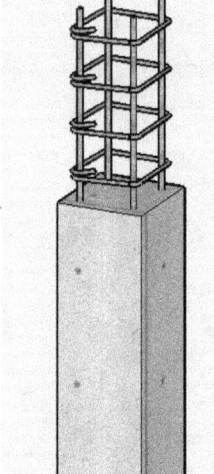

Solution)

Factor Loads

P_u = 1.2 DL + 1.6 LL =

Select Column Dimension

$$P_u \leq \phi P_n = \phi \alpha [\, 0.85 f_c' (A_g - A_s) + F_y A_s \,]$$

$\rho = (\quad) \quad \therefore A_s = (\quad) A_g$

(   ) ≤ (   )(   )[0.85 (   )(A_g − A_g) + (   )(   ) A_g]

$A_g \geq$

Select a square $\sqrt{\rule{2cm}{0pt}}$ = (   ) in → use (   )   (Round up to next inch.)

use ☐ (A_g =   in²)

Select Longitudinal Bars

$$P_u \leq \phi P_n = \phi \alpha [\, 0.85 f_c' (A_g - A_s) + F_y A_s \,]$$

(   ) ≤ (   )(   )[0.85 (   )(− A_s) + (   ) A_s]

A_s = (   )

from Table A.4, use ☐ -#   bars (A_s =   in²)

DESIGN OF COLUMNS

Design of Ties

   a. Use #3 ties for #10 or smaller longitudinal bars.
   b. Use #4 ties for larger than #10 longitudinal bars.

Spacing:

16 × diameter of longitudinal bar		
48 × diameter of tie		
Least lateral dimension of column		

use #   @

Check Code Requirements

Item	Value	Note	Judgment
Minimum Steel Ratio	1%	$\rho = \dfrac{A_s}{A_g} =$	
Maximum Steel Ratio	8%	$\rho =$ < 8%	
Min. Number of Bars	4 bars	> 4 bars	
Minimum Size of Ties		Checked already.	
Tie Spacing		Checked already.	
Lateral Support of Longitudinal Bars		Every corner and alternate longitudinal bar must be laterally supported by a tie. Unsupported bars must be within 6 inches clear from the supported bars.	
Clear Spacing of Longitudinal Bars	Larger of $(1'', d_b)$	*Larger* of (1", $d_b =$ in.) = in. Clear Spacing= 	

Sketch Results

DESIGN OF COLUMNS

Workshop 7-2a

Using the appropriate interaction curves, determine the value of P_n for the short tied column shown if $e_x = 10$ in. Use $f_c' = 4$ ksi, and $F_y = 60$ ksi

Solution

$e/h =$

$\rho_g = \dfrac{A_s}{A_g} =$

$\gamma =$

Plot a straight line from the origin to the intersection of assumed values of R_n and K_n such that $R_n/K_n =$ the e/h value of ( ). (say, and , respectively).

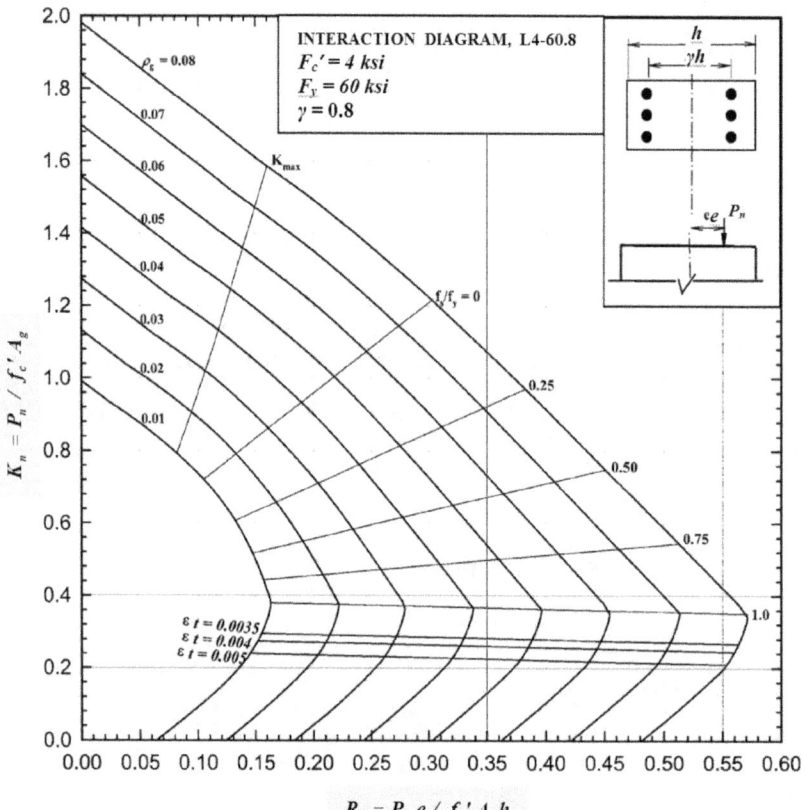

COLUMNS 3.8.3 – Nominal load-moment strength interaction diagram, L4-60.8

For $\rho_g =$, read the value of R_n.

$R_n =$

$R_n = P_n e / f_c' A_g h =$ or, $P_n = R_n f_c' A_g h / e$

$P_n =$

DESIGN OF COLUMNS

Workshop 7-2b

Using the appropriate interaction curves, determine the value of P_n for the short tied column shown if e_x = 15 in. Use f_c' = 4 ksi, and F_y = 60 ksi

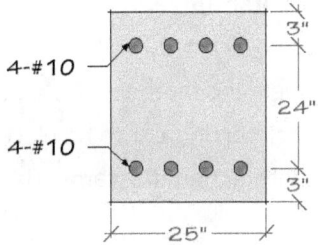

Solution

$e/h =$

$\rho_g = \dfrac{A_s}{A_g} =$

$\gamma =$

Plot a straight line from the origin to the intersection of assumed values of R_n and K_n such that $R_n/K_n =$ the e/h value of (   ). (say,   and   , respectively).

For $\rho_g =$, read the value of R_n.

$R_n =$

$R_n = P_n e / f_c' A_g h =$ or, $P_n = R_n f_c' A_g h / e$

$P_n =$

Workshop 7-2c

Using the appropriate interaction curves, determine the value of P_n for the short tied column shown if e_x = 20 in. Use f_c' = 4 ksi, and F_y = 60 ksi

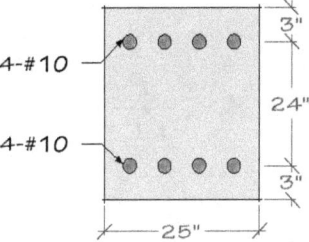

Solution

$e/h =$

$\rho_g = \dfrac{A_s}{A_g} =$

$\gamma =$

Plot a straight line from the origin to the intersection of assumed values of R_n and K_n such that $R_n/K_n =$ the e/h value of (   ). (say,   and   , respectively).

For $\rho_g =$, read the value of R_n.

$R_n =$

$R_n = P_n e / f_c' A_g h =$ or, $P_n = R_n f_c' A_g h / e$

$P_n =$

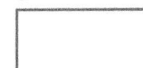

DESIGN OF COLUMNS

Workshop 7-3a

The short 20"x20" tied column is used to support the following loads and bending moment: P_D = 150k, P_L=160k, M_D=95 k-ft and M_L = 110 k-ft. Select reinforcing bar to be placed in its end faces only using sppropriate ACI column interaction diagrams. Use f_c' = 4 ksi and F_y = 60 ksi

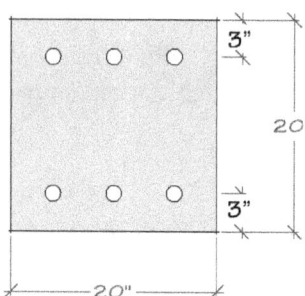

Solution

Factor Loads

$P_u = 1.2\ DL + 1.6\ LL =$

$P_n = \dfrac{P_u}{\Phi} =$

$M_u = 1.2\ DL + 1.6\ LL =$

$M_n = \dfrac{M_u}{\Phi} =$

Design Parameters

$e = \dfrac{M_n}{P_n} =$ $\qquad\qquad\qquad \gamma =$

$K_n = \dfrac{P_n}{f_c' A_g} =$ $\qquad\qquad R_n = \dfrac{P_n e}{f_c' A_g h} =$

Determine ρ-value from γ-value (using interaction diagrams)

	γ-value	ρ-value
$x_1 =$		$y_1 =$
$x =$		$y =$?
$x_2 =$		$y_2 =$

$y = y_1 + \dfrac{y_2 - y_1}{x_2 - x_1}(x - x_1) =$

Determine Steel Reinforcement

$A_s = \rho\ (b \times h) =$

DESIGN OF COLUMNS

Workshop 7-3b

The short 20"x20" tied column is used to support the following loads and bending moment: P_D = 140k, P_L=120k, M_D=100 k-ft and M_L = 120 k-ft. Select reinforcing bar to be placed in its end faces only using sppropriate ACI column interaction diagrams. Use f_c' = 4 ksi and F_y = 60 ksi

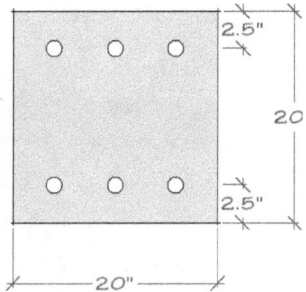

Solution

Factor Loads

$P_u = 1.2\ DL + 1.6\ LL =$

$P_n = \dfrac{P_u}{\Phi} =$

$M_u = 1.2\ DL + 1.6\ LL =$

$M_n = \dfrac{M_u}{\Phi} =$

Design Parameters

$e = \dfrac{M_n}{P_n} =$ 	 $\gamma =$

$K_n = \dfrac{P_n}{f_c' A_g} =$ 	 $R_n = \dfrac{P_n e}{f_c' A_g h} =$

Determine ρ-value from γ-value (using interaction diagrams)

γ-value	ρ-value
$x_1 =$	$y_1 =$
$x =$	$y =$?
$x_2 =$	$y_2 =$

$y = y_1 + \dfrac{y_2 - y_1}{x_2 - x_1}(x - x_1) =$

Determine Steel Reinforcement

$A_s = \rho\ (b \times h) =$

8. FOUNDATIONS

8.1 Introduction

Foundation (or footings) are structural members that transmit column or wall loads to the underlying soil below the structure. All soils compress noticeably when loaded and cause the supported superstructure to settle. Footings are designed to transmit these loads to the soil without exceeding its safe bearing capacity, to prevent excessive settlement of the structure to a tolerable limit, to minimize differential settlement, and to prevent sliding and overturning. The settlement depends upon the intensity of the load, type of soil, and foundation level. Where possibility of differential settlement occurs, the different footings should be designed in such a way to settle independently of each other. Foundation design involves a soil study to establish the most appropriate type of foundation and a structural design to determine footing dimensions and required amount of reinforcement. Because compressive strength of the soil is generally much weaker than that of the concrete, the contact area between the soil and the footing is much larger than that of the columns and walls. The closer a foundation is to the ground surface, the more economical it will be to construct. There are two reasons, however, that may keep the designer from using very shallow foundations. First, it is necessary to locate the bottom of a footing below the ground freezing level to avoid vertical movement or heaving of the footing as the soil freezes and expands in volume. This depth varies from about 3 ft to 6 ft in the northern states and less in the southern states. Second, it is necessary to excavate a sufficient distance so that a satisfactory bearing material is reached, and this distance may on occasion be quite a few feet. Reinforced concrete is considered as the most appropriate construction material admirably suited for footings and is widely used for both reinforced concrete and structural steel buildings, bridges, towers, and other structures.

FOUNDATIONS

8.2 Pressure Distribution below Foundations

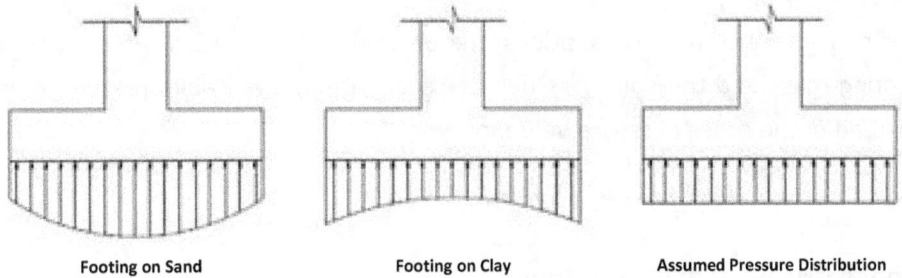

Footing on Sand Footing on Clay Assumed Pressure Distribution

The distribution of soil pressure under a footing is a function of the type of soil, the relative rigidity of the soil and the footing, and the depth of foundation at level of contact between footing and soil. A concrete footing on sand will have a pressure distribution shown above. When a rigid footing is resting on sandy soil, the sand near the edges of the footing tends to displace laterally when the footing is loaded. This tends to decrease in soil pressure near the edges, whereas soil away from the edges of footing is relatively confined. As the footing is loaded, the soil under the footing deflects in a bowl-shaped depression, relieving the pressure under the middle of the footing. For design purposes, it is common to assume the soil pressures are linearly distributed. The pressure distribution will be uniform if the centroid of the footing coincides with the resultant of the applied loads.

8.3 Allowable Bearing Capacity of Soil

The maximum intensity of loading at the base of a foundation which causes shear failure of soil is called ultimate bearing capacity of soil, denoted by q_u. The intensity of loading that the soil carries without causing shear failure and without causing excessive settlement is called allowable bearing capacity of soil, denoted by q_a. It should be noted that q_a is a service load stress. The allowable bearing capacity of soil is obtained by dividing the ultimate bearing capacity of soil by a factor of safety on the order of 2.50 to 3.0.

Gross Soil Pressure

The allowable soil pressure for soil may be either gross or net pressure permitted on the soil directly under the base of the footing. The gross pressure represents the total stress in the soil created by all the loads above the base of the footing. These loads include:
1. column service loads;
2. the weight of the footing; and
3. the weight of the soil on the top of the footing, or

$$q_{gross} = q_{soil} + q_{footing} + q_{column}$$

Net Soil Pressure

For moment and shear calculations, the upward and downward pressures of the footing mass and the soil mass get cancelled. Thus, a net soil pressure is used instead of the gross pressure value, or

$$q_{net} = q_{gross} - q_{footing} - q_{soil}$$

Concentrically loaded Footings

If the resultant of the loads acting at the base of the footing coincides with the centroid of the footing area, the footing is concentrically loaded and a uniform distribution of soil pressure is assumed in design, as shown in Figure 11.4. The magnitude of the pressure intensity is given by

$$Q = P/A$$

where, A is the bearing area of the footing, and P is the applied load.

8.4 Depth of Foundation

The depth to which foundations shall be carried is to satisfy the following:

a. Ensuring adequate bearing capacity.
b. In the case of clay soils, footings are to penetrate below the zone where shrinkage and swelling due to seasonal weather changes are likely to cause appreciable movement.
c. The footing should be located sufficiently below maximum scouring depth.
d. The footing should be located away from top soils containing organic materials.
e. The footing should be located away from unconsolidated materials such as garbage. All footings shall extend to a depth of at least 0.50 meter below natural ground level. On rock or such other weather-resisting natural ground, removal of the top soil may be all that is required. In such cases, the surface shall be cleaned, so as to provide a suitable bearing. Usually footings are located at depths of 1.5 to 2.0 meters below natural ground level.

FOUNDATIONS

8.5 Foundation Types

Among the several types of reinforced concrete footings in common use are the wall, isolated, combined, raft, and pile-cap types. These are briefly introduced in this section; the remainder of the chapter is used to provide more detailed information about the simpler types of this group. The type of footing chosen for a particular structure is affected by the following:

1. The bearing capacity of the underlying soil.
2. The magnitude of the column loads.
3. The position of the water table.
4. The depth of foundations of adjacent buildings.

Footings may be classified as deep or shallow. If depth of the footing is equal to or greater than its width, it is called deep footing; otherwise it is called shallow footing. Shallow footings comprise the following types:

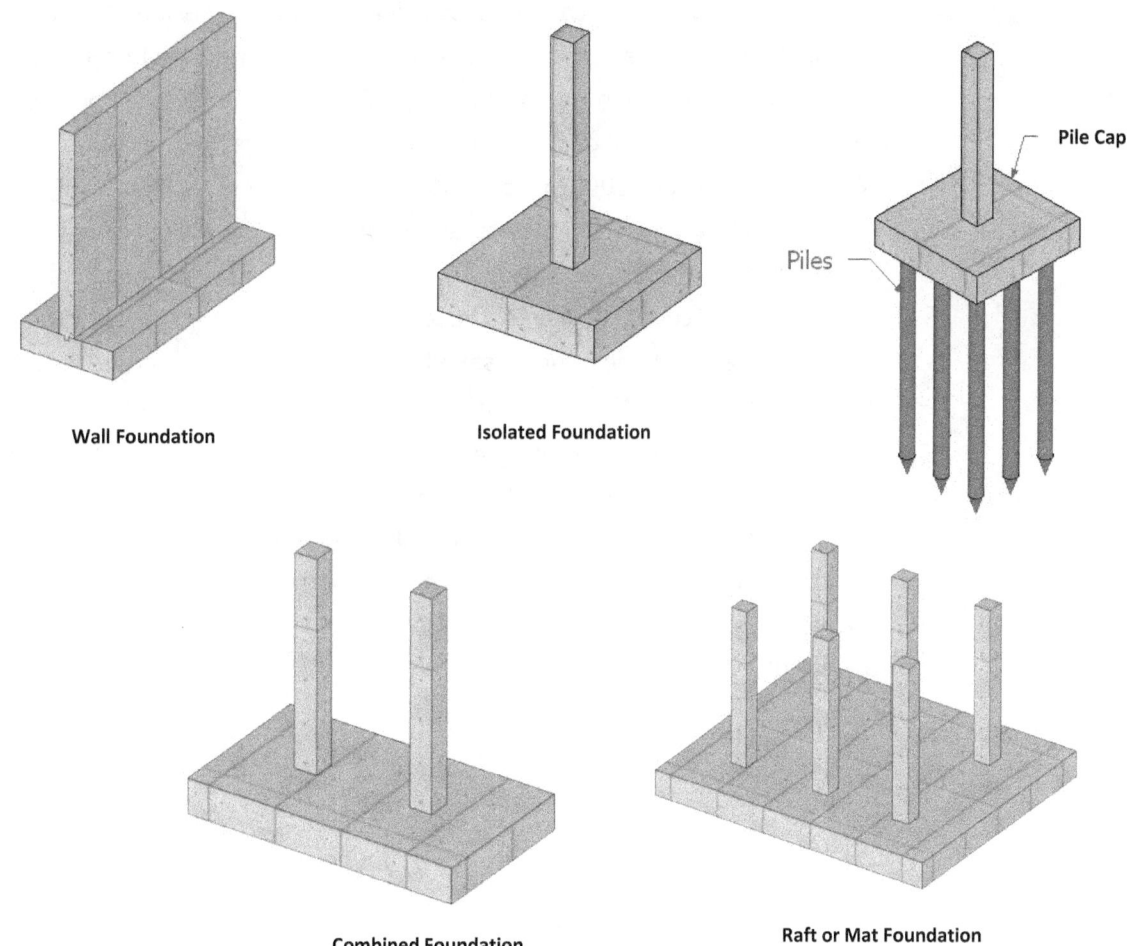

8.6 Wall Foundation

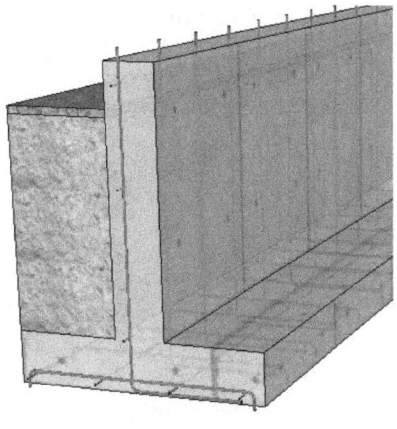
Wall Foundation

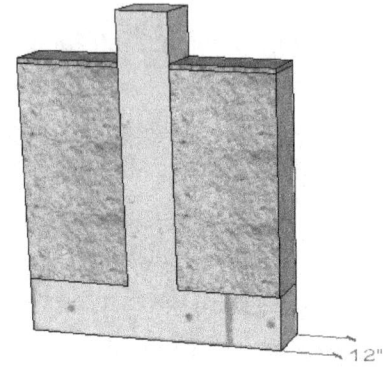
A Typical 12"-wide Piece

The design of wall footings is conveniently handled by using 12-in. widths of the wall, as shown above. Such a practice is followed for the design of a wall footing. It should be noted that the depth of a footing above the bottom reinforcing bars may be no less than 6 in. for footings on soils and 12 in. for those on piles. Thus, total minimum practical depths are at least 10 in. for regular spread footings and 16 in. for pile caps. 3000 psi and 4000 psi concretes are commonly used for footings and are generally quite economical. Occasionally, when it is very important to minimize footing depths and weights, stronger concretes may be used. For most cases, however, the extra cost of higher-strength concrete will appreciably exceed the money saved with the smaller concrete volume. The exposure category of the footing may control the concrete strength. ACI requires that concrete exposed to sulfate have minimum f_c' values of 4000 psi or 4500 psi, depending on the sulfur concentration in the soil. The determination of a footing depth is a trial-and-error problem. The designer assumes an effective depth, d, computes the d required for shear, tries another d, computes the d required for shear, and so on, until the assumed value and the calculated value are within about 1 in. of each other. Two trials are usually sufficient. The upward soil pressure under the wall footing tends to bend the footing into the deformed shape shown. The footings will be designed as shallow beams for the moments and shears involved. In beams where loads are usually only a few hundred pounds per foot and spans are fairly large, sizes are almost always proportioned for moment. In footings,

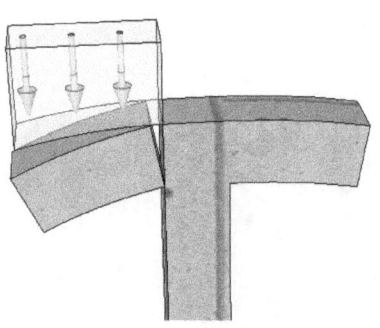
Critical Section for Bending

loads from the supporting soils may run several thousand pounds per foot and spans are relatively short. As a result, shears will almost always control depths. The simple principles of beam action apply to wall footings with only minor modifications. If bending moments were computed from these forces, the maximum moment would take place at the middle of the width. For footings under concrete walls, it is satisfactory to compute the moment at the face of the wall. To compute the bending moments and shears in a footing, it is necessary to compute only the net upward pressure, q_u, caused by the factored wall loads above. In other words, the weight of the footing and soil on top of the footing can be neglected. These items cause an upward pressure equal to their downward weights, and they cancel each other for purposes of computing shears and moments. If a wall footing is loaded until it fails in shear, the failure will not occur on a vertical plane at the wall face but rather at an angle of approximately 45° with the wall. Apparently the diagonal tension is opposed by the compression caused by the downward wall load and the upward soil pressure. Therefore, for nonprestressed sections, shear may be calculated at a distance d from the face of the wall. The use of stirrups in footings is usually considered impractical and uneconomical. For this reason, the effective depth of wall footings is selected so that V_u is limited to the design shear strength, ϕV_c, that the concrete can carry without web reinforcing.

8.7 Isolated Footings

An isolated footing is used to support the load on a single column. It is usually either square or rectangular in plan. It represents the simplest, most economical type and most widely used footing. Whenever possible, square footings are provided so as to reduce the bending moments and shearing forces at their critical sections. Isolated footings are used in case of light column loads, when columns are not closely spaced, and in case of good homogeneous soil. Under the effect of upward soil pressure, the footing bends in a dish shaped form. An isolated footing must, therefore, be provided by two sets of reinforcement bars placed on top of the other near the bottom of the footing. In case of property line restrictions, footings may be designed for eccentric loading or combined footing is used as an alternative to isolated footing.

One-way Shear (or, Beam Shear)
Two shear conditions must be considered in column footings, regardless of their shapes. The first of these is one-way or beam shear, which is the same as that considered in wall footings in the preceding section. The beam shear checking for an isolated footing must be performed in both directions of the footing.

FOUNDATIONS

Failure Modes of Isolated Footings

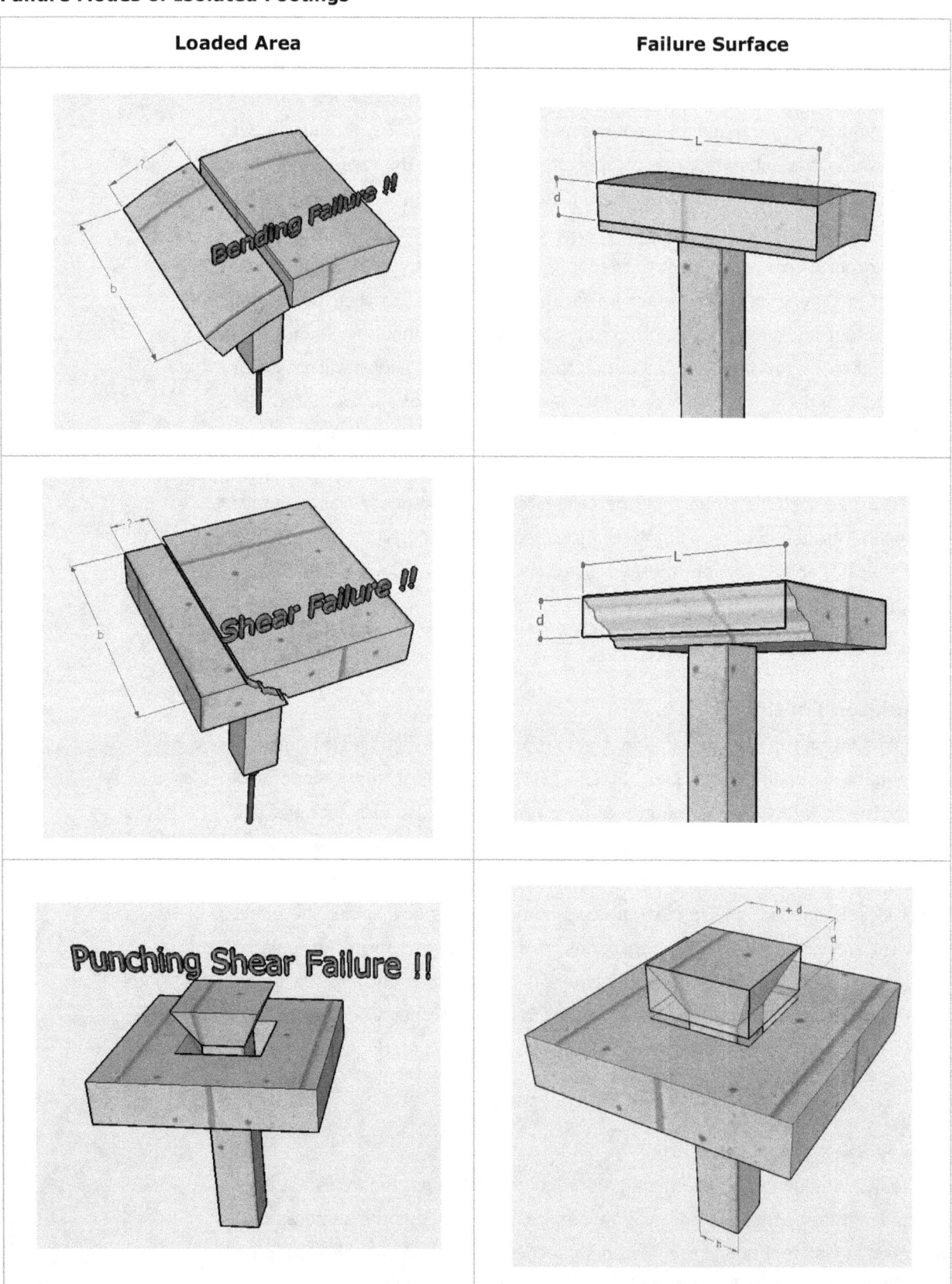

Punching Shear

Two-way shear, popularly known as punching shear, is critical in flat slab, footings, pile-caps and two-way slabs carrying concentrated load. For relatively low value of the ratio of length of load to length of slab, the two-way bending action is predominant giving  rise to two-way shear as in case of column footing. The two-way action in the slabs under point loads give rise to a peculiar punching shear stress failure of slab/footing in the vicinity and around the concentrated loads, with potential diagonal cracking along the surface of a truncated cone, or a pyramid, around the concentrated load. Tests have shown that the shear strength of slab/footing under two-way action (punching shear strength) depends upon the tensile strength of concrete and effective depth of slab/footing and propagates at a distance "*d/2*" from the face of concentrated load (column). It is interesting to note that earlier it was envisaged that punching shear failure takes place at the face of point load/column. It is now changed to a distance "*d/2*" based on experimental results.

FOUNDATIONS

Case Study 8-1

A wall footing, as shown in the figure, supports a 12-in.-wide reinforced concrete wall with a dead load, **DL** = 20 k/ft and a live load, **LL** = 15 k/ft. The bottom of the footing is 4 ft below the final grade, the soil weight is 100 pcf and the allowable soil pressure, q_a = 4 ksf. Use f_c' = 3 ksi, and f_y = 60 ksi. Check the adequacy of the wall foundation.

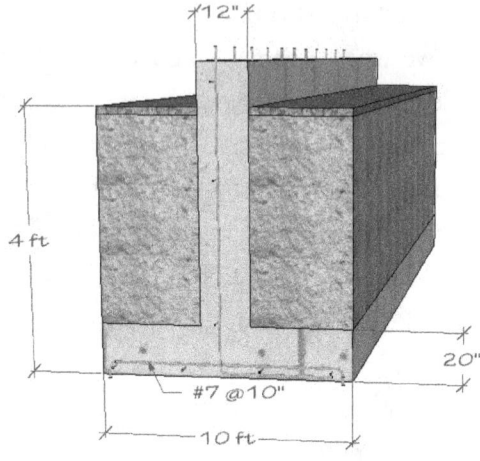

Solution)

1. **Soil Pressure Check** (use unfactored load)

Weight of the footing	
Weight of soil on the footing	
Dead Load	
Live Load	
Total Load	

2. **Footing Check** (use factored load)

Factored Load, P_u =

Bearing Pressure, q_u =

FOUNDATIONS

Check for shear

Shear Force caused by soli pressure

$V_u =$

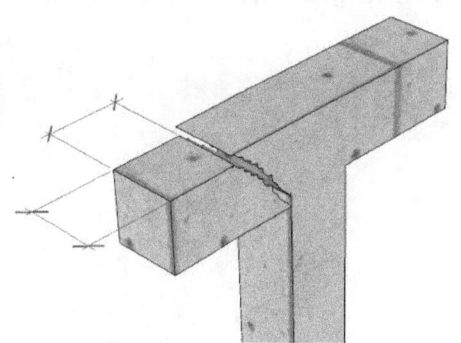

Shear Resistance by Concrete *(No stirrup is practical in footings!!)*

$$V_c = \phi\left(2\sqrt{f_c'}\right) A_c = \phi\left(2\sqrt{f_c'}\right)(b \times d)$$

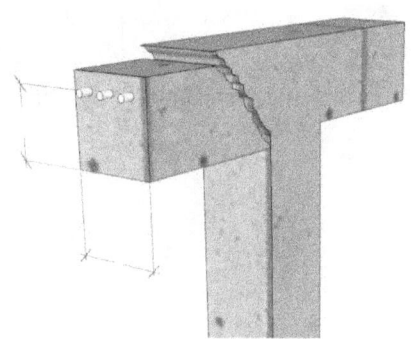

Concrete Shear Check $V_u \leq V_c$

(OK or NG)

FOUNDATIONS

Check for Moment

Bending Moment caused by soil pressure

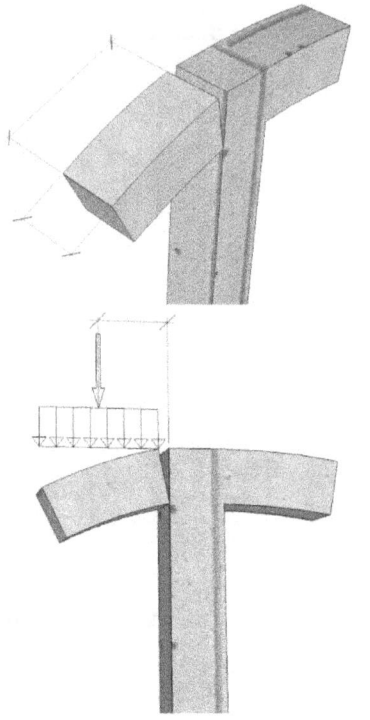

P =

e =

M_u = P x e =

Moment Strength (Beam Action)

Moment Check $M_u \leq \phi M_n$

(OK or NG)

Workshop 8-1a

A wall footing, as shown in the figure, supports a 18-in.-wide reinforced concrete wall with a dead load, **DL** = 25 k/ft and a live load, **LL** = 15 k/ft. The bottom of the footing is to be 5 ft below the final grade, the soil weight is 100 pcf and the allowable soil pressure, q_a = 4 ksf. Use f_c' = 3 ksi, and f_y = 50 ksi. Check the adequacy of the wall foundation.

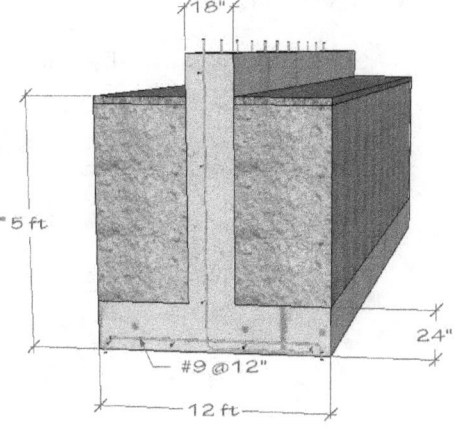

Solution)

1. Soil Pressure Check (use unfactored load)

Weight of the footing	
Weight of soil on the footing	
Dead Load	
Live Load	
Total Load	

2. Footing Check (use factored load)

Factored Load, P_u =

Bearing Pressure, q_u =

FOUNDATIONS

Check for shear

Shear Force caused by soli pressure

$V_u =$

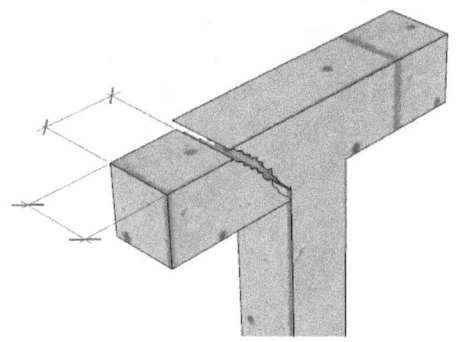

Shear Resistance by Concrete *(No stirrup is practical in footings!!)*

$$V_c = \phi\left(2\sqrt{f_c'}\right) A_c = \phi\left(2\sqrt{f_c'}\right)(b \times d)$$

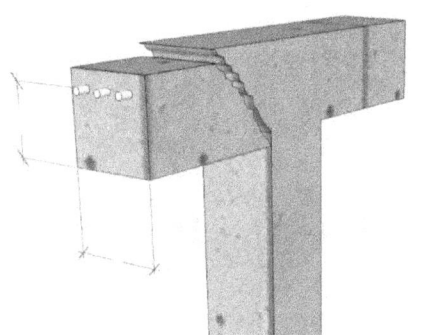

Concrete Shear Check $V_u \leq V_c$

(OK or NG)

Check for Moment

Bending Moment caused by soil pressure

P =

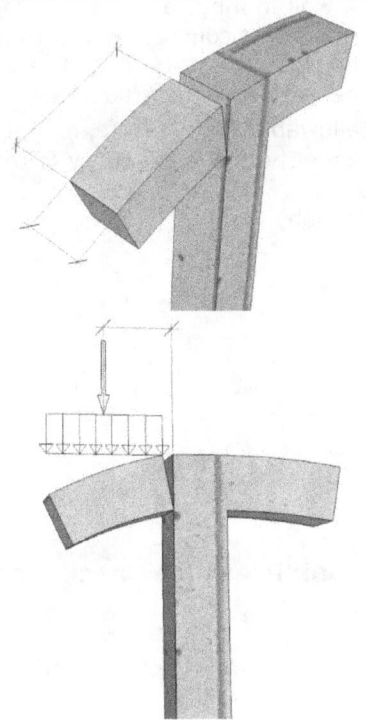

e =

M_u = P x e =

Moment Strength (Beam Action)

Moment Check $M_u ≤ \phi M_n$

(OK or NG)

FOUNDATIONS

Workshop 8-1b

A wall footing, as shown in the figure, supports a 12-in.-wide reinforced concrete wall with a dead load, **DL** = 15 k/ft and a live load, **LL** = 10 k/ft. The bottom of the footing is to be 5 ft below the final grade, the soil weight is 100 pcf and the allowable soil pressure, q_a = 4 ksf. Use f_c' = 3 ksi, and f_y = 60 ksi. Check the adequacy of the wall foundation.

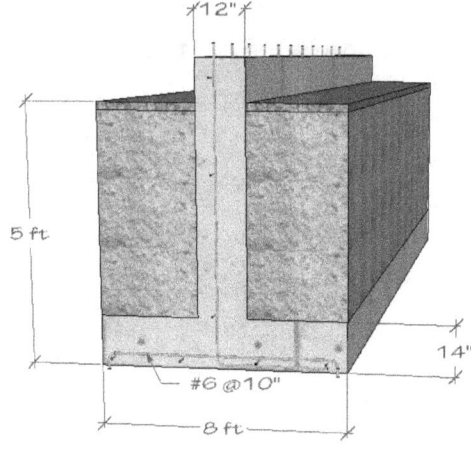

Solution)

---

1. Soil Pressure Check (use unfactored load)

Weight of the footing	
Weight of soil on the footing	
Dead Load	
Live Load	
Total Load	

2. Footing Check (use factored load)

Factored Load, P_u =

Bearing Pressure, q_u =

FOUNDATIONS

Check for shear

Shear Force caused by soli pressure

$V_u =$

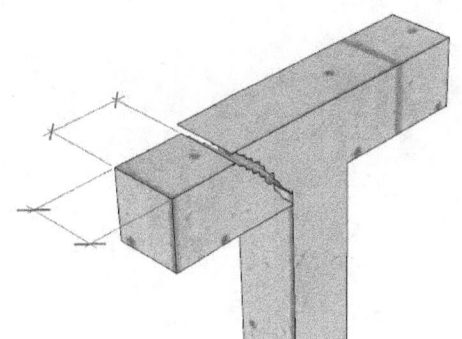

Shear Resistance by Concrete *(No stirrup is practical in footings!!)*

$$V_c = \phi\left(2\sqrt{f_c'}\right)A_c = \phi\left(2\sqrt{f_c'}\right)(b \times d)$$

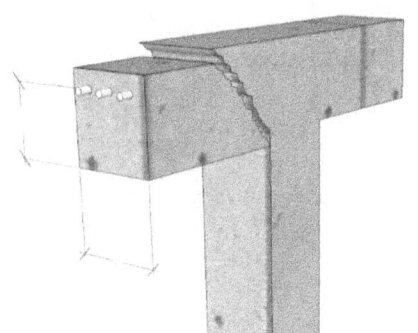

Concrete Shear Check $V_u \leq V_c$

(OK or NG)

Check for Moment

Bending Moment caused by soil pressure

P =

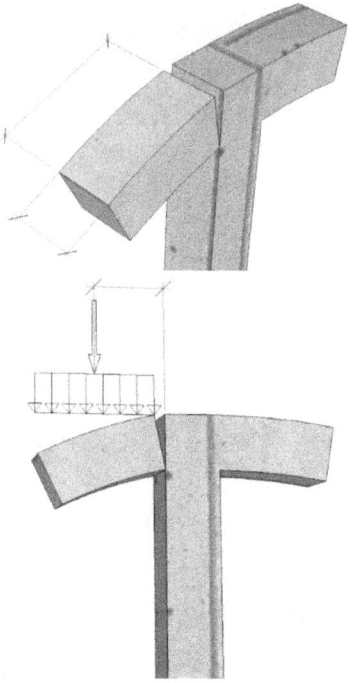

e =

M_u = P x e =

Moment Strength (Beam Action)

Moment Check $M_u \leq \phi M_n$

(OK or NG)

FOUNDATIONS

Workshop 8-1c
A wall footing, as shown in the figure, supports a 18-in. wide reinforced concrete wall with a dead load, **DL** = 20 k/ft and a live load, **LL** = 10 k/ft. The bottom of the footing is to be 6 ft below the final grade, the soil weight is 100 pcf and the allowable soil pressure, q_a = 4 ksf. Use f_c' = 3 ksi, and f_y = 60 ksi. Check the adequacy of the wall foundation.

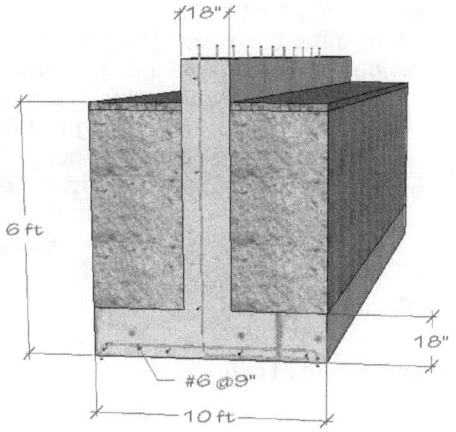

Solution)

FOUNDATIONS

Case Study 8-2

Determine the size of the 24 in thick square isolated footing using the design data given below and then check the adequacy of it.
1. The 24" square column supports **DL**=250 k and **LL**=170 k.
2. The base of the footing is 6 ft below grade.
3. The soil weight is 100 pcf.
4. The allowable soil pressure, q_a = 5 ksf.
5. 7#9 bars are used in both directions.
6. Use f_c' = 3 ksi, and f_y = 60 ksi.

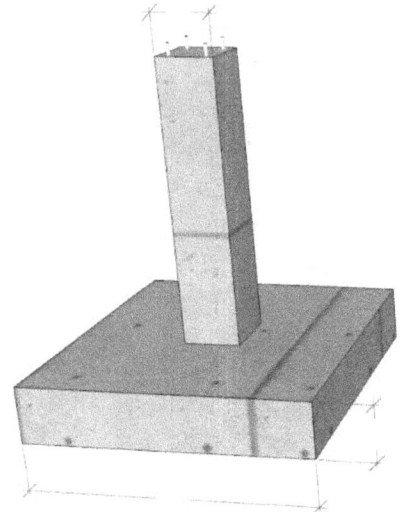

Solution)

Size of Footing

Weight of footing =

Weight of soil on the footing =

Therefore, the effective soil pressure, q_e

q_e =

Area of Footing Required =

Bearing Pressure

Factored Load, P_u =

Bearing Pressure, q_u =

FOUNDATIONS

Design Moment

P =

M_u =

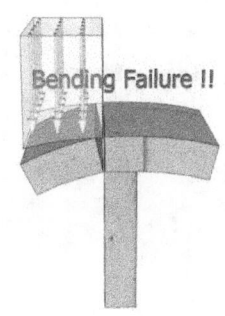

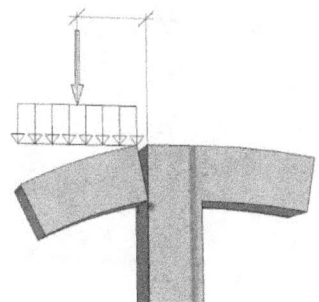

Bending Strength of Footing

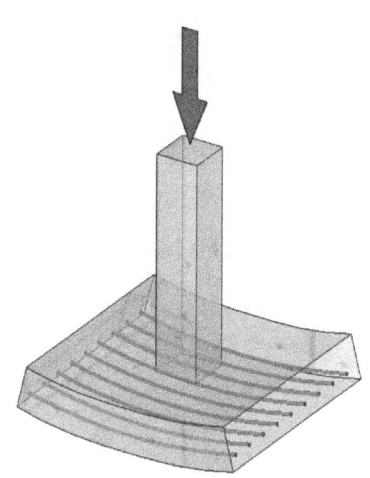

FOUNDATIONS

One-Way Shear *(or **beam shear** at a distance **d** from face of wall)*

   Shear Force

      V_{u1} = (loaded area x soil pressure)

      =

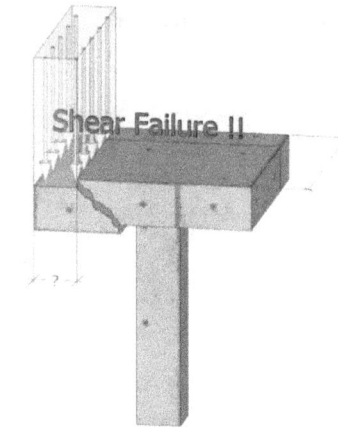

   Shear Strength

      $V_{u1} \leq V_{c1}$ *(No stirrup is practical in footings!!)*

$$V_{c1} = \phi\left(2\sqrt{f_c'}\right)(b \times d) =$$

Two-Way Shear *(or **punching shear** at a distance **d/2** from face of wall)*

   Shear Force

      V_{u2} = (soil pressure x area)

      =

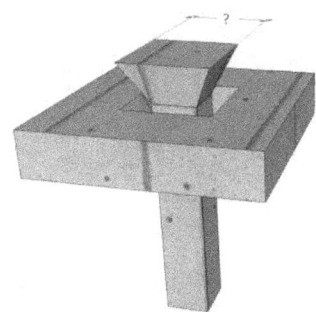

   Shear Strength

      $V_{u2} \leq V_{c2}$ *(No stirrup is practical in footings!!)*

$$V_{c2} = \phi\left(4\sqrt{f_c'}\right)(l \times d) =$$

FOUNDATIONS

Workshop 8-2a
Determine the size of the 18 in thick square isolated footing using the design data given below and then check the adequacy of it.
1. The 12" square column supports **DL** = 120 k and **LL** = 80 k.
2. The base of the footing is 4 ft below grade.
3. The soil weight is 100 pcf.
4. The allowable soil pressure, q_a = 4 ksf.
5. 6#8 bars are used in both directions.
6. Use f_c' = 4 ksi, and f_y = 50 ksi.

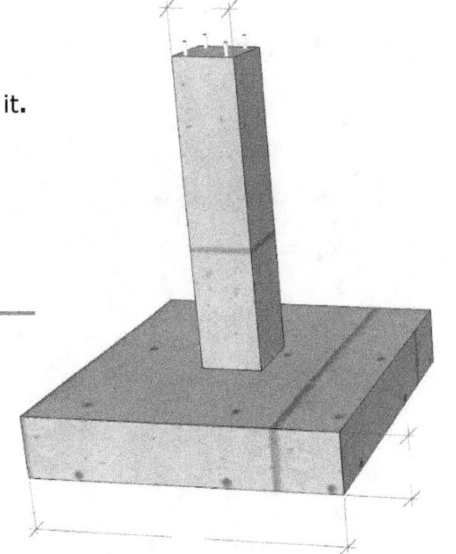

Solution)

Size of Footing

    Weight of footing =

    Weight of soil on the footing =

    Therefore, the effective soil pressure, q_e

    q_e =

    Area of Footing Required =

Bearing Pressure

    Factored Load, P_u =

    Bearing Pressure, q_u =

FOUNDATIONS

Design Moment

$P =$

$M_u =$

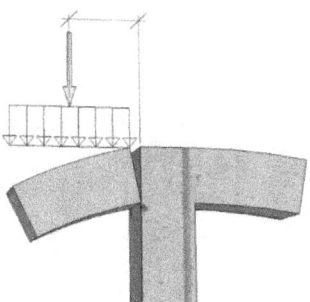

Bending Strength of Footing

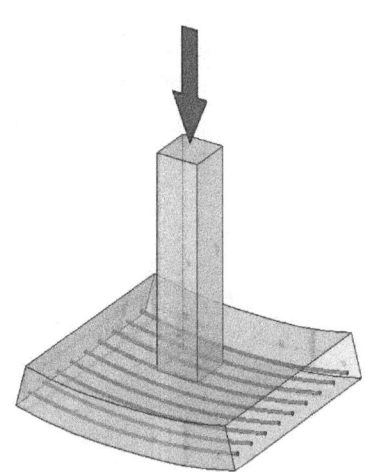

FOUNDATIONS

One-Way Shear *(or **beam shear** at a distance **d** from face of wall)*

Shear Force

V_{u1} = (loaded area x soil pressure)

=

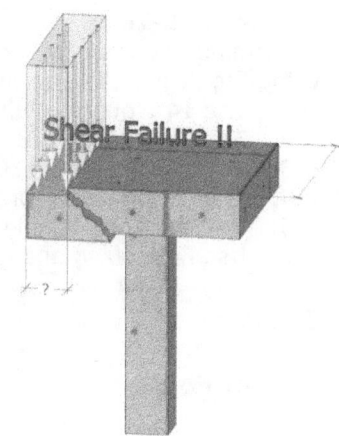

Shear Strength

$V_{u1} \leq V_{c1}$ *(No stirrup is practical in footings!!)*

$$V_{c1} = \phi\left(2\sqrt{f_c'}\right)(b \times d) =$$

Two-Way Shear *(or **punching shear** at a distance **d/2** from face of wall)*

Shear Force

V_{u2} = (soil pressure x area)

=

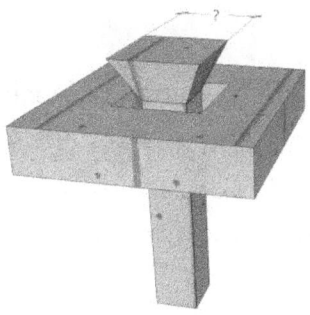

Shear Strength

$V_{u2} \leq V_{c2}$ *(No stirrup is practical in footings!!)*

$$V_{c2} = \phi\left(4\sqrt{f_c'}\right)(l \times d) =$$

FOUNDATIONS

Workshop 8-2b
Determine the size of the 24 in thick square isolated footing using the design data given below and then check the adequacy of it.
1. The 14" square column supports **DL** = 150 k and **LL** = 120 k.
2. The base of the footing is 4 ft below grade.
3. The soil weight is 110 pcf.
4. The allowable soil pressure, q_a = 4 ksf.
5. 7#7 bars are used in both directions.
6. Use f_c' = 4 ksi, and f_y = 60 ksi.

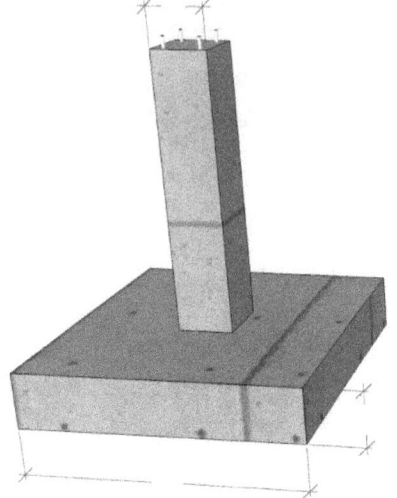

Solution)

Size of Footing

Weight of footing =

Weight of soil on the footing =

Therefore, the effective soil pressure, q_e

$q_e =$

Area of Footing Required =

Bearing Pressure

Factored Load, P_u =

Bearing Pressure, q_u =

FOUNDATIONS

Design Moment

$P =$

$M_u =$

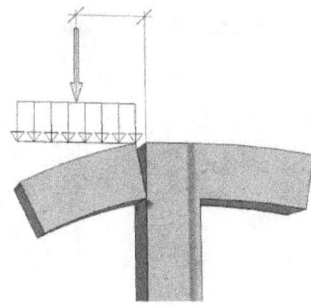

Bending Strength of Footing

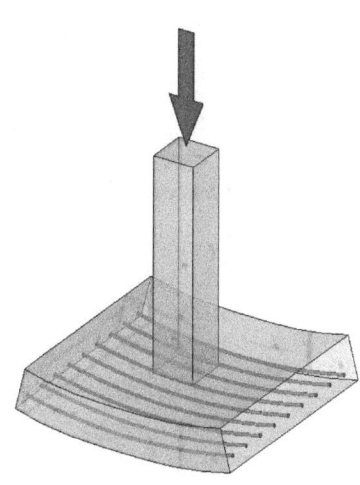

FOUNDATIONS

One-Way Shear *(or **beam shear** at a distance **d** from face of wall)*

   Shear Force

   V_{u1} = (loaded area x soil pressure)

   =

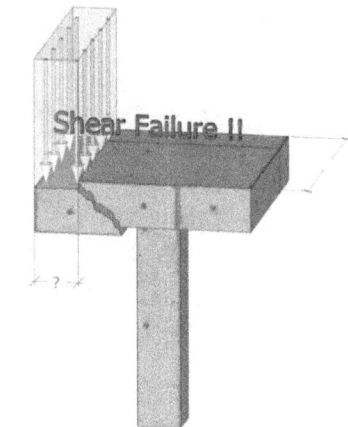

   Shear Strength

   $V_{u1} \leq V_{c1}$ *(No stirrup is practical in footings!!)*

   $V_{c1} = \phi \left(2\sqrt{f_c'} \right)(b \times d) =$

Two-Way Shear *(or **punching shear** at a distance **d/2** from face of wall)*

   Shear Force

   V_{u2} = (soil pressure x area)

   =

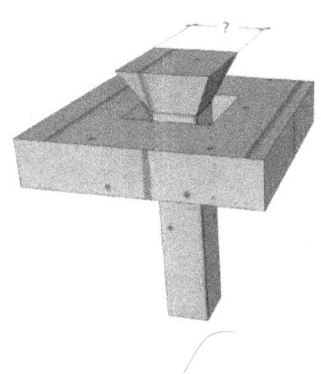

   Shear Strength

   $V_{u2} \leq V_{c2}$ *(No stirrup is practical in footings!!)*

   $V_{c2} = \phi \left(4\sqrt{f_c'} \right)(l \times d) =$

Case Study 8-3

Design a square isolated footing for a 16" square column that supports a dead load, D = 200 k and a live load, L = 160 k. The base of the footing is 5 ft below grade, the soil weight is 100 pcf and the allowable soil pressure, q_a = 5 ksf. Use f_c' = 3 ksi, and f_y = 60 ksi.

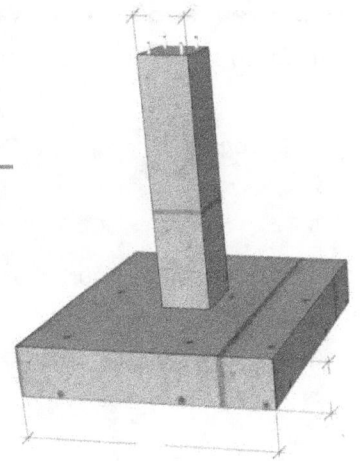

Solution)

Bearing Pressure Calculation

Assume a 24-in.-thick footing.

Weight of footing =

Weight of soil on the footing =

Therefore, the effective soil pressure,

q_e =

Area of Footing Required =

Factored Load, P_u =

Bearing Pressure, q_u =

$d_{assumed}$ =

FOUNDATIONS

Depth required for One-Way Shear
(or **beam shear** at a distance d from face of wall)

Loaded Area =

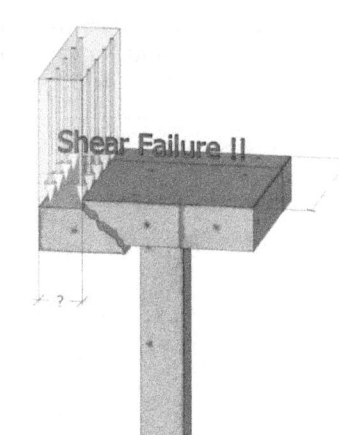

V_{u1} = (soil pressure x area) =

$V_{u1} \leq V_{c1}$ (No stirrup is practical in footings!!)

$V_{u1} \leq V_{c1} = \phi\left(2\sqrt{f_c'}\right)(b \times d) =$

Therefore, $d_{required\ 1} \geq$

Depth required for Two-Way Shear
(or **punching shear** at a distance $d/2$ from face of wall)

V_{u2} = (soil pressure x area)

Loaded Area =

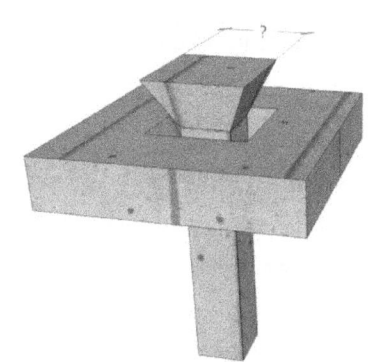

V_{u2} = (soil pressure x area) =

$V_{u2} \leq V_{c2}$ (No stirrup is practical in footings!!)

$l =$

$V_{u2} \leq V_{c1} = \phi\left(4\sqrt{f_c'}\right)(l \times d) =$

Therefore, $d_{required\ 2} \geq$

FOUNDATIONS

Design Moment

$P_u =$

$M_u =$

Steel Ratio

$$R_n = \frac{M_u}{\phi\, bd^2} =$$

$$\rho = \frac{0.85 f'_c}{F_y}\left(1 - \sqrt{1 - \frac{2R_n}{0.85 f'_c}}\right)$$

$\rho =$

Minimum Steel Ratio

$$A_{s,min} = \frac{3\sqrt{f'_c}}{f_y} b_w d \geq \frac{200}{f_y} b_w d \qquad\qquad \text{(or, use Table 5.)}$$

Steel Area

$A_s =$

FOUNDATIONS

Workshop 8-3
Design a square isolated footing for a 12" square column that supports a dead load, **D** = 100 k and a live load, **L** = 120 k. The base of the footing is 5 ft below grade, the soil weight is 100 pcf and the allowable soil pressure, q_a = 5 ksf. Use f_c' = 3 ksi, and f_y = 60 ksi.

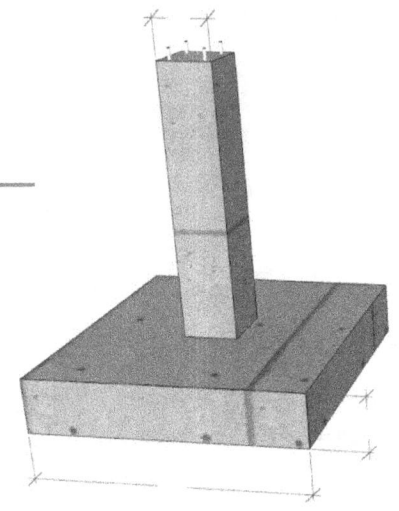

Solution)

Bearing Pressure Calculation

Assume a 24-in.-thick footing.

Weight of footing =

Weight of soil on the footing =

Therefore, the effective soil pressure,

q_e =

Area of Footing Required =

Factored Load, P_u =

Bearing Pressure, q_u =

$d_{assumed}$ =

FOUNDATIONS

Depth required for One-Way Shear
(or **beam shear** at a distance d from face of wall)

Loaded Area =

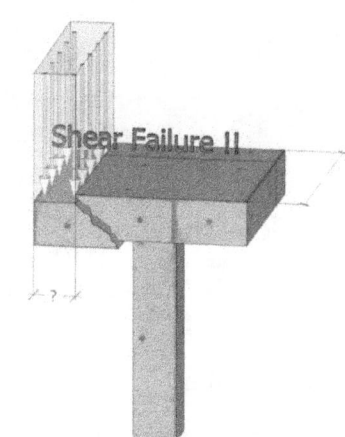

V_{u1} = (soil pressure x area) =

$V_{u1} \leq V_{c1}$ (No stirrup is practical in footings!!)

$V_{u1} \leq V_{c1} = \phi\left(2\sqrt{f_c'}\right)(b \times d) =$

Therefore, $d_{required\ 1} \geq$

Depth required for Two-Way Shear
(or **punching shear** at a distance $d/2$ from face of wall)

V_{u2} = (soil pressure x area)

Loaded Area =

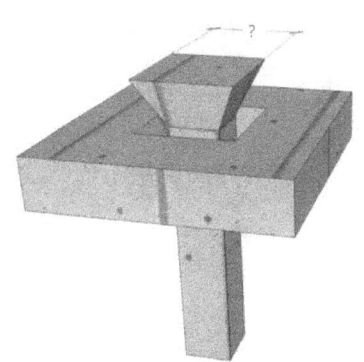

V_{u2} = (soil pressure x area) =

$V_{u2} \leq V_{c2}$ (No stirrup is practical in footings!!)

$l =$

$V_{u2} \leq V_{c1} = \phi\left(4\sqrt{f_c'}\right)(l \times d) =$

Therefore, $d_{required\ 2} \geq$

FOUNDATIONS

Design Moment

$P_u =$

$M_u =$

Steel Ratio

$$R_n = \frac{M_u}{\phi b d^2} =$$

$$\rho = \frac{0.85 f_c'}{F_y}\left(1 - \sqrt{1 - \frac{2R_n}{0.85 f_c'}}\right)$$

$\rho =$

Minimum Steel Ratio

$$A_{s,min} = \frac{3\sqrt{f'_c}}{f_y} b_w d \geq \frac{200}{f_y} b_w d \qquad \text{(or, use Table 5.)}$$

Steel Area

$A_s =$

FOUNDATIONS

Case Study 8.4

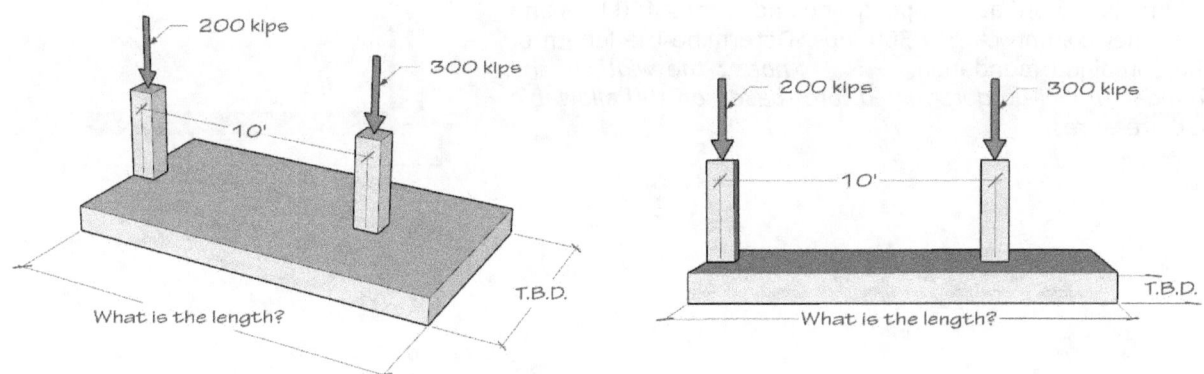

A combined foundation is supporting two 1'x1' columns. One column is located at a property line and carries 200 kips and the other column carries 300 kips. Determine the length of the combined foundation. (*note : the width of the foundation will be determined later based on the allowable soil pressure.*)

Workshop 8.4a

A combined foundation is supporting two columns. One column is located at a property line and carries 400 kips and the other column carries 500 kips. Determine the length of the combined foundation. (note : the width of the foundation will be determined later based on the allowable soil pressure.)

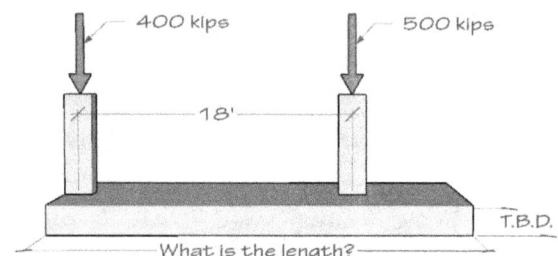

Workshop 8.4b

A combined foundation is supporting two 1'x1' columns. One column is located at a property line and carries 300 kips and the other column carries 400 kips. Determine the length of the combined foundation.

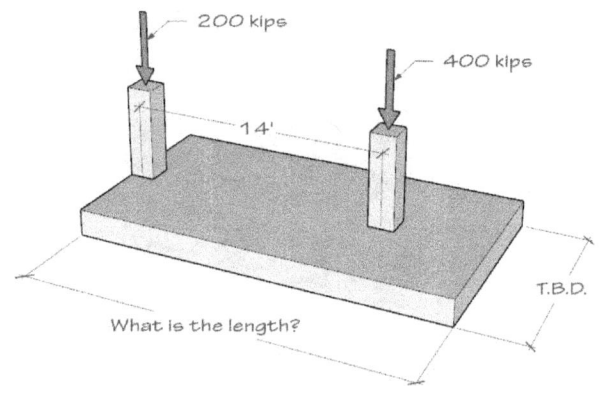

8.8 Retaining Walls

Introduction

In general, retaining walls can be divided into two major categories:

A. gravity type and
B. cantilever type.

Whichever type is used, there will be 3 forces involved that must be in equilibrium:

1. The **gravity loads** of the concrete and any soil on top of the footing.
2. The **lateral loads** from the soil.
3. The **bearing resistance** of the soil.

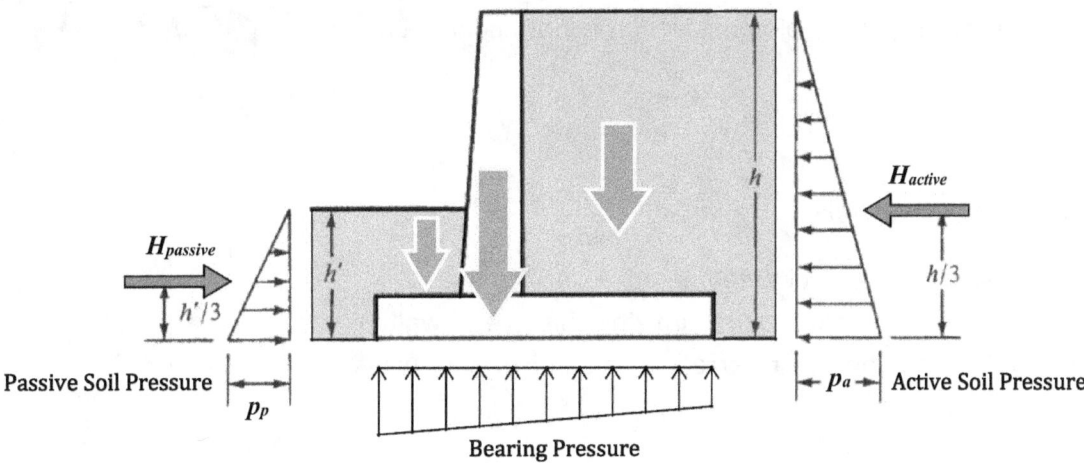

Design Consideration

In designing retaining walls, an engineer must assume some of their dimensions. Called proportioning, such assumptions allow the engineer to check trial sections of the walls for stability. If the stability checks yield undesirable results, the sections can be changed and rechecked. In the case of ordinary retaining walls, water table problems and hence hydrostatic pressure are not encountered. Facilities for drainage from the retained soils are always provided.

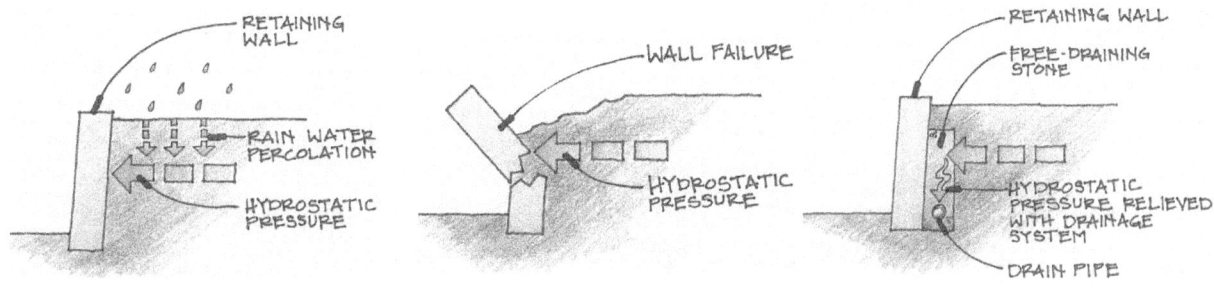

Types of Retaining Walls

Conventional retaining walls can generally be classified into four varieties:

1. Gravity retaining walls
2. Semi-gravity retaining walls
3. Cantilever retaining walls
4. Counterfort retaining walls

(1) Gravity retaining walls

Gravity retaining walls are constructed with plain concrete or stone masonry. They depend for stability on their own weight and any soil resting on the footing. This type of construction is not economical for high walls.

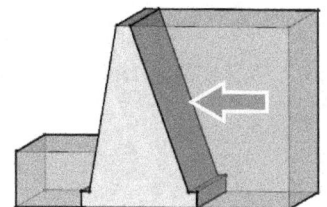

(2) Semi-gravity retaining walls

In many cases, a small amount of steel may be used for the construction of gravity walls, thereby minimizing the size of wall sections. Such walls are generally referred to as semi-gravity walls.

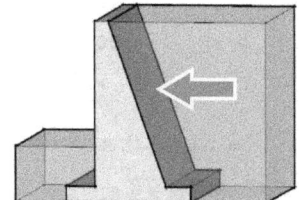

(3) Cantilever retaining walls

Cantilever retaining walls are made of reinforced concrete that consists of a thin stem and a base slab (footing). This type of wall is economical to a height of about 8 m (25 ft).

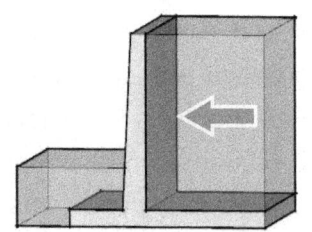

(4) Counterfort retaining walls

Counterfort retaining walls are similar to cantilever walls. At regular intervals, however, they have thin vertical concrete slabs known as counterforts that tie the wall and the base slab together. The purpose of the counterforts is to reduce the shear and the bending moments.

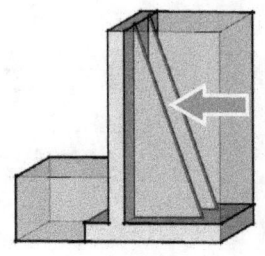

Design Procedure for Retaining Walls

To design retaining walls properly, an engineer must know the basic parameters – the unit weight, angle of friction, and cohesion of the soil retained behind the wall and the soil below the footing. Knowing the properties of the soil behind the wall enables the engineer to determine the lateral pressure distribution that has to be designed for.

There are **two phases** in the design of a conventional retaining wall:

First, with the lateral earth pressure known, the **structure as a whole** is checked for stability. The structure is examined for possible overturning, sliding, and bearing capacity failures.

Second, each **component of the structure** is checked for strengths, and the steel reinforcement of each component is determined.

Check Retaining Walls as a whole

A retaining wall may fail in any of the following ways:

1. It may **overturn** about its toe.
2. It may **slide** along its base.
3. It may fail due to the loss of **bearing capacity** of the soil supporting the base.
4. It may undergo **deep-seated shear failure**.
5. It may go through **excessive settlement**.

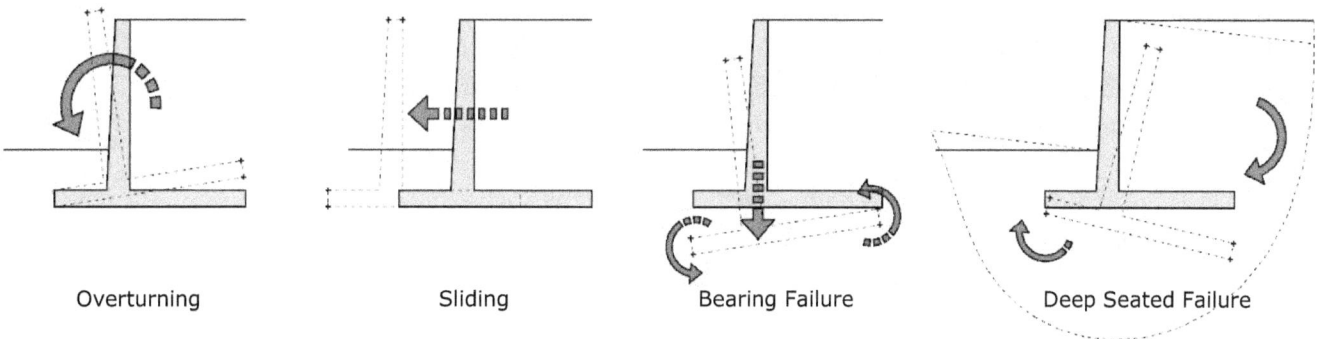

Overturning　　　　Sliding　　　　Bearing Failure　　　　Deep Seated Failure

FOUNDATIONS

Check for Overturning

Based on the assumption that the Rankine active pressure is acting along a vertical plane drawn through the heel of the structure. The factor of safety against overturning about the toe – that is, about point C may be expressed as:

$$F.S. = \frac{\Sigma M_{stabilizing}}{\Sigma M_{overturning}} < 2$$

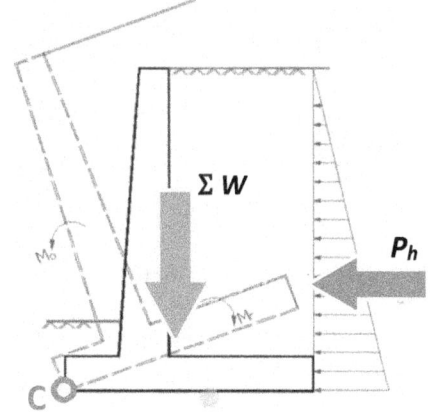

The usual minimum desirable value of the factor of safety with respect to overturning is **2** to **3**. The overturning moment is:

$$\Sigma M_{overturning} = P_h (H/3)$$

Check for Sliding along the Base

The factor of safety against sliding may be expressed by the equation:

$$F.S. = \frac{\mu \Sigma W}{P_h} < 1.5$$

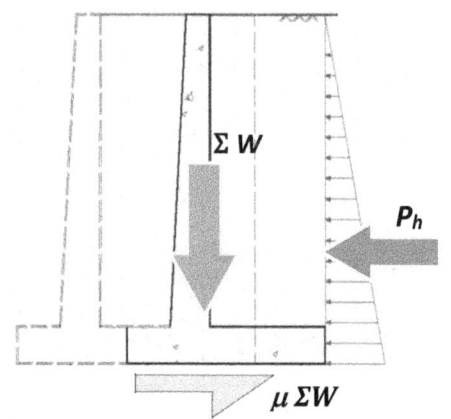

The only horizontal force that will tend to cause the wall to slide (a driving force) is the horizontal component of the active force P_a. In many cases, the passive force P_p is ignored in calculating the factor of safety with respect to sliding.

A minimum factor of safety of **1.5** against sliding is generally required. If the desired value of FS (sliding) is not achieved, several alternatives may be investigated:

1. Increase the width of the base slab (i.e., the heel of the footing).
2. Use a key to the base slab.

FOUNDATIONS

Check for Bearing Capacity Failure

The nature of variation of the vertical pressure transmitted by the footing into the soil is shown in the following Figure. Note that q_{toe} is the maximum and q_{heel} is the minimum pressures occurring at the ends of the toe and heel sections, respectively. The magnitudes of q_{toe} and q_{heel} can be determined in the following manner:

$$\bar{x} = \frac{\Sigma M_{stabilizing} - \Sigma M_{overturning}}{W}$$

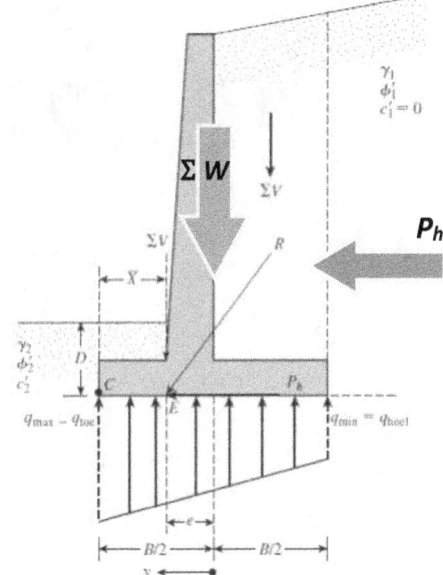

Hence, the eccentricity of the resultant R may be expressed as:

$$e = \frac{B}{2} - \bar{x}$$

The pressure distribution under the footing may be determined by using simple principles from the mechanics of materials.

$$q = \frac{W}{A} \pm \frac{W(e)}{I} y$$

Note that ΣW includes the weight of the concrete and soil and. When the value of the eccentricity e becomes greater than $B/6$, $qmin$ becomes negative. Thus, there will be some tensile stress at the end of the heel section. This stress is not desirable, because the tensile strength of soil is very small. If the analysis of a design shows that $e > B/6$, the design should be reproportioned and calculations redone.

Once the ultimate bearing capacity of the soil has been calculated by, the factor of safety against bearing capacity failure can be determined. Generally, a factor of safety of 3 is required.

FOUNDATIONS

Design of Components of Retaining Walls

Once the approximate size of the retaining wall has been established, the stem, heel, and toe can be designed in detail. Each of these components will be designed individually as a cantilever sticking out of a central mass, as shown.

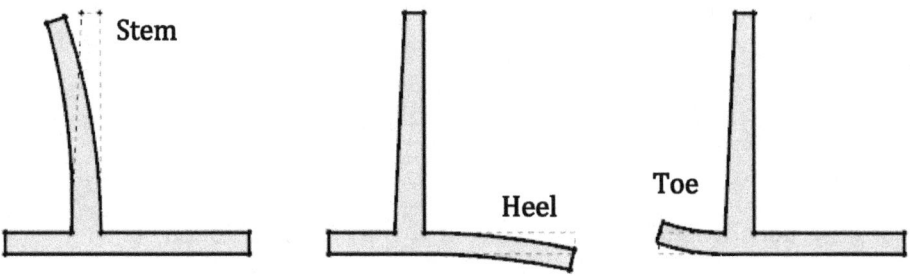

Stem Design

The values of shear and moment at the base of the stem resulting from lateral earth pressures are computed and used to determine the stem thickness and necessary reinforcing. Because the lateral pressures are considered to be live load forces, a load factor of 1.6 is used. It will be noted that the bending moment requires the use of vertical reinforcing bars on the soil side of the

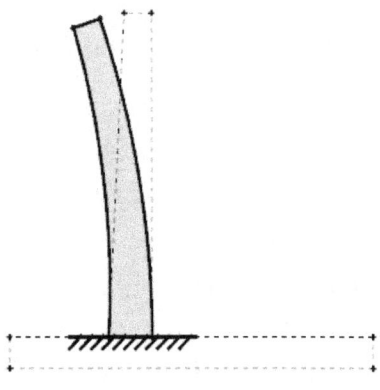

stem. The major changes in temperature occur on the front or exposed face of the stem. For this reason, most of the horizontal reinforcing (perhaps two-thirds) should be placed on that face with just enough vertical steel used to support the horizontal bars.

Heel Design

Lateral earth pressure tends to cause the retaining wall to rotate about its toe. This action tends to pick up the heel into the backfill. Thus, the backfill pushes down on the heel cantilever, causing tension in its top. Although it is true that there is some upward soil pressure from the bottom of the footing, many designers choose to neglect it because it is relatively small. The downward loads tend to push the heel of the footing down, and the necessary upward reaction to hold it attached to the stem is provided by the vertical tensile steel in the stem, which is extended down into the footing. Because the reaction in the direction of the shear does not introduce compression into the heel part of the footing in the region of the stem, it is not permissible to determine V_u at a distance d from the face of the stem, as provided in Section 11.1.3.1 of the ACI Code. Because the load here consists of the weights of soil and concrete, a load factor of 1.2 is used for making the calculations.

Toe Design

The toe is assumed to be a beam cantilevered from the front face of the stem. The loads include the weight of the cantilever slab and the upward soil pressure beneath. Usually any backfill on top of the toe is neglected (as though it has been eroded). The upward soil pressure is the major force applied to the toe. Because this pressure is primarily caused by the lateral force H, a load factor of 1.6 is used for the calculations. The maximum moment for design is taken at the face of the stem, whereas the maximum shear for design is assumed to occur at a distance d from the face of the stem because the reaction in the direction of the shear does introduce compression into the toe of the footing.

Case Study 8.5

Complete the design of the cantilever retaining wall shown. Use $f_c' = 3$ ksi, $F_y = 60$ ksi, $q_a = 4$ ksf, and the coefficient of sliding friction, μ equals 0.50 for concrete on soil. Use ρ approximately equal to 0.18 f_c'/F_y to maintain reasonable deflection control.

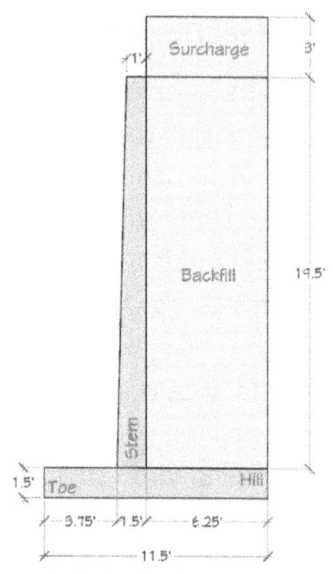

Lateral Soil Pressures

Surcharge	$0.32 (100) (3) = 96$ psf
Backfill	$0.32 (100) (21) = 672$ psf

Lateral Forces

Surcharge	$(96)(21) = 2016$ lb
Backfill	$\frac{1}{2} (672)(21) = 7056$ lb

Overturning Moment (unfactored load)

Surcharge	$2016 (10.5') = 21168$ lb-ft
Backfill	$7052 (7') = 48392$ lb-ft
Total	$= 70560$ lb-ft

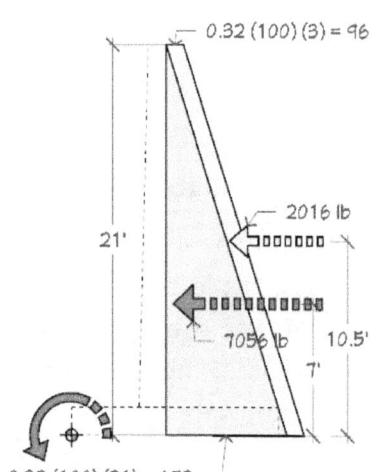

Gravity Loads

Soil	$(100)(19.5+3)(6.5) = 14062$ lb
Stem 1	$(150)(19.5)(1) = 2925$ lb
Stem 2	$\frac{1}{2} (150)(19.5)(0.5) = 731$ lb
Footing	$(150)(11.5)(1.5) = 2588$ lb
	Total $= 20306$ lb

Stabilizing Moment

Soil	14062 lb $(8.37') = 117699$ lb-ft
Stem 1	2925 lb $(4.75') = 13894$ lb-ft
Stem 2	731 lb $(4.08') = 2982$ lb-ft
Footing	2588 lb $(5.75') = 14881$ lb-ft
	Total $= 149456$ lb-ft

$$\text{F.S.} = \frac{149456}{70560} = 2.12 > 2 \quad \text{O.K.}$$

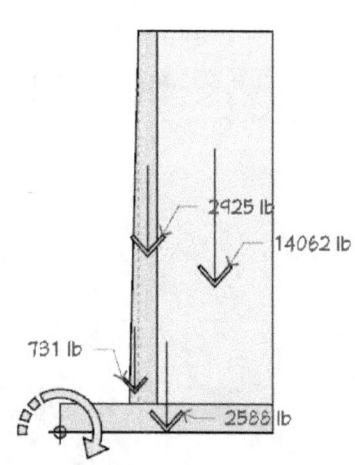

FOUNDATIONS

Sliding Force

Lateral Force   2016 + 7056 = 9072 lb

Friction Force

Soil Friction μW = (0.5)(20306) = 10153 lb

$$F.S. = \frac{10153}{9072} = 1.12 < 1.5 \quad N.G.$$

1. Increase the width of the base slab (i.e., the heel of the footing).
2. Use a key to the base slab.

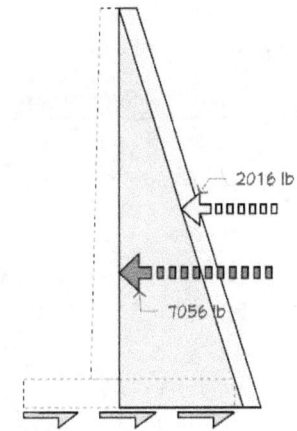

Soil Bearing Pressure

Location of **W** $\bar{x} = \dfrac{149456 - 70560}{20306} = 3.89'$

Eccentricity Moment, **M**

$20306 \left(\dfrac{11.5}{2} - 3.89\right) = 20306 \,(1.86') = 37769$

Soil Pressure $q = \dfrac{P}{A} \pm \dfrac{M}{I} y$

$I = \dfrac{b\,d^3}{12} = \dfrac{1\,(11.5)^3}{12} = 126.74 \text{ ft}^4$

$q = \dfrac{20306}{11.5} \pm \dfrac{37769}{126.74} \, 5.75$

$q = 1766 \pm 1714$ $q = 3480$ or 52 psf

< 4000 psf   O.K.

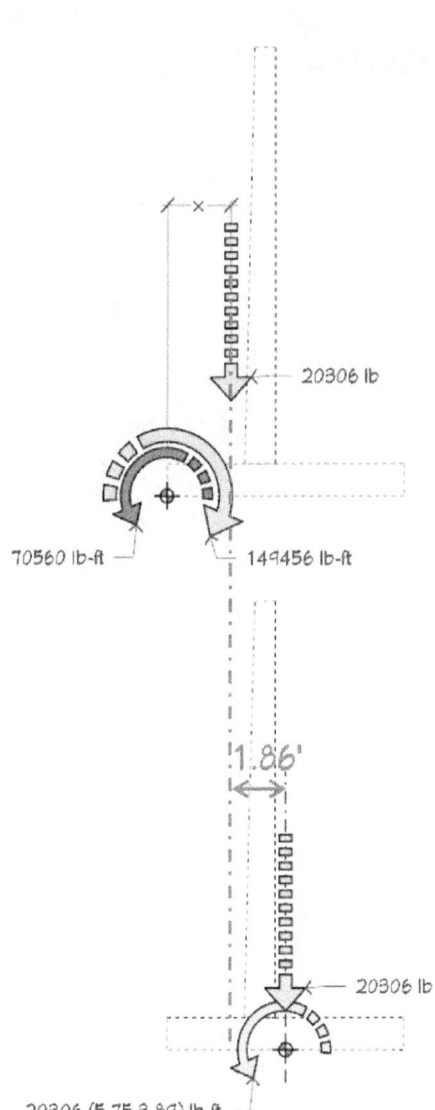

FOUNDATIONS

Design of Stem

Design Bending Moment

9734 (6.5') + 2995 (9.75') = 92472 lb-ft

$$\rho_{approx} = \frac{0.18 \, f'_c}{F_y} = \frac{0.18 \, (3000)}{60000} = 0.009$$

$$\frac{M_u}{\phi b d^2} = 482.6 \quad \text{(from Table 7-5)}$$

$(12)d^2 = \dfrac{12 \, (92472)}{0.9 \, (482.6)} = 2555 \qquad d = 14.59"$

h = 14.59" + 2" + 0.5" = 17.09"   Say, h = 18" (d = 15.5")

$$\frac{M_u}{\phi b d^2} = \frac{12 \, (92472)}{0.9 (12)(15.5)^2} = 427.7 \qquad \rho = 0.00786 \quad \text{(from Table 7-5)}$$

$A_s = \rho \, bd = 0.00786 \, (12)(15.5) = 1.46 \text{ in}^2$

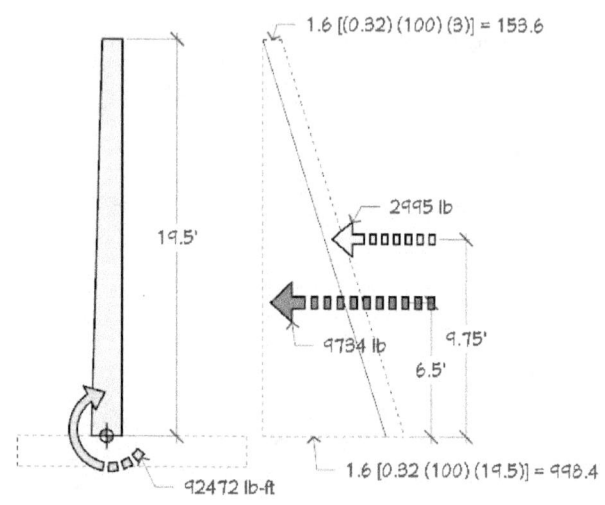

Design of Stem

Design Shear

$V_u = 9734 + 2995 = 12729 \text{ lb}$

Shear Strength of Concrete

$$\boxed{V_c = \phi \, 2\sqrt{f'_c} \, b_w d}$$

$V_c = 0.75 \, 2\sqrt{3000} \, (120 \times 15.5) = 15281 \text{ lb} > V_u = 12729 \text{ lb} \quad \text{O.K.}$

Note: Actually, V_u at a distance d from the top of the footing may be used but for simplicity V_u at the top face was used.

Design of Heel

Design Bending Moment

$M_u = (16500 + 2251)(\tfrac{1}{2} 6.25') = 58597 \text{ lb-ft}$

$$\frac{M_u}{\phi b d^2} = \frac{12 \, (58596)}{0.9(12)(20.5)^2} = 155$$

$\rho = \rho_{min} = 0.00267$ (from Table 7-5)

$$\rho_{min \, 1} = \frac{3\sqrt{f'_c}}{F_y} = \frac{3\sqrt{3000}}{60000} = 0.00273$$

$$\rho_{min \, 2} = \frac{200}{F_y} = \frac{200}{60000} = 0.0033 \quad \longleftarrow \text{Controls}$$

$A_s = \rho \, bd = 0.0033(12)(20.5) = 0.82 \text{ in}^2 \qquad \text{Use, #8@11"} \; (A_s = 0.86 \text{ in}^2)$

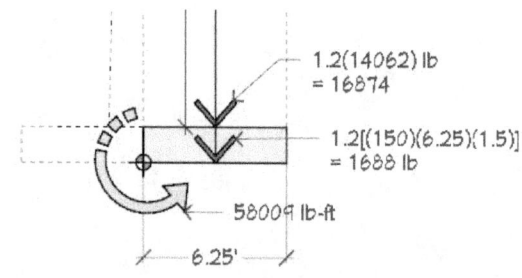

FOUNDATIONS

Design of Heel Note: This load is caused mainly by the weights of soil and concrete,
a load factor of 1.2 is used.

Design Shear

$V_u = 1.2\,[(100)(6.25)(22.5)] + 1.2\,[(150)(6.25)(1.5)]$

$\quad = 1.2\,(14062) + 1.2\,(1406)$

$\quad = 18563\ \text{lb}$

Shear Strength of Concrete

$$\boxed{V_c = \phi\ 2\sqrt{f'_c}\ b_w d}$$

$V_c = 0.75\ 2\sqrt{3000}\ (12 \times 14.5) = 14295\ \text{lb}\ < V_u = 18563\ \text{lb}\quad \text{N.G.}$

Try, h = 24" (d = 20.5")

$V_c = 0.75\ 2\sqrt{3000}\ (12 \times 20.5) = 20210\ \text{lb}\ > V_u = 18563\ \text{lb}\quad \text{O.K.}$

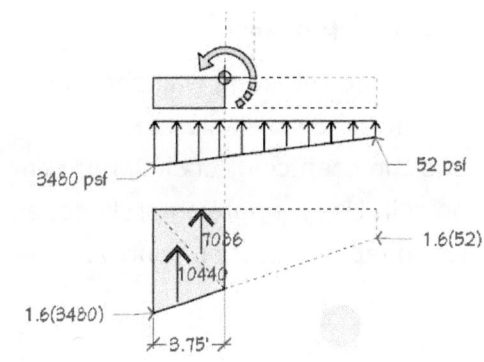

Design of Heel

Design Bending Moment

$M_u = (16500+2251)(\tfrac{1}{2} 6.25') = 58597\ \text{lb-ft}$

$\dfrac{M_u}{\phi b d^2} = \dfrac{12\,(58596)}{0.9(12)(20.5)^2} = 155$

$\rho = \rho_{min} = 0.00267$ (from Table 7-5)

$\rho_{min\,1} = \dfrac{3\sqrt{f'_c}}{F_y} = \dfrac{3\sqrt{3000}}{60000} = 0.00273$

$\rho_{min\,2} = \dfrac{200}{F_y} = \dfrac{200}{60000} = 0.0033$ ⟵ Controls

$A_s = \rho\ bd = 0.0033(12)(20.5) = 0.82\ \text{in}^2$ Use, #8@11" (A_s= 0.86 in²)

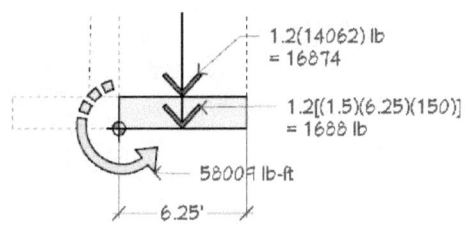

Design of Toe

Note: This pressure is primarily caused by the lateral force,
a load factor of 1.6 is used.

Design Shear $V_u = 10440 + 7086 = 17526\ \text{lb} < \phi V_n = 20210\ \text{lb}\quad \text{O.K.}$

Note: Actually, V_u at a distance d from the top of the footing may be used but
for simplicity V_u at the top face was used.

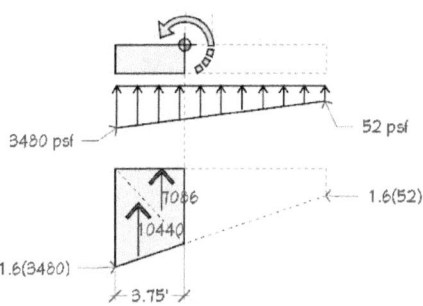

Design Bending Moment

$M_u = (10440)(\tfrac{2}{3} 3.75') + (7086)(\tfrac{1}{3} 3.75') = 34958\ \text{lb-ft}$

$\dfrac{M_u}{\phi b d^2} = \dfrac{12\,(34958)}{0.9(12)(20.5)^2} = 92\qquad \rho = \rho_{min} = 0.0033$ (as in Heel)

Workshop 8.5a

Check the retaining wall shown for overturning, sliding and bearing pressure failures. Use $f_c' = 3$ ksi, $F_y = 60$ ksi, $q_a = 5$ ksf, and the coefficient of sliding friction, μ equals 0.50 for concrete on soil. Use ρ approximately equal to 0.18 f_c'/F_y to maintain reasonable deflection control.

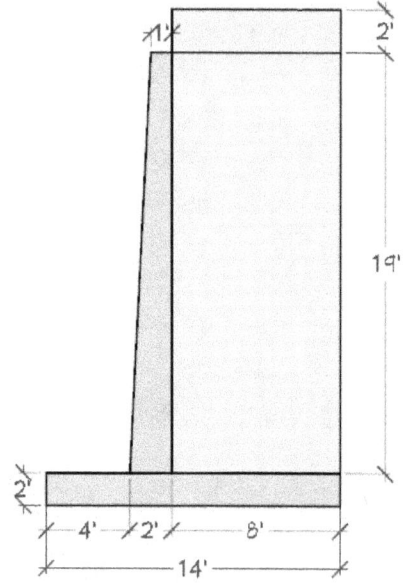

FOUNDATIONS

Workshop 8.5b

Check the retaining wall shown for overturning, sliding and bearing pressure failures. Use $f_c' = 3$ ksi, $F_y = 60$ ksi, $q_a = 4$ ksf, and the coefficient of sliding friction, μ equals 0.50 for concrete on soil. Use ρ approximately equal to $0.18\, f_c'/F_y$ to maintain reasonable deflection control.

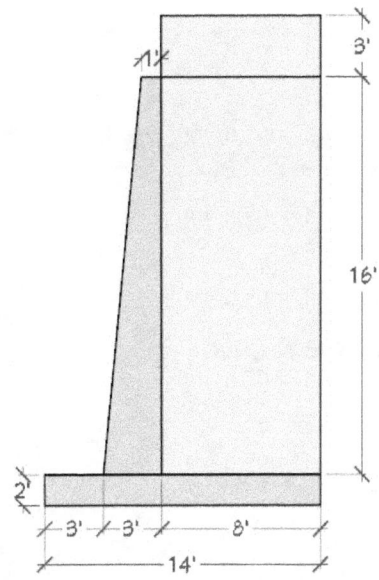

APPENDIX

CHAPTER A

APPENDIX

APPENDIX

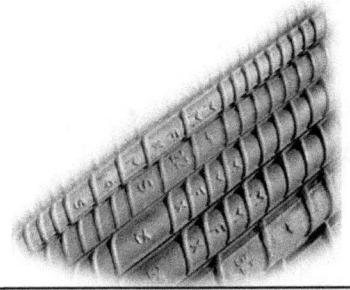  

Table 1. Reinforcing Bar Properties

Bar Size	Area (in^2)	Weight (lbs./ft.)	Diameter (in.)	Perimeter (in.)
#3	0.11	0.376	0.375	1.178
#4	0.20	0.668	0.500	1.571
#5	0.31	1.043	0.625	1.963
#6	0.44	1.502	0.750	2.356
#7	0.60	2.044	0.875	2.749
#8	0.79	2.670	1.000	3.142
#9	1.00	3.400	1.128	3.544
#10	1.27	4.303	1.270	3.990
#11	1.56	5.313	1.410	4.430
#14	2.26	7.650	1.693	5.320
#18	4.00	13.600	2.257	7.091

Typical specification: ASTM A615 Grade 60 Deformed Bars

Table 2. Areas of Groups of Standard Reinforcing Bars

Bar Size	Number of Bars							
	1	2	3	4	5	6	7	8
#3	0.11	0.22	0.33	0.44	0.55	0.66	0.77	0.88
#4	0.20	0.39	0.59	0.78	0.98	1.17	1.37	1.56
#5	0.31	0.61	0.92	1.22	1.53	1.83	2.14	2.44
#6	0.44	0.88	1.32	1.77	2.21	2.65	3.09	3.53
#7	0.60	1.20	1.80	2.41	3.01	3.61	4.21	4.81
#8	0.79	1.57	2.36	3.14	3.93	4.71	5.50	6.28
#9	1.00	2.00	3.00	4.00	5.00	6.00	7.00	8.00
#10	1.27	2.53	3.80	5.06	6.33	7.59	8.86	10.12
#11	1.56	3.12	4.69	6.25	7.81	9.37	10.94	12.50
#14	2.25	4.50	6.75	9.00	11.25	13.50	15.75	18.00
#18	4.00	8.00	12.00	16.00	20.00	24.00	28.00	32.00

Typical specification: ASTM A615 Grade 60 Deformed Bars

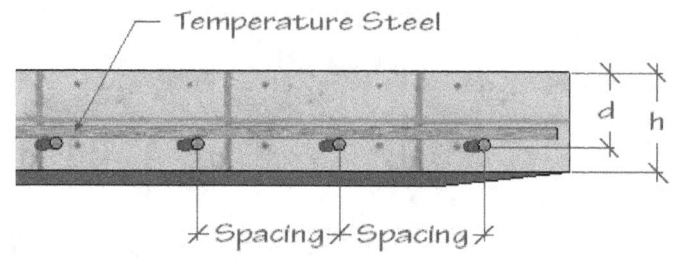

Table 3. Area of Bars in Slabs (in²/ft.)						
Spacing (in.)	Bar Size						
	#3	#4	#5	#6	#7	#8	#9
3	0.44	0.79	1.23	1.77	2.41	3.14	4.00
3 1/2	0.38	0.67	1.05	1.51	2.06	2.69	3.43
4	0.33	0.59	0.92	1.33	1.80	2.36	3.00
4 1/2	0.29	0.52	0.82	1.18	1.60	2.09	2.66
5	0.27	0.47	0.74	1.06	1.44	1.88	2.40
5 1/2	0.24	0.43	0.67	0.96	1.31	1.71	2.18
6	0.22	0.39	0.61	0.88	1.20	1.57	2.00
6 1/2	0.20	0.36	0.57	0.82	1.11	1.45	1.84
7	0.19	0.34	0.53	0.76	1.03	1.35	1.71
7 1/2	0.18	0.31	0.49	0.71	0.96	1.26	1.60
8	0.17	0.29	0.46	0.66	0.90	1.18	1.50
9	0.15	0.26	0.41	0.59	0.80	1.05	1.33
10	0.13	0.24	0.37	0.53	0.72	0.94	1.20
12	0.11	0.20	0.31	0.44	0.60	0.79	1.00
Typical specification: ASTM A615 Grade 60 Deformed Bars						

Table 4. Minimum Web Width (in.) for Beams with Inside Exposure						
Bar Size	Number of Bars						
	2	3	4	5	6	7	8
#4	6.8	8.3	9.8	11.3	12.8	14.3	15.8
#5	6.9	8.5	10.2	11.8	13.4	15.0	16.7
#6	7.0	8.8	10.5	12.3	14.0	15.8	17.5
#7	7.2	9.0	10.9	12.8	14.7	16.5	18.4
#8	7.3	9.3	11.3	13.3	15.3	17.3	19.3
#9	7.6	9.8	12.1	14.3	16.6	18.8	21.1
#10	7.8	10.4	12.9	15.5	18.0	20.5	23.1
#11	8.1	10.9	13.8	16.6	19.4	22.2	25.0
#14	8.9	12.3	15.7	19.0	22.4	25.8	29.2
#18	10.6	15.1	19.6	24.1	28.6	33.1	37.7
Typical specification: Minimum Widths were calculated using #3 stirrups.						

APPENDIX

Table 5. Steel Ratio (ρ) for tensilely reinforced rectangular beams

	$f_c' = 3$ ksi	$f_c' = 4$ ksi	$f_c' = 5$ ksi	$f_c' = 6$ ksi	
	0.0371	0.0495	0.0582	0.0655	$\rho_{balanced}$
$F_y = 40$ ksi	0.0050	0.0050	0.0053	0.0058	ρ_{min}
	0.0203	0.0271	0.3190	0.0359	ρ_{max}
	0.0275	0.0367	0.0432	0.0486	$\rho_{balanced}$
$F_y = 50$ ksi	0.0040	0.0040	0.0042	0.0046	ρ_{min}
	0.0163	0.0217	0.0255	0.0287	ρ_{max}
	0.0214	0.0285	0.0335	0.0377	$\rho_{balanced}$
$F_y = 60$ ksi	0.0033	0.0033	0.0035	0.0039	ρ_{min}
	0.0135	0.0181	0.0213	0.0239	ρ_{max}
	0.0155	0.0207	0.0243	0.0274	$\rho_{balanced}$
$F_y = 75$ ksi	0.0027	0.0027	0.0028	0.0031	ρ_{min}
	0.0108	0.0145	0.0170	0.0191	ρ_{max}

Table 6. Minimun Thickness of Beams or One-Way Slab

	Members not supporting partitions to be damaged by large deflection			
	Simply Supported	One End continuous	Both Ends continuous	Cantilever
Solid one-way slab	$l/20$	$l/24$	$l/28$	$l/10$
Beams / Ribbed one-way slab	$l/16$	$l/18.5$	$l/21$	$l/8$

(Note : Span Length l is in inches.)

APPENDIX

Table 7-1. Steel Ratio Table

fy = 40000 psi   fc' = 3000 psi   UOG SU Dr. Hong

ρ	M/Φbd²	ρ	M/Φbd²	ρ	M/Φbd²	ρ	M/Φbd²	ρ	M/Φbd²	ρ	M/Φbd²
0.0020	78.75	0.0051	195.84	0.0082	306.91	0.0113	411.94	0.0144	510.95	0.0175	603.92
0.0021	82.62	0.0052	199.52	0.0083	310.39	0.0114	415.23	0.0145	514.04	0.0176	606.82
0.0022	86.48	0.0053	203.19	0.0084	313.86	0.0115	418.51	0.0146	517.13	0.0177	609.71
0.0023	90.34	0.0054	206.85	0.0085	317.33	0.0116	421.79	0.0147	520.21	0.0178	612.60
0.0024	94.19	0.0055	210.51	0.0086	320.80	0.0117	425.05	0.0148	523.28	0.0179	615.48
0.0025	98.04	0.0056	214.16	0.0087	324.25	0.0118	428.32	0.0149	526.35	0.0180	618.35
0.0026	101.9	0.0057	217.8	0.0088	327.7	0.0119	431.6	0.0150	529.4	0.0181	621.2
0.0027	105.7	0.0058	221.4	0.0089	331.1	0.0120	434.8	0.0151	532.5	0.0182	624.1
0.0028	109.5	0.0059	225.1	0.0090	334.6	0.0121	438.1	0.0152	535.5	0.0183	626.9
0.0029	113.4	0.0060	228.7	0.0091	338.0	0.0122	441.3	0.0153	538.6	0.0184	629.8
0.0030	117.2	0.0061	232.3	0.0092	341.4	0.0123	444.5	0.0154	541.6	0.0185	632.6
0.0031	121.0	0.0062	235.9	0.0093	344.9	0.0124	447.8	0.0155	544.6	0.0186	635.5
0.0032	124.8	0.0063	239.5	0.0094	348.3	0.0125	451.0	0.0156	547.7	0.0187	638.3
0.0033	128.6	0.0064	243.1	0.0095	351.7	0.0126	454.2	0.0157	550.7	0.0188	641.1
0.0034	132.4	0.0065	246.7	0.0096	355.1	0.0127	457.4	0.0158	553.7	0.0189	643.9
0.0035	136.2	0.0066	250.3	0.0097	358.5	0.0128	460.6	0.0159	556.7	0.0190	646.7
0.0036	139.9	0.0067	253.9	0.0098	361.9	0.0129	463.8	0.0160	559.7	0.0191	649.5
0.0037	143.7	0.0068	257.5	0.0099	365.3	0.0130	467.0	0.0161	562.7	0.0192	652.3
0.0038	147.5	0.0069	261.1	0.0100	368.6	0.0131	470.2	0.0162	565.7	0.0193	655.1
0.0039	151.2	0.0070	264.6	0.0101	372.0	0.0132	473.3	0.0163	568.6	0.0194	657.9
0.0040	155.0	0.0071	268.2	0.0102	375.4	0.0133	476.5	0.0164	571.6	0.0195	660.7
0.0041	158.7	0.0072	271.7	0.0103	378.7	0.0134	479.7	0.0165	574.6	0.0196	663.5
0.0042	162.5	0.0073	275.3	0.0104	382.1	0.0135	482.8	0.0166	577.5	0.0197	666.2
0.0043	166.2	0.0074	278.8	0.0105	385.4	0.0136	486.0	0.0167	580.5	0.0198	669.0
0.0044	169.9	0.0075	282.4	0.0106	388.7	0.0137	489.1	0.0168	583.5	0.0199	671.8
0.0045	173.6	0.0076	285.9	0.0107	392.1	0.0138	492.3	0.0169	586.4	0.0200	674.5
0.0046	177.4	0.0077	289.4	0.0108	395.4	0.0139	495.4	0.0170	589.3	0.0201	677.3
0.0047	181.1	0.0078	292.9	0.0109	398.7	0.0140	498.5	0.0171	592.3	0.0202	680.0
0.0048	184.8	0.0079	296.4	0.0110	402.0	0.0141	501.6	0.0172	595.2	0.0203	682.7
0.0049	188.5	0.0080	299.9	0.0111	405.3	0.0142	504.7	0.0173	598.1	0.0204	685.4
0.0050	192.2	0.0081	303.4	0.0112	408.6	0.0143	507.8	0.0174	601.0	0.0205	688.2

minimum for flexure: 0.0050

APPENDIX

Table 7-2. Steel Ratio Table

| fy = | 40000 psi | | fc' = | 4000 psi | | | | | | UOG | Dr. Hong |

ρ	M/Φbd²	ρ	M/Φbd²	ρ	M/Φbd²	ρ	M/Φbd²	ρ	M/Φbd²	ρ	M/Φbd²
0.0020	79.06	0.0060	231.53	0.0100	376.47	0.0140	513.88	0.0180	643.76	0.0220	766.12
0.0021	82.96	0.0061	235.24	0.0101	380.00	0.0141	517.22	0.0181	646.92	0.0221	769.08
0.0022	86.86	0.0062	238.96	0.0102	383.52	0.0142	520.56	0.0182	650.06	0.0222	772.04
0.0023	90.76	0.0063	242.66	0.0103	387.04	0.0143	523.88	0.0183	653.20	0.0223	774.99
0.0024	94.64	0.0064	246.36	0.0104	390.55	0.0144	527.21	0.0184	656.34	0.0224	777.94
0.0025	98.53	0.0065	250.06	0.0105	394.06	0.0145	530.53	0.0185	659.47	0.0225	780.88
0.0026	102.4	0.0066	253.8	0.0106	397.6	0.0146	533.8	0.0186	662.6	0.0226	783.8
0.0027	106.3	0.0067	257.4	0.0107	401.1	0.0147	537.2	0.0187	665.7	0.0227	786.8
0.0028	110.2	0.0068	261.1	0.0108	404.6	0.0148	540.5	0.0188	668.8	0.0228	789.7
0.0029	114.0	0.0069	264.8	0.0109	408.0	0.0149	543.8	0.0189	672.0	0.0229	792.6
0.0030	117.9	0.0070	268.5	0.0110	411.5	0.0150	547.1	0.0190	675.1	0.0230	795.5
0.0031	121.7	0.0071	272.1	0.0111	415.0	0.0151	550.4	0.0191	678.2	0.0231	798.4
0.0032	125.6	0.0072	275.8	0.0112	418.5	0.0152	553.6	0.0192	681.3	0.0232	801.4
0.0033	129.4	0.0073	279.5	0.0113	422.0	0.0153	556.9	0.0193	684.4	0.0233	804.3
0.0034	133.3	0.0074	283.1	0.0114	425.4	0.0154	560.2	0.0194	687.4	0.0234	807.2
0.0035	137.1	0.0075	286.8	0.0115	428.9	0.0155	563.5	0.0195	690.5	0.0235	810.1
0.0036	141.0	0.0076	290.4	0.0116	432.3	0.0156	566.7	0.0196	693.6	0.0236	813.0
0.0037	144.8	0.0077	294.0	0.0117	435.8	0.0157	570.0	0.0197	696.7	0.0237	815.8
0.0038	148.6	0.0078	297.7	0.0118	439.2	0.0158	573.3	0.0198	699.8	0.0238	818.7
0.0039	152.4	0.0079	301.3	0.0119	442.7	0.0159	576.5	0.0199	702.8	0.0239	821.6
0.0040	156.2	0.0080	304.9	0.0120	446.1	0.0160	579.8	0.0200	705.9	0.0240	824.5
0.0041	160.0	0.0081	308.6	0.0121	449.6	0.0161	583.0	0.0201	708.9	0.0241	827.3
0.0042	163.8	0.0082	312.2	0.0122	453.0	0.0162	586.2	0.0202	712.0	0.0242	830.2
0.0043	167.6	0.0083	315.8	0.0123	456.4	0.0163	589.5	0.0203	715.0	0.0243	833.1
0.0044	171.4	0.0084	319.4	0.0124	459.8	0.0164	592.7	0.0204	718.1	0.0244	835.9
0.0045	175.2	0.0085	323.0	0.0125	463.2	0.0165	595.9	0.0205	721.1	0.0245	838.8
0.0046	179.0	0.0086	326.6	0.0126	466.6	0.0166	599.2	0.0206	724.2	0.0246	841.6
0.0047	182.8	0.0087	330.2	0.0127	470.0	0.0167	602.4	0.0207	727.2	0.0247	844.4
0.0048	186.6	0.0088	333.8	0.0128	473.4	0.0168	605.6	0.0208	730.2	0.0248	847.3
0.0049	190.4	0.0089	337.4	0.0129	476.8	0.0169	608.8	0.0209	733.2	0.0249	850.1
0.0050 (minimum for flexure)	194.1	0.0090	340.9	0.0130	480.2	0.0170	612.0	0.0210	736.2	0.0250	852.9
0.0051	197.9	0.0091	344.5	0.0131	483.6	0.0171	615.2	0.0211	739.2	0.0251	855.8
0.0052	201.6	0.0092	348.1	0.0132	487.0	0.0172	618.4	0.0212	742.2	0.0252	858.6
0.0053	205.4	0.0093	351.6	0.0133	490.4	0.0173	621.6	0.0213	745.2	0.0253	861.4
0.0054	209.1	0.0094	355.2	0.0134	493.8	0.0174	624.8	0.0214	748.2	0.0254	864.2
0.0055	212.9	0.0095	358.8	0.0135	497.1	0.0175	627.9	0.0215	751.2	0.0255	867.0
0.0056	216.6	0.0096	362.3	0.0136	500.5	0.0176	631.1	0.0216	754.2	0.0256	869.8
0.0057	220.4	0.0097	365.9	0.0137	503.8	0.0177	634.3	0.0217	757.2	0.0257	872.6
0.0058	224.1	0.0098	369.4	0.0138	507.2	0.0178	637.4	0.0218	760.2	0.0258	875.4
0.0059	227.8	0.0099	372.9	0.0139	510.5	0.0179	640.6	0.0219	763.2	0.0259	878.2

APPENDIX

Table 7-3. Steel Ratio Table

fy =	50000 psi		fc' =	3000 psi						UOG	Dr. Hong
ρ	$M/\Phi bd^2$	ρ	$M/\Phi bd^2$	ρ	$M/\Phi bd^2$	ρ	$M/\Phi bd^2$	ρ	$M/\Phi bd^2$	ρ	$M/\Phi bd^2$
0.0020	98.04	0.0051	242.25	0.0082	377.04	0.0113	502.41	0.0144	618.35		
0.0021	102.84	0.0052	246.75	0.0083	381.23	0.0114	506.29	0.0145	621.94		
0.0022	107.63	0.0053	251.23	0.0084	385.41	0.0115	510.17	0.0146	625.51		
0.0023	112.41	0.0054	255.71	0.0085	389.58	0.0116	514.04	0.0147	629.07		
0.0024	117.18	0.0055	260.17	0.0086	393.75	0.0117	517.90	0.0148	632.63		
0.0025	121.94	0.0056	264.63	0.0087	397.90	0.0118	521.75	0.0149	636.17		
0.0026	126.7	0.0057	269.1	0.0088	402.0	0.0119	525.6	0.0150	639.7		
0.0027	131.4	0.0058	273.5	0.0089	406.2	0.0120	529.4	0.0151	643.2		
0.0028	136.2	0.0059	277.9	0.0090	410.3	0.0121	533.2	0.0152	646.7		
0.0029	140.9	0.0060	282.4	0.0091	414.4	0.0122	537.0	0.0153	650.2		
0.0030	145.6	0.0061	286.8	0.0092	418.5	0.0123	540.8	0.0154	653.7		
0.0031	150.3	0.0062	291.2	0.0093	422.6	0.0124	544.6	0.0155	657.2		
0.0032	155.0	0.0063	295.5	0.0094	426.7	0.0125	548.4	0.0156	660.7		
0.0033	159.7	0.0064	299.9	0.0095	430.8	0.0126	552.2	0.0157	664.2		
0.0034	164.3	0.0065	304.3	0.0096	434.8	0.0127	555.9	0.0158	667.6		
0.0035	169.0	0.0066	308.6	0.0097	438.9	0.0128	559.7	0.0159	671.1		
0.0036	173.6	0.0067	313.0	0.0098	442.9	0.0129	563.4	0.0160	674.5		
0.0037	178.3	0.0068	317.3	0.0099	447.0	0.0130	567.2	0.0161	677.9		
0.0038	182.9	0.0069	321.7	0.0100	451.0	0.0131	570.9	0.0162	681.4		
0.0039	187.5	0.0070	326.0	0.0101	455.0	0.0132	574.6	0.0163	684.8		
0.0040 (minimum for flexure)	192.2	0.0071	330.3	0.0102	459.0	0.0133	578.3				
0.0041	196.8	0.0072	334.6	0.0103	463.0	0.0134	582.0				
0.0042	201.4	0.0073	338.9	0.0104	467.0	0.0135	585.7				
0.0043	205.9	0.0074	343.2	0.0105	471.0	0.0136	589.3				
0.0044	210.5	0.0075	347.4	0.0106	474.9	0.0137	593.0				
0.0045	215.1	0.0076	351.7	0.0107	478.9	0.0138	596.6				
0.0046	219.6	0.0077	355.9	0.0108	482.8	0.0139	600.3				
0.0047	224.2	0.0078	360.2	0.0109	486.8	0.0140	603.9				
0.0048	228.7	0.0079	364.4	0.0110	490.7	0.0141	607.5				
0.0049	233.2	0.0080	368.6	0.0111	494.6	0.0142	611.2				
0.0050	237.7	0.0081	372.8	0.0112	498.5	0.0143	614.8				

APPENDIX

Table 7-4. Steel Ratio Table

| fy = | 50000 psi | | fc' = | 4000 psi | | | | | | UOG U | Dr. Hong |

ρ	M/Φbd²	ρ	M/Φbd²	ρ	M/Φbd²	ρ	M/Φbd²	ρ	M/Φbd²	ρ	M/Φbd²
0.0020	98.53	0.0051	245.44	0.0082	385.28	0.0113	518.06	0.0144	643.76	0.0175	762.41
0.0021	103.38	0.0052	250.06	0.0083	389.67	0.0114	522.22	0.0145	647.70	0.0176	766.12
0.0022	108.22	0.0053	254.67	0.0084	394.06	0.0115	526.38	0.0146	651.63	0.0177	769.82
0.0023	113.06	0.0054	259.28	0.0085	398.44	0.0116	530.53	0.0147	655.56	0.0178	773.51
0.0024	117.88	0.0055	263.88	0.0086	402.81	0.0117	534.67	0.0148	659.47	0.0179	777.20
0.0025	122.70	0.0056	268.47	0.0087	407.17	0.0118	538.81	0.0149	663.38	0.0180	780.88
0.0026	127.5	0.0057	273.1	0.0088	411.5	0.0119	542.9	0.0150	667.3	0.0181	784.6
0.0027	132.3	0.0058	277.6	0.0089	415.9	0.0120	547.1	0.0151	671.2	0.0182	788.2
0.0028	137.1	0.0059	282.2	0.0090	420.2	0.0121	551.2	0.0152	675.1	0.0183	791.9
0.0029	141.9	0.0060	286.8	0.0091	424.6	0.0122	555.3	0.0153	678.9	0.0184	795.5
0.0030	146.7	0.0061	291.3	0.0092	428.9	0.0123	559.4	0.0154	682.8	0.0185	799.2
0.0031	151.5	0.0062	295.9	0.0093	433.2	0.0124	563.5	0.0155	686.7	0.0186	802.8
0.0032	156.2	0.0063	300.4	0.0094	437.5	0.0125	567.6	0.0156	690.5	0.0187	806.4
0.0033	161.0	0.0064	304.9	0.0095	441.8	0.0126	571.6	0.0157	694.4	0.0188	810.1
0.0034	165.8	0.0065	309.5	0.0096	446.1	0.0127	575.7	0.0158	698.2	0.0189	813.7
0.0035	170.5	0.0066	314.0	0.0097	450.4	0.0128	579.8	0.0159	702.1	0.0190	817.3
0.0036	175.2	0.0067	318.5	0.0098	454.7	0.0129	583.8	0.0160	705.9	0.0191	820.9
0.0037	180.0	0.0068	323.0	0.0099	459.0	0.0130	587.9	0.0161	709.7	0.0192	824.5
0.0038	184.7	0.0069	327.5	0.0100	463.2	0.0131	591.9	0.0162	713.5	0.0193	828.1
0.0039	189.4	0.0070	332.0	0.0101	467.5	0.0132	595.9	0.0163	717.3	0.0194	831.6
0.0040	194.1	0.0071	336.5	0.0102	471.8	0.0133	600.0	0.0164	721.1	0.0195	835.2
0.0041	198.8	0.0072	340.9	0.0103	476.0	0.0134	604.0	0.0165	724.9	0.0196	838.8
0.0042	203.5	0.0073	345.4	0.0104	480.2	0.0135	608.0	0.0166	728.7	0.0197	842.3
0.0043	208.2	0.0074	349.9	0.0105	484.5	0.0136	612.0	0.0167	732.5	0.0198	845.9
0.0044	212.9	0.0075	354.3	0.0106	488.7	0.0137	616.0	0.0168	736.2	0.0199	849.4
0.0045	217.6	0.0076	358.8	0.0107	492.9	0.0138	620.0	0.0169	740.0	0.0200	852.9
0.0046	222.2	0.0077	363.2	0.0108	497.1	0.0139	624.0	0.0170	743.7	0.0201	856.5
0.0047	226.9	0.0078	367.6	0.0109	501.3	0.0140	627.9	0.0171	747.5	0.0202	860.0
0.0048	231.5	0.0079	372.1	0.0110	505.5	0.0141	631.9	0.0172	751.2	0.0203	863.5
0.0049	236.2	0.0080	376.5	0.0111	509.7	0.0142	635.9	0.0173	755.0	0.0204	867.0
0.0050	240.8	0.0081	380.9	0.0112	513.9	0.0143	639.8	0.0174	758.7	0.0205	870.5

minimum for flexure: 0.0040

APPENDIX

Table 7-5. Steel Ratio Table

| fy = | 60000 psi | | fc' = | 3000 psi | | | | | | UOG | Dr. Hong |

ρ	M/Φbd²	ρ	M/Φbd²	ρ	M/Φbd²	ρ	M/Φbd²
0.0020	117.18	0.0051	287.64	0.0082	444.54	0.0113	587.87
0.0021	122.89	0.0052	292.91	0.0083	449.37	0.0114	592.26
0.0022	128.58	0.0053	298.17	0.0084	454.19	0.0115	596.65
0.0023	134.27	0.0054	303.42	0.0085	459.00	0.0116	601.02
0.0024	139.93	0.0055	308.65	0.0086	463.79	0.0117	605.37
0.0025	145.59	0.0056	313.86	0.0087	468.57	0.0118	609.71
0.0026	151.2	0.0057	319.1	0.0088	473.3	0.0119	614.0
0.0027	156.9	0.0058	324.3	0.0089	478.1	0.0120	618.4
0.0028	162.5	0.0059	329.4	0.0090	482.8	0.0121	622.7
0.0029	168.1	0.0060	334.6	0.0091	487.5	0.0122	626.9
0.0030	173.6	0.0061	339.7	0.0092	492.3	0.0123	631.2
0.0031	179.2	0.0062	344.9	0.0093	496.9	0.0124	635.5
0.0032	184.8	0.0063	350.0	0.0094	501.6	0.0125	639.7
0.0033	190.3	0.0064	355.1	0.0095	506.3	0.0126	643.9
0.0034	195.8	0.0065	360.2	0.0096	510.9	0.0127	648.1
0.0035	201.4	0.0066	365.3	0.0097	515.6	0.0128	652.3
0.0036	206.9	0.0067	370.3	0.0098	520.2	0.0129	656.5
0.0037	212.3	0.0068	375.4	0.0099	524.8	0.0130	660.7
0.0038	217.8	0.0069	380.4	0.0100	529.4	0.0131	664.9
0.0039	223.3	0.0070	385.4	0.0101	534.0	0.0132	669.0
0.0040	228.7	0.0071	390.4	0.0102	538.6	0.0133	673.1
0.0041	234.1	0.0072	395.4	0.0103	543.1	0.0134	677.3
0.0042	239.5	0.0073	400.4	0.0104	547.7	0.0135	681.4
0.0043	244.9	0.0074	405.3	0.0105	552.2	0.0136	685.4
0.0044	250.3	0.0075	410.3	0.0106	556.7		
0.0045	255.7	0.0076	415.2	0.0107	561.2		
0.0046	261.1	0.0077	420.1	0.0108	565.7		
0.0047	266.4	0.0078	425.1	0.0109	570.1		
0.0048	271.7	0.0079	429.9	0.0110	574.6		
0.0049	277.1	0.0080	434.8	0.0111	579.0		
0.0050	282.4	0.0081	439.7	0.0112	583.5		

minimum for flexure: 0.0033

APPENDIX

Table 7-6. Steel Ratio Table

| | fy = | 60000 psi | | fc' = | 4000 psi | | | | | UOG | Dr. Hong |

ρ	M/Φbd²	ρ	M/Φbd²	ρ	M/Φbd²	ρ	M/Φbd²	ρ	M/Φbd²	ρ	M/Φbd²
0.0020	117.88	0.0051	292.23	0.0082	456.40	0.0113	610.40	0.0144	754.22	0.0175	887.87
0.0021	123.67	0.0052	297.68	0.0083	461.53	0.0114	615.20	0.0145	758.69	0.0176	892.01
0.0022	129.44	0.0053	303.13	0.0084	466.64	0.0115	619.99	0.0146	763.15	0.0177	896.14
0.0023	135.20	0.0054	308.56	0.0085	471.75	0.0116	624.76	0.0147	767.60	0.0178	900.26
0.0024	140.95	0.0055	313.99	0.0086	476.84	0.0117	629.53	0.0148	772.04	0.0179	904.37
0.0025	146.69	0.0056	319.40	0.0087	481.93	0.0118	634.28	0.0149	776.47	0.0180	908.47
0.0026	152.4	0.0057	324.8	0.0088	487.0	0.0119	639.0	0.0150	780.9	0.0181	912.6
0.0027	158.1	0.0058	330.2	0.0089	492.1	0.0120	643.8	0.0151	785.3		
0.0028	163.8	0.0059	335.6	0.0090	497.1	0.0121	648.5	0.0152	789.7		
0.0029	169.5	0.0060	340.9	0.0091	502.2	0.0122	653.2	0.0153	794.1		
0.0030	175.2	0.0061	346.3	0.0092	507.2	0.0123	657.9	0.0154	798.4		
0.0031	180.9	0.0062	351.6	0.0093	512.2	0.0124	662.6	0.0155	802.8		
0.0032	186.6	0.0063	357.0	0.0094	517.2	0.0125	667.3	0.0156	807.2		
0.0033	192.2	0.0064	362.3	0.0095	522.2	0.0126	672.0	0.0157	811.5		
0.0034	197.9	0.0065	367.6	0.0096	527.2	0.0127	676.6	0.0158	815.8		
0.0035	203.5	0.0066	372.9	0.0097	532.2	0.0128	681.3	0.0159	820.2		
0.0036	209.1	0.0067	378.2	0.0098	537.2	0.0129	685.9	0.0160	824.5		
0.0037	214.8	0.0068	383.5	0.0099	542.1	0.0130	690.5	0.0161	828.8		
0.0038	220.4	0.0069	388.8	0.0100	547.1	0.0131	695.1	0.0162	833.1		
0.0039	225.9	0.0070	394.1	0.0101	552.0	0.0132	699.8	0.0163	837.3		
0.0040	231.5	0.0071	399.3	0.0102	556.9	0.0133	704.4	0.0164	841.6		
0.0041	237.1	0.0072	404.6	0.0103	561.8	0.0134	708.9	0.0165	845.9		
0.0042	242.7	0.0073	409.8	0.0104	566.7	0.0135	713.5	0.0166	850.1		
0.0043	248.2	0.0074	415.0	0.0105	571.6	0.0136	718.1	0.0167	854.4		
0.0044	253.8	0.0075	420.2	0.0106	576.5	0.0137	722.6	0.0168	858.6		
0.0045	259.3	0.0076	425.4	0.0107	581.4	0.0138	727.2	0.0169	862.8		
0.0046	264.8	0.0077	430.6	0.0108	586.2	0.0139	731.7	0.0170	867.0		
0.0047	270.3	0.0078	435.8	0.0109	591.1	0.0140	736.2	0.0171	871.2		
0.0048	275.8	0.0079	441.0	0.0110	595.9	0.0141	740.7	0.0172	875.4		
0.0049	281.3	0.0080	446.1	0.0111	600.8	0.0142	745.2	0.0173	879.6		
0.0050	286.8	0.0081	451.3	0.0112	605.6	0.0143	749.7	0.0174	883.7		

minimum for flexure: 0.0033

COLUMNS 3.2.1 – Nominal load-moment strength interaction diagram, R4-60.6

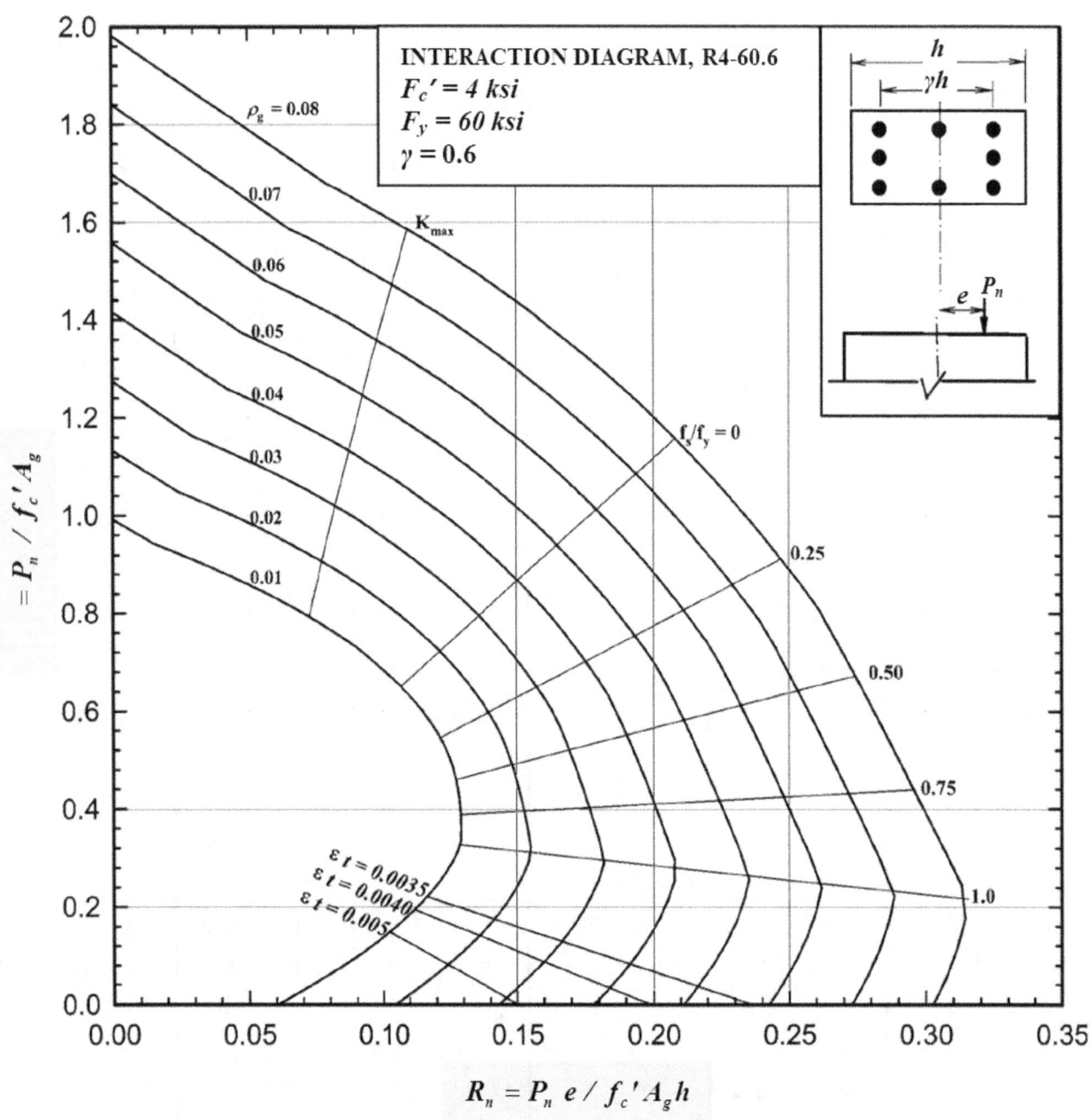

COLUMNS 3.2.2 – Nominal load-moment strength interaction diagram, R4-60.7

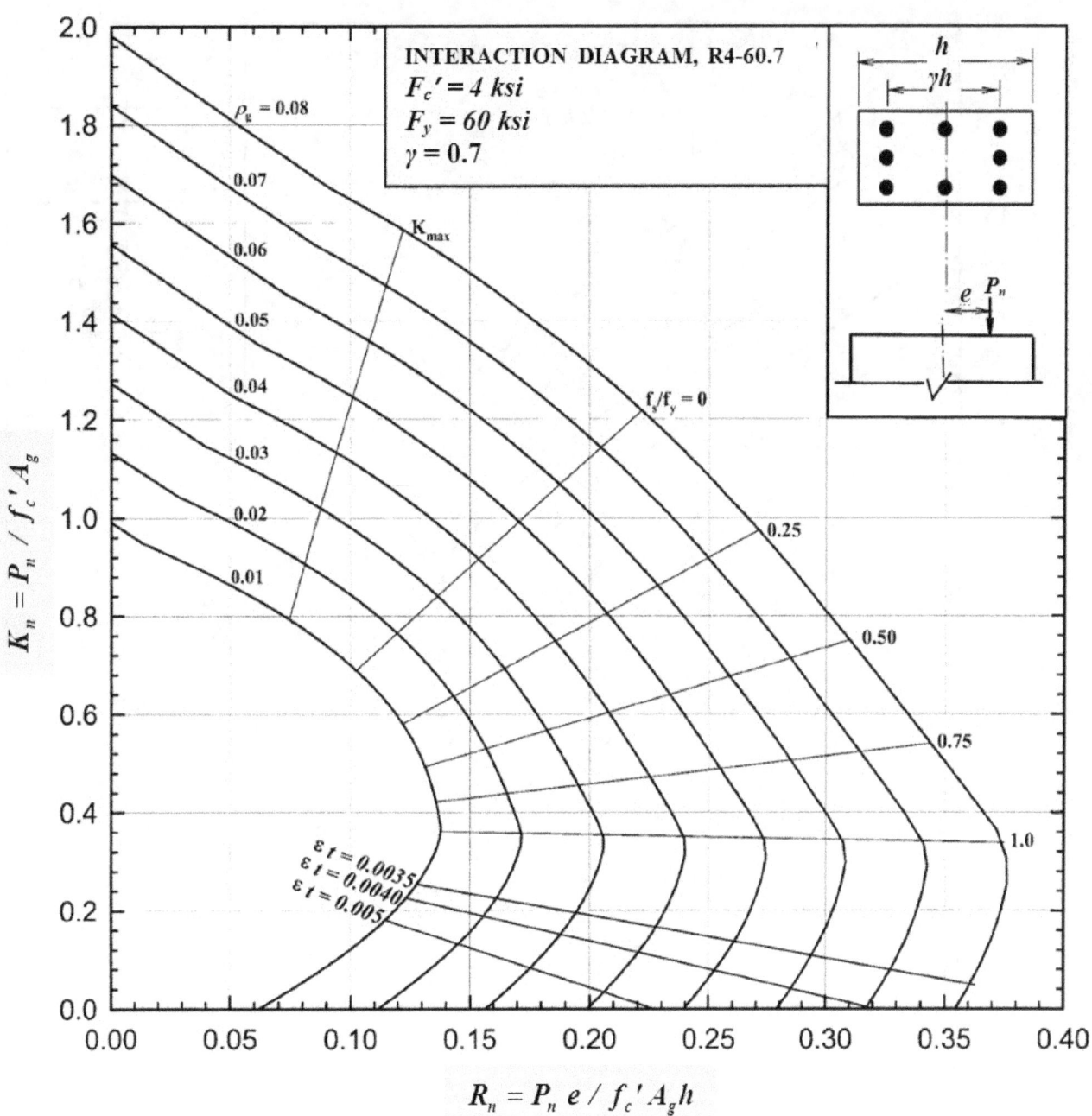

COLUMNS 3.2.3 – Nominal load-moment strength interaction diagram, R4-60.8

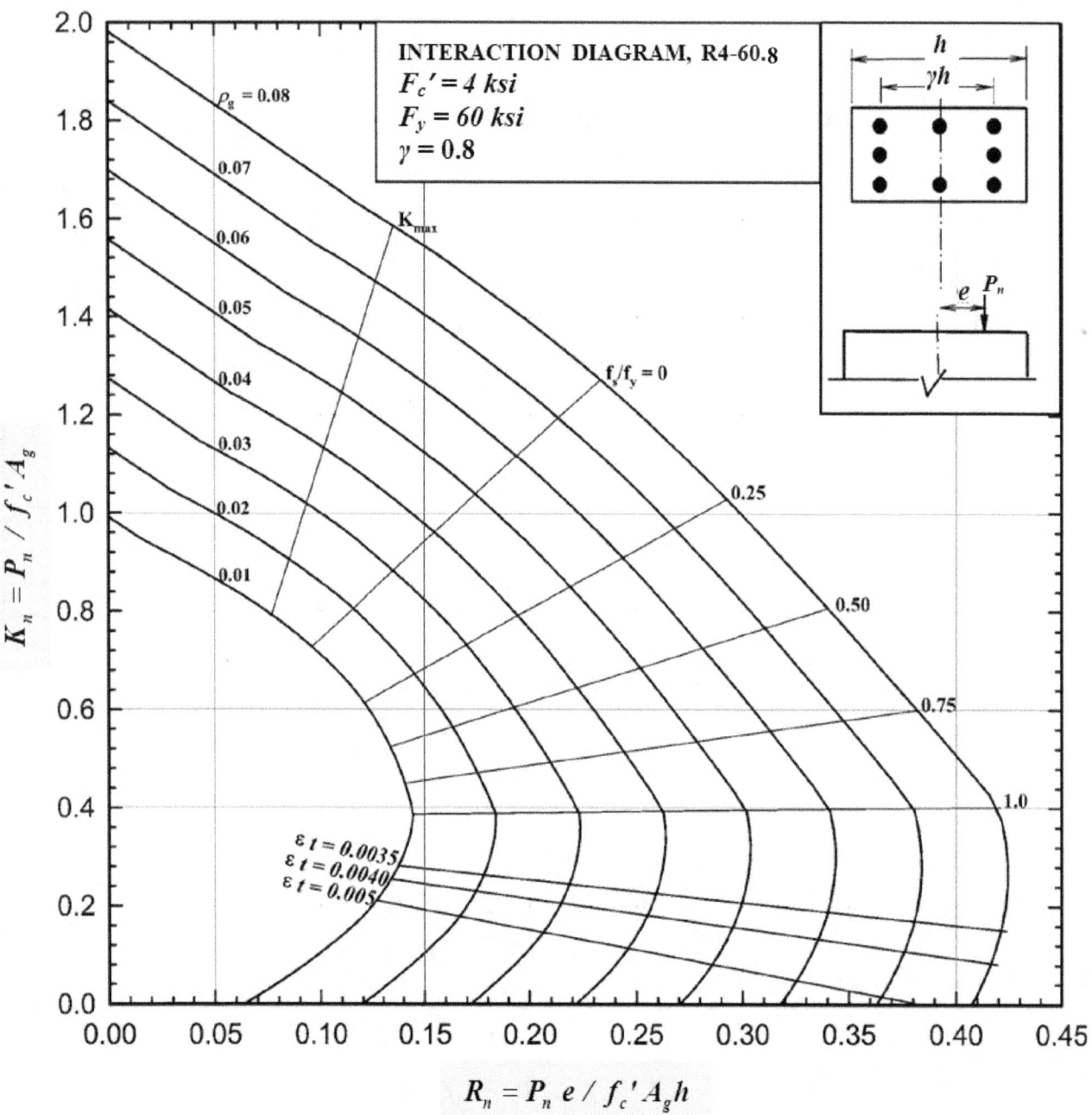

COLUMNS 3.2.4 – Nominal load-moment strength interaction diagram, R4-60.9

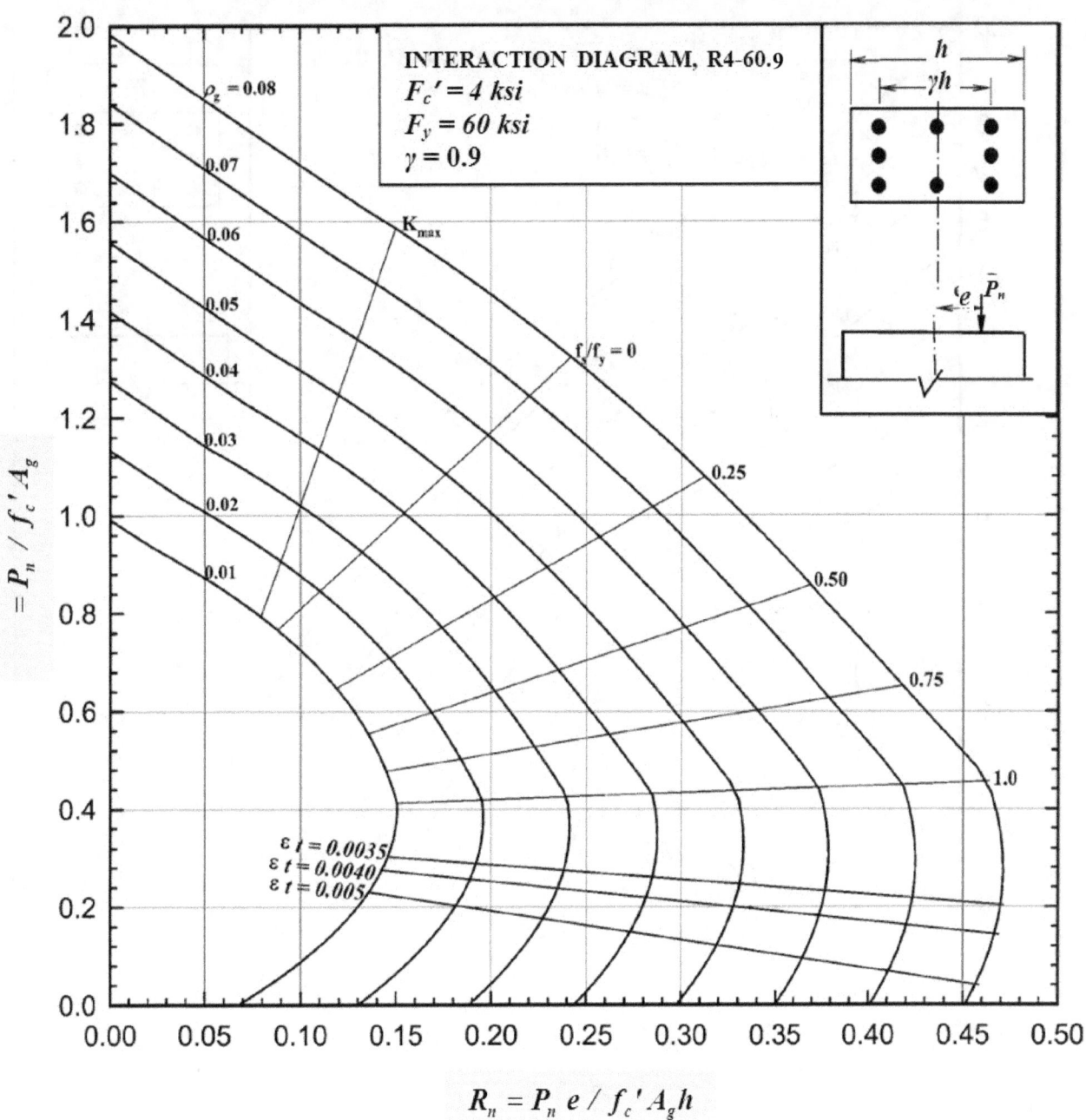

COLUMNS 3.8.1 – Nominal load-moment strength interaction diagram, L4-60.6

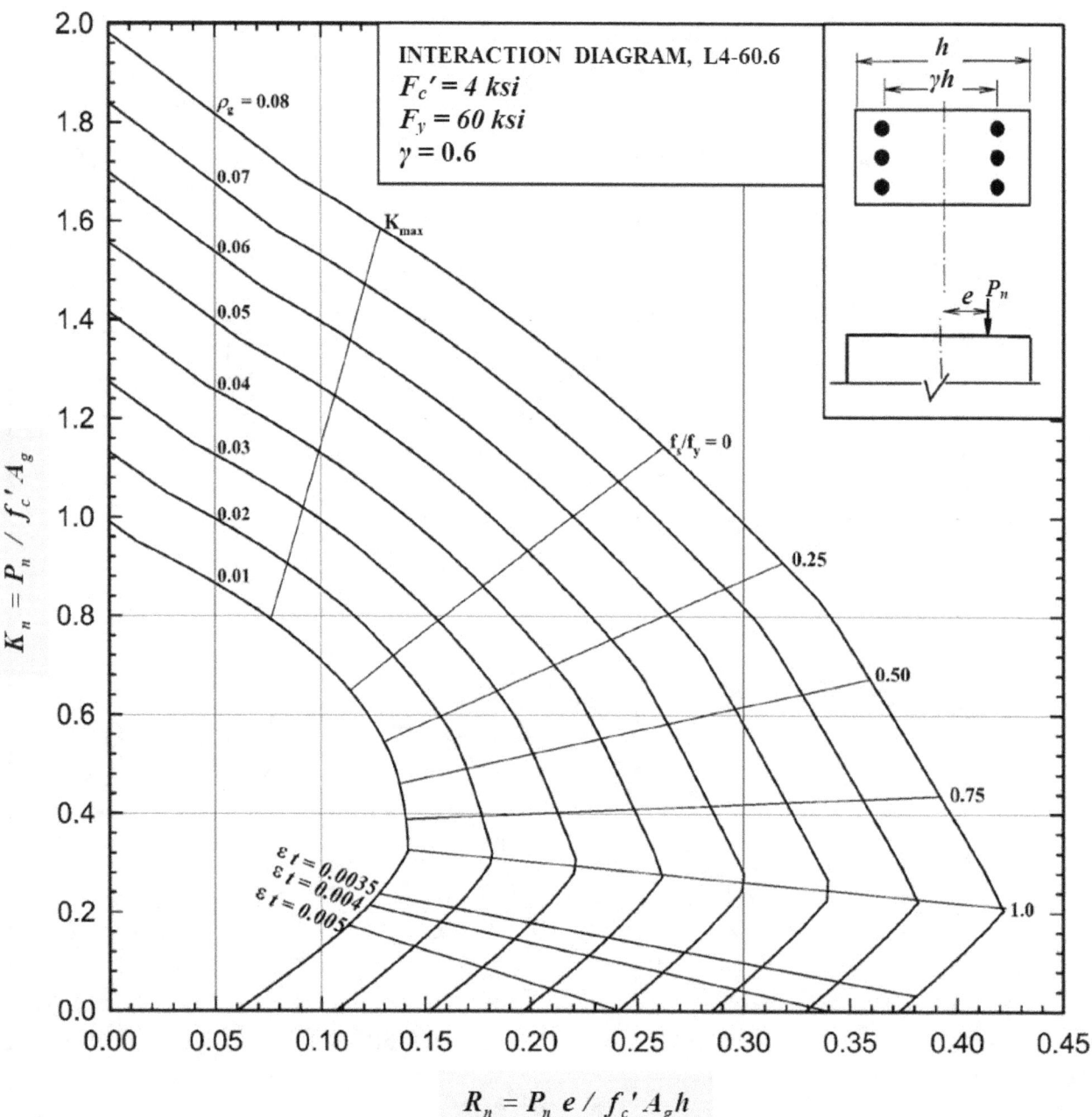

COLUMNS 3.8.2 – Nominal load-moment strength interaction diagram, L4-60.7

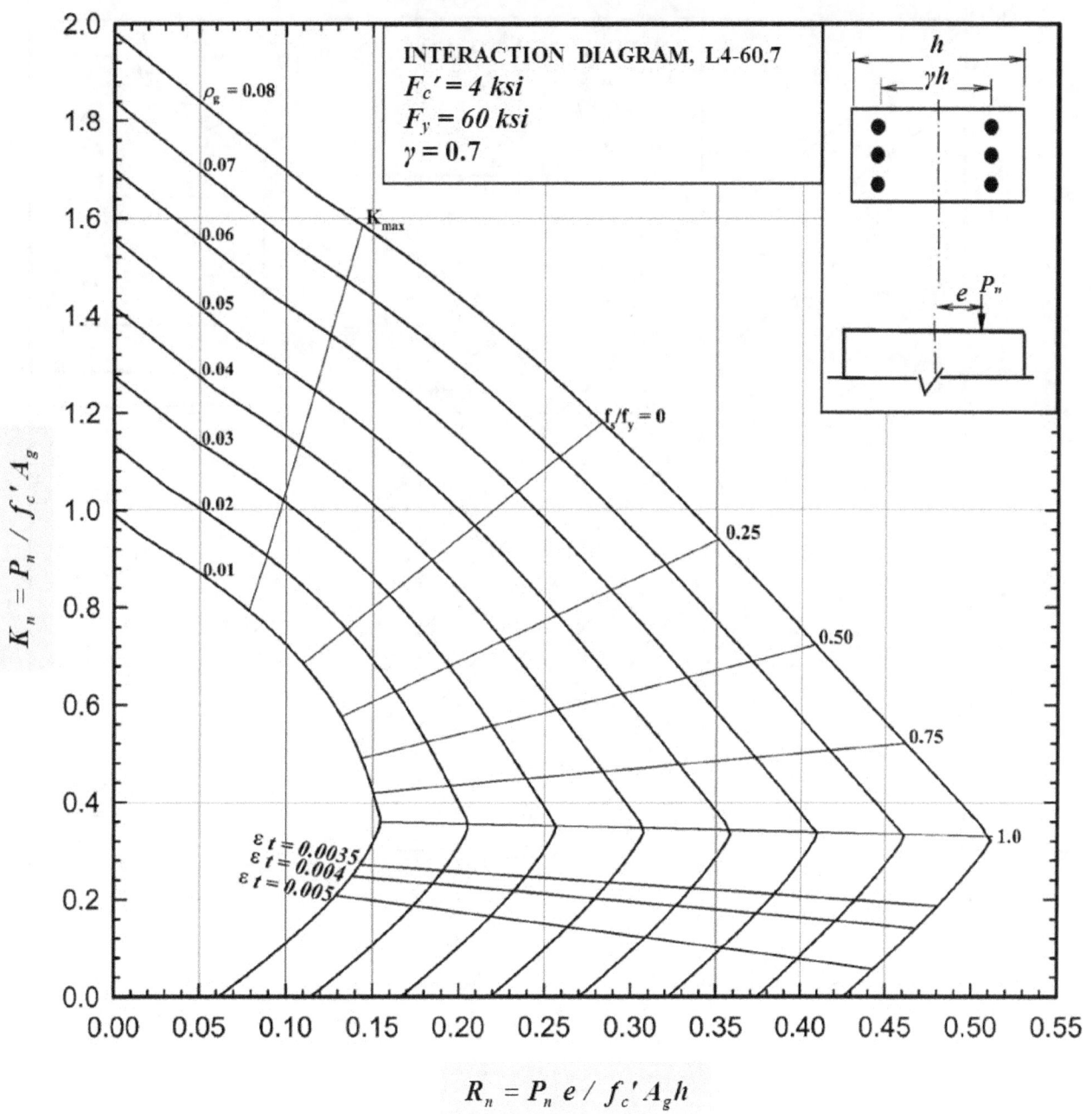

COLUMNS 3.8.3 – Nominal load-moment strength interaction diagram, L4-60.8

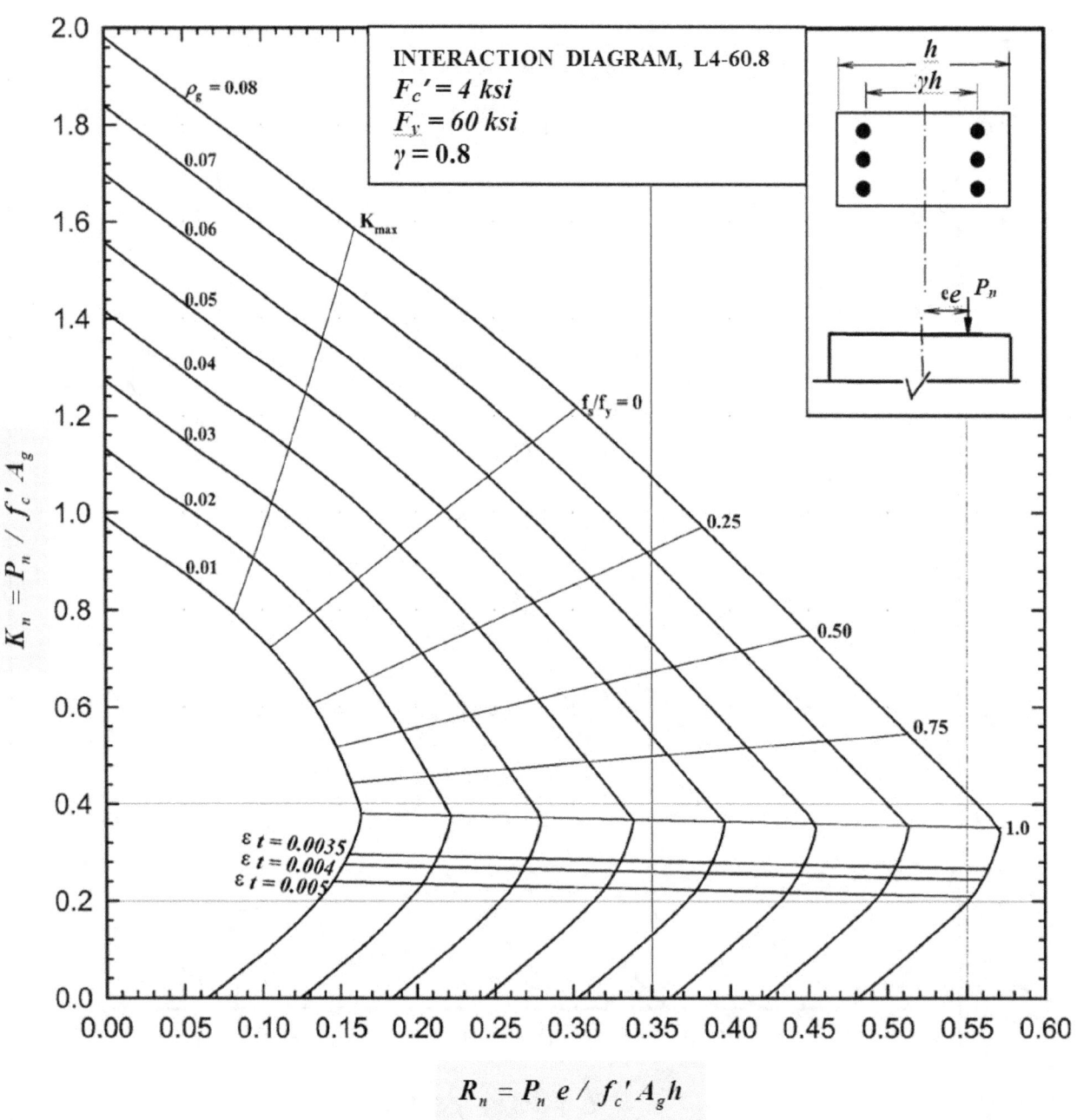

COLUMNS 3.8.4 – Nominal load-moment strength interaction diagram, L4-60.9

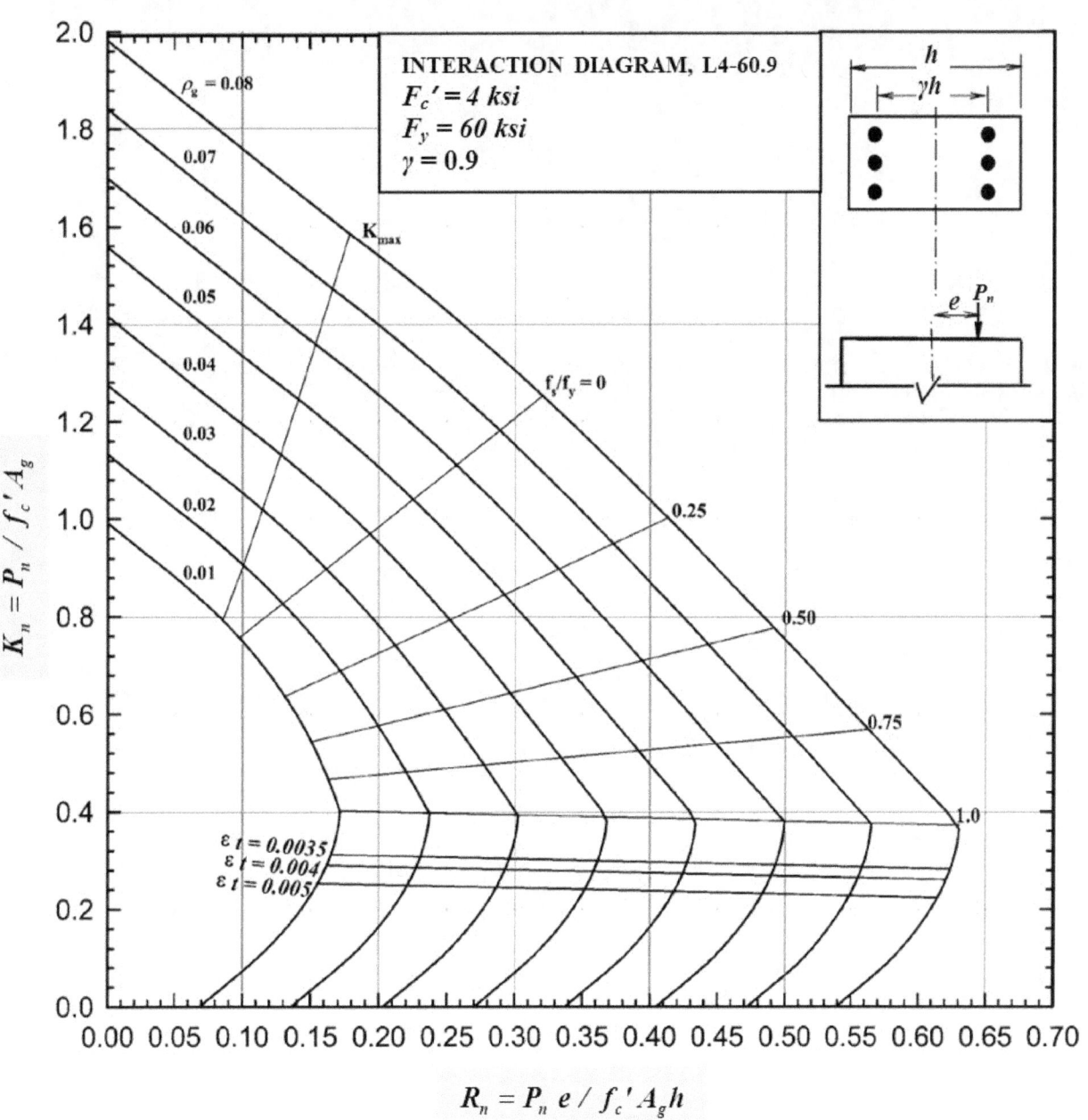

www.ingramcontent.com/pod-product-compliance
Lightning Source LLC
Chambersburg PA
CBHW081419230426
43668CB00016B/2284